The Early Days of Radio Broadcasting

The Early Days
of Radio Broadcasting

by
George H. Douglas

McFarland & Company, Inc., Publishers
Jefferson, North Carolina, and London

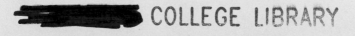

Library of Congress Cataloguing-in-Publication Data

Douglas, George H., 1934–
  The early days of radio broadcasting.

  Bibliography: p. 215.
  Includes index.
  1. Radio broadcasting—United States—History.
2. Radio programs—United States—History.   3. Radio
supplies industry—United States—History.   I. Title.
HE8698.D68   1987   384.54'0973   86-43090

ISBN 0-89950-285-7 (acid-free natural paper) ∞

Printed in the United States of America.

McFarland   Box 611   Jefferson NC 28640

Table of Contents

Acknowledgments

I am grateful to a number of individuals and institutions whose talents and resources have made this book possible. I am especially grateful to two of my colleagues at the University of Illinois, Professors Francis W. Weeks and Robert W. Mayer, who read the manuscript in its entirety and gave me the benefit of their recollections from the days of the crystal set. I am also grateful for the advice given me by Professor John Frayne of the English Department and Professors William L. Everitt, Millard McVey and Paul Hudson of the Department of Electrical Engineering, each of whom was helpful at earlier stages of this project.

For aid in researching the book I should also like to thank Diane Carothers, Communications Librarian of the University of Illinois, whose efforts aided me in developing and expanding the bibliography. I should also like to thank Charles P. Furlong of the Westinghouse Broadcasting and Cable Company, Pamela Haslam of the Media Relations Department of CBS, Ruth Shoemaker of the General Electric Company, and Frieda Schubert of RCA, who generously supplied many of the pictures used in this book. I should like to thank Paul Bartlett and Bill Pabst, who kindly spoke to me about the development of radio on the West Coast.

Needless to say, no book of this kind could be produced without the help of numerous institutions and repositories of information. I should especially like to mention the Broadcast Pioneer's Library at the National Association of Broadcasters, the Oral History Collection of the Columbia University Library, the Library of the National Broadcasting Company, the Museum of Broadcasting, the University of Illinois Library, the Newberry Library, the New Jersey Historical Society, the New York Historical Society and the Museum of the City of New York.

Introduction

This book is an informal history of the early years of radio broadcasting in the United States. The period covered is that between 1920 and 1930, although occasional reference is necessarily made to the infant years of radio before 1920 and to the great golden age of radio that began about 1930. My reason for concentrating on the 1920s is to focus more sharply than earlier histories on the years when radio was rapidly growing into a large American industry, dealing with as many aspects of this growth as possible in some depth. Thus my story is not simply of the development of radio as a form of entertainment, a business or a technology, but of the entire panorama of radio as it relates to broadcasting—that is, the political, financial, manufacturing and entertainment developments of this great industry in its formative years.

Even though much of this story has been told before, it is impossible to overestimate the importance of the electric media of communication in American life. Americans have been wildly enthusiastic about all such forms of communication since the invention of the telegraph by Samuel F.B. Morse in the 1840s. Nearly all of the early electric media, as soon as their usefulness became clearly manifest, were warmly welcomed by a people who had a vast land of open spaces to span, a circumstance unknown to most of the highly settled and civilized nations of Europe. Americans have, perhaps, reached the point where they take the electric means of communication for granted, almost to the extent that any tampering with them—such as the breakup of the giant American Telephone & Telegraph Company in 1984—is the cause of nervous anxiety. Clearly these media have become such a deeply ingrained part of the American way of life that we can't even imagine being without them.

One obvious reason for focusing on the gestation years of commercial broadcasting in the United States is that it teaches a great deal about the style and cultural significance of present-day radio and television. It is conceivable that both radio and television could have developed along lines different from those with which Americans are familiar. Radio (and by implication television) might have developed into a public monopoly as it did in many other countries. The program offerings might have been considerably better than those which America has enjoyed; they might also have been considerably worse. Or they might have been just different. But the story of precisely how and why radio developed the way it did continues to be a fascinating one.

And since the story is fascinating, I have tried as much as possible to tell it in narrative terms, with a strong emphasis on the human drama involved. A good number of histories of radio have been written, although far fewer in the last several decades than in the early years themselves, but my reading finds most of them to be indiscriminately overloaded with information and chaotically organized, so that the general reader needs to struggle to orient himself in a vast and confusing terrain. I have tried to cover the territory in considerable detail but without sacrificing continuity and drama. The result, I hope, will be of interest to both the specialist and the general reader.

Radio, as we all know, was not a strictly American phenomenon, but the development of the radio industry on the American shore is a thrilling story — one which occasions some nostalgia for a time when Americans were gifted with success and when the country had a native genius for making things work.

1. KDKA

On election day, November 2, 1920, at 8 o'clock P.M. EST, a newly established radio station in East Pittsburgh, Pennsylvania, owned by the Westinghouse Electric and Manufacturing Company, began reporting election returns in the race between Warren G. Harding and James M. Cox. History books tell us that this was the beginning of radio broadcasting as we know it today.

The truth is, it has never been easy to decide when radio broadcasting really began. A Detroit amateur station 8MK (later WWJ) began regular broadcasting of a sort two months before KDKA. Station 2ZK in New Rochelle, New York, made an attempt to broadcast music regularly in 1916. Even earlier, in 1912, Station KQW in San Jose, California, carried on a broadcast schedule with some regularity, and it had been on the air sporadically since 1909. Lee H. De Forest, one of the pioneers of radio, claims to have begun it all as early as 1907 when he "distributed sweet melody broadcast" over New York City and out to sea — a claim that clearly cannot be challenged.

What, then, was so novel or special about station KDKA? What novel thing did they do from the rooftop of the Westinghouse plant at Pittsburgh on that election evening at the beginning of the 1920s? For one thing, the station was the first to be specifically licensed by the United States government for the purpose of operating a general broadcasting service. But that trivial point by itself would doubtless deserve only a footnote in the pages of history. There was something even more earthshaking about KDKA. What had really happened was that the Westinghouse Company had decided to bring broadcasting out of the experimental phase — radio had hitherto been a plaything for tinkerers and scientific dabblers — and into the American home. KDKA was started with the idea that it might encourage the sale, not of a few, but of thousands of receiving sets for homes within the listening range of the station. It has been estimated that in 1920 there were some 5,000 to 10,000 receivers able to pick up the KDKA signal, but almost all of those were owned by amateur enthusiasts. The Westinghouse Company was no longer thinking of these piddling few amateurs. From the executive offices came the order to build radio receiving sets for the multitudes, for the man in the street, perhaps for the little old lady who just wanted to listen to music on the radio without having to know anything about a radio set except how to turn it on and off. Radio was to become the possession of everyman, not the specialist or expert.

1

From a commercial standpoint radio was far from an infant in 1920. Indeed, there were already giants and conglomerates in the field, most notably the Radio Corporation of America (RCA), which had been formed in 1919 as successor to the American Marconi Company. Westinghouse, which had been a leader in the industry during World War I, saw much of its business being stolen away by RCA, and by the other two giants in the field, the General Electric Corporation and the American Telephone & Telegraph Company. Now Westinghouse was looking for something it could call its own. RCA had a virtual monopoly on ship-to-shore radio and transatlantic communication, but wasn't the slightest bit interested in radio broadcasting as we think of it today. To be sure, RCA had its visionaries, one being young David Sarnoff, who had been strongly urging the company to make radio into a "household utility." But in 1920 Sarnoff was a voice crying in the wilderness, and his visionary schemes had been regularly rebuffed.

The technology was there had RCA wanted to use it. And it was there in the laboratories of GE and AT&T. They could have gotten into the radio broadcasting business had they so chosen, but they believed that there were bigger fish to fry elsewhere. AT&T, for example, had every reason to be interested in transmitting the human voice over the airwaves as part of their regular telephone operations. Transmitting the human voice by telephone wires between New York and San Francisco had proven unsatisfactory, the quality of the transmission being poor and unreliable. So, yes, radio telephony was of interest to them. But not radio broadcasting. RCA, on the other hand, was committed to radio telegraphy, and nearly all of its operations revolved around the transmission of those dot-dash bleeps of the Morse code that had been the form of long-distance communication since the days of Samuel F.B. Morse, but which of late had also been beamed into the atmosphere. To RCA the sending out of things like music or the human voice was mere frivolity — ice cream for the select few. It was not big business stuff. And RCA was the epitome of big business.

To understand where radio was in 1920 it is necessary to follow the road it had already come. To the mind of the general public, radio was still in its infancy. However, to those who had been working in the field for a long time, radio was already old hat by 1920. There had been literally hundreds of advances in the radio field between the 1890s and 1920, but for commercial purposes they seemed to have become a tangled web. Everybody in the field was aware that vast possibilities lay ahead, but what would they be?

The establishment of regular broadcasting on KDKA in the fall of 1920 was not so much an innovation as it was a turning point, a realization of a simple truth to which people had been blind. Radio had been around for a long time, but its commercial uses were severely restricted. Outside the few giant companies, it did not reach out to the multitudes, but only to a small corps of hobbyists and aficionados who took private delight in attempting to pull weak and elusive signals from the night air. It was there as a gold mine for the monopolistic combines of RCA and AT&T, but for the typical American it remained in the domain of the arcane and mysterious.

Most Americans of 1920 were vaguely aware that this strange new art went back at least to 1897, when a young Italian inventor named Guglielmo Marconi obtained his first patent for radio receiving and transmitting devices. As a scientific idea the possibility of transmission of sounds through the atmosphere went still back further in the nineteenth century—perhaps the idea was one devoutly to be wished ever since the invention of the telegraph in the 1840s.

Radio was of necessity a child of both scientific and technological genius. During the last half of the nineteenth century there was a passionate interest among European scientists in the question of how light passed from one object to another. A number of theories appeared, but in 1864, a brilliant young Scotsman named James Clerk Maxwell delivered a paper before the Royal Society entitled "A Dynamical Theory of Electro-Magnetic Field," which showed that electromagnetic waves must exist and that obviously they could be propagated through space.

Following up on this theory was the German scientist Heinrich Hertz, who succeeded in producing these waves under laboratory conditions. By 1887 Hertz had found that by creating intense charges of positive and negative electricity and discharging them across an air gap in the form of an electric spark, he could create, so to speak, waves in space—very much like the kinds of waves set up in a pond when a stone is thrown into the water. In his experiments Hertz had shown how these waves were set in motion and how they could be detected, but he was so consumed by the various scientific ramifications of his experiments that he failed to follow up on their practical implications. Nevertheless, the practical implications were there, and scientists everywhere began talking about these amazing "Hertzian waves"; it was believed to be only a matter of time before Hertz's discoveries would be brought to good account.

Of the many scientists and inventors intrigued by Hertzian waves, none was more obsessed and insistent than Guglielmo Marconi, who had been intrigued by a paper on Hertzian waves and retired to the privacy of his family villa to experiment with them. Marconi was still in his teens when he began his experiments in the early 1890s, and to the dismay of his family he gave up all thoughts of a career or profession to fool around with what looked to everybody else like a collection of meaningless wires, batteries and electrical doodads. Marconi got a certain amount of sympathy from his Irish-born mother, an intrepid lady who had gone to Italy as a teenager and fallen in love with a rich Italian widower many years older than herself. Marconi's father was skeptical from the outset, and in time even Signora Marconi had her doubts about young Guglielmo, one of those single-minded geniuses who crop up in the pages of history and who are so totally enraptured by the objects of their obsession that they give no thoughts even to the ordinary business of sustaining life.

Retiring to a third-floor room at the family's Villa Grifone outside of Bologna, Guglielmo grew thinner and paler as he plunged forward in his work, often never opening the door to his room to pick up the meal trays his mother silently laid on the floor. Even when he did come down to join the family at dinner, he seemed to be distracted, preoccupied, often bringing along strange diagrams and calculations that looked like hieroglyphics. Marconi's father, hoping the boy would select a career as a military officer or some other suitable gentlemanly occupation, became disgruntled as the months and even years rolled by without any sign that these complicated diagrams and elecrical gadgets would ever come to anything.

At last, after years of heartbreaking failure, success began to come, and when it came it was astonishing and magical. Even the elder Marconi sat up and took notice. Using Hertzian waves, young Marconi could ring a bell on the other side of a room, or even downstairs. It took no superhuman intelligence to see that here was an effect that had never before been seen in the history of science.

But an even more important achievement was in the offing. The invention for which Marconi deserves his place in the history books was his discovery of a process that would allow the transmission of *intelligible* signals across space. He produced an improved Hertzian wave apparatus that could be interrupted in such a way as to send out the dots and dashes of the Morse code. Then, at another point a few feet away, he set up an iron filings coherer, in which a small pile of iron filings was made to pass—or not pass—a local electric current. He found that when he shunted the sparking contacts of his receiver, the Morse signals sent out by his transmitter were exactly reproduced by the electric currents passing through the coherer. This was proof positive that actual messages could be transmitted through the air and received in the same form elsewhere—the origin of wireless radio.

By a process of trial and error Marconi also discovered that the best way to get oscillatory electrical motions into the air was by means of an upright wire connected with the ground; the higher the wire, the better the result. He also discovered that the best receiver was a second upright wire similarly connected to the ground and raised as high as possible in the air. Shortly after this discovery, and by means of the filings coherer, Marconi was able to send messages for distances up to two miles. Later this was extended to four and then eight miles, and by 1895, the distances were impressive enough that Marconi was convinced that he had invented a workable and profitable device. By now his father was also convinced that Guglielmo's invention was far more than just an idle child's toy, and he suggested that it was time to disseminate information about these developments.

The Marconis now wrote to the Minister of Post and Telegraph of the Italian government, but were rebuffed: The Italian government was just not interested in this gentleman's playtoy. Frustrated, Signora Marconi took a strong hand in the matter. Firmly convinced that back in her native British isles the public officials would not be such dunderheads, she packed up her somber and sallow young son with all his equipment and set sail for England.

And yes, England was the place to go. Not that there weren't dunderheads there also; indeed, when young Marconi arrived in England with a big box full of wires, batteries, dials, oscillators and the like, he was taken, in spite of his patrician appearance, for some kind of anarchist or troublemaker, and all his equipment was seized and smashed by customs

officers. Of course the whole invention was now in Marconi's head, and he very shortly reconstructed all the equipment needed to put on a demonstration for English officials.

The higher English officials were not fools. The Marconis called on Sir William Preece, Chief Engineer of Telegraphs of the British Post Office, a man quite prepared to appreciate what Marconi had done since he himself had been experimenting with wireless, although with only modest success. Tests were first conducted in rooms of the London Post Office in Queen Victoria Street. A signal was sent to St. Martin's-le-Grand, a distance of a few hundred yards. Some weeks later, communication was established on the Salisbury Plain over a distance of 1¾ miles. By May of 1897, Marconi had managed to transmit signals a distance of 8 miles between Lavernock and Brean Down, both on the Bristol Channel.

Meanwhile Marconi had been consulting with patent attorneys, and on July 2, 1897, he received an English patent for his equipment. Almost immediately thereafter—for the British were not at all slow to perceive the vast possibilities of this device as a means of communicating with distant places and with ships at sea—a powerful group of backers joined Marconi to form the Wireless Telegraph and Signal Company, Ltd., later to be called Marconi's Wireless Telegraph Company, Ltd., which company subsequently acquired all of Marconi's patents, offering the inventor half of the stock and £15,000 in cash.

Now lost forever to Marconi was the tranquil environment of his family villa, with its grape arbors and its gentle rolling hills. Much against his will he was precipitated into a world of international capital and business, all of which committed him to a life of strenuous activity for which he was neither prepared nor temperamentally suited.[1]

Despite his dislike of commercialism, Marconi was convinced that the wireless telegraph was an invention of many practical applications, so he moved quickly to exploit his invention financially. In doing so he was far more than a self-seeking inventor; he believed in his invention and spent as much time as he could improving it and studying wider and wider applications. In 1899 he sent a message across the English Channel, and in 1901 he managed to send a wireless signal from Poldu in Cornwall that was received near St. John's, Newfoundland, on an aerial held aloft by a kite in a gale of wind. These signals had crossed the Atlantic Ocean—a distance of 1,800 miles.

Transatlantic communication by radio would continue to be erratic and unreliable for a number of years, but Marconi's fame spread quickly around the world and to the governments of all the major nations, who saw in it an invaluable aid in communicating with ships at sea. Not only did the British Navy show a keen interest in these possibilities, but shortly the navies of other countries expressed interest as well—the United States, Germany, even Marconi's native Italy, which only a few years ago had laughed at the young inventor.

As early as 1899 a distress signal had been sent from the lightship *East Goodwin*, and shortly afterwards, wireless telegraphy was used by ships to summon help or to communicate other urgent messages. In 1909, the S.S. *Republic* foundered off New York, and all passengers were saved by the use of wireless. An even more famous incident that dramatized the value of radio communication to the general public was the sinking of the *Titanic* on its maiden voyage in 1912. Investigation of the accident showed that if it had not been for radio, many more, if not all, of the passengers on this vessel might have been lost. It was also shown that a fuller use of the radio equipment already available would have saved a great many more lives: A ship very near to the *Titanic* had turned off its radio receiver at midnight, just a few minutes before the *Titanic*'s fatal rendezvous with a deadly iceberg. If there had been any doubt before, the general public now knew that radio was no playboy's diversion, but a technical device of inestimable value.

Nearly all of Marconi's interests during the first decade of his company's development were with the improvement of *radiotelegraphy*, that is, with the transmission of dot-dash Morse code messages. There was much to do in improving this service: fighting the deadly static, overcoming vast distances, setting up a complicated network of senders and receivers. In overcoming these technical obstacles Marconi was being outflanked by others whose concern was broadening the communication possibilities of radio to include *radiotelephony*, that is, the transmission of the human voice and other sounds, even music.

At this point the drama shifts to America, where a whole army of pioneers would shortly be setting to work. The first figure of any importance was Canadian-born Reginald Aubrey Fessenden, who had worked as the chief chemist at the Edison Laboratory in West Orange, New Jersey, and in 1893 became a professor of electrical engineering at Western University (now the University of Pittsburgh). While at Pittsburgh he had, like many others of his day, experimented with Hertzian rays. In 1900 the Weather Service of the U.S. Department of Agriculture employed him at $3,000 a year to explore the possibilities of sending weather information by radio.

It wasn't long before Fessenden was thinking seriously about the problem of transmitting the human voice over the radio. Obviously the spark system of transmission in use by Marconi and his followers would be of no value to the aims of radiotelephony, so Fessenden began thinking along other lines. In the Marconi system, waves were radiated in short bursts of rapidly diminishing amplitude repeated at very short intervals. Fessenden conceived the idea of radiating a continuous series of waves, all of equal amplitude.

To obtain the kind of continuous wave transmission that he wanted, Fessenden had to have a radio frequency alternator. Unfortunately there was no suitable alternator available. Fessenden approached the General Electric Company with the idea, and the company assigned the job to a member of its engineering staff, Swedish-born Ernst F.W. Alexanderson. The highest frequency available to Fessenden was about 500 cycles per second, but what was needed was something more like 50,000 cycles (50kHz). Alexanderson was up to the task, and eventually produced the alternator. Indeed, Alexanderson was himself on the road to being one of radio's greatest pioneers: Giant 200 kw

Two of radio's early pioneers, Guglielmo Marconi (left) and Ernst F.W. Alexanderson, shown here at a General Electric banquet in the 1920s. Alexanderson's alternator would give Marconi's radio signal the big boost it needed to become commercially feasible. (Photo courtesy General Electric.)

alternators of his devising made reliable long-distance radio transmission possible by World War I and finally allowed American companies to break the monopoly of the British Marconi Company.

Using the new alternator that Alexanderson had built for him, an output modulated with a carbon microphone, and his electrolytic detector, Fessenden in 1902 succeeded for the first time in transmitting the human voice over the air.

Over the next several years Fessenden strove to improve his invention, and on Christmas Eve, 1906, made the first real "radio program" of voice and music. Using a 1kW Alexanderson alternator on a wavelength of 7,000m (42kHz), Fessenden's program consisted of the voice of a woman singing, a violin solo and an address. There would be a certain amount of justice in saying that radio as we know it today stems from that Christmas Eve broadcast of 1906.

But Fessenden's apparatus was a long way from being practical. Were it not for the magic and mystery of it all, none of the hearers of Fessenden's early program would have thought of the whole business as anything more than a scratchy little sound box. For radio telephony to grow into something useful a lot of help was needed. And help was already on the way in the person of America's most important early radio pioneer, a recent Ph.D. from Yale named Lee H. De Forest.

De Forest styled himself "the Father of Radio," perhaps a grandiose title when one considers the contributions of Marconi and Fessenden, but there is some aptness in the title when one considers that no other inventor contributed more technical advances to radio over a longer period of time than Lee De Forest. During the infant days of radio between 1902 and 1906 he pioneered over thirty patents, and in the years to follow he was granted over two hundred. Technically his greatest claim to fame was the invention of the Audion tube, the offspring of which became the heart and soul of radio, the keystone of twentieth-century electronics.

Lee De Forest had been born in a small parsonage in Council Bluffs, Iowa, in 1873 (one year before Marconi). His early life was spent in the deep South, where his clergyman father had been called as head of tiny Talladega College, maintained by the church for black students. In the South the De Forests were not looked upon as benefactors but as northern troublemakers and intellectual carpetbaggers, so Lee grew up in isolation from his schoolmates and neighbors. This isolation may have been responsible for his later infatuation with communication in all its forms.

Lee's father wanted him to enter the clergy, and he prepared for that vocation from an early age. He read the Bible from cover to cover, and made every effort to involve himself in the instruction of his father's college. An even more important influence on his life, however, was his mother, who sang and played the piano at musicals arranged for the benefit of the college students. De Forest remained a zealous music lover throughout his life, which perhaps explains his compelling interest in the musical potential of radio from his first association with that medium.

An even stronger calling than the ministry, however, was the world of invention, so recently an object of public attention through the work of men like Thomas Alva Edison. During his high school years De Forest spent long hours poring through copies of the *Patent Office Gazette* and its numerous schematic drawings and technical notations. His knowledge was sufficiently extensive by 1893 that he was able to pass the entrance examinations to the Sheffield Scientific School at Yale. De Forest stayed on at Yale to take his Ph.D., which he earned in 1899 with a dissertation entitled, "Reflection of Hertzian Waves from the Ends of Parallel Wires." By this time he had become deeply enmeshed in research into wireless and was in the forefront of those seeking to make improvements in the Marconi system. He plunged forward in a number of directions with frenetic intensity. De Forest was not, and would never be, a great theoretical scientist. He was too restless and impatient for that; but he would become a great wide-ranging inventor of the Edison variety.

With his Ph.D. finished De Forest took a job with the Western Electric Company in Chicago, shortly managing to have himself transferred to the telephone department. In 1902 De Forest moved to New York, and with the backing of a Wall Street financier named Albert M. White, formed the American De Forest Wireless Telegraphy Company. White and De Forest were interested in becoming competitors to the Marconi Company, and very shortly they made a big splash by landing a plump contract with the War Department to erect two experimental coast stations for military communications. Shortly thereafter De Forest was also building ship-to-shore stations for the Navy. The company opened a plant to build radio equipment in Newark, New Jersey, and the products sold briskly, turning a handsome profit for De Forest, White and their backers.

Profits from the De Forest Wireless Company began rolling in immediately, for Albert White was a flamboyant promoter. In 1902 the very latest model automobile cruised the streets of New York carrying a De Forest-made apparatus, its spark gap crackling in the air to the amazement of transfixed bystanders. Every afternoon this car would cruise down Wall Street, where it would telegraph the day's closing prices into the atmosphere, presumably to those who had receivers — surely few, or none, in the beginning. In no time, however, the company was capitalized at $15,000,000 and briskly selling both stock *and* radio equipment.

With White doing the promoting, Lee De Forest was left free to do the sorts of things he wanted: carry on experiments in improving radio transmission and reception. Fessenden had already shown that voice and music could be transmitted through the air waves, but he had not really moved his equipment out of a crude experimental stage. Meanwhile De Forest had been studying a new idea that had been held over from some earlier experiments of Thomas Edison. In 1883, while studying the problem of the tendency of the early incandescent lamps to blacken with use, Edison discovered that current could be transferred through the space between the glowing hot filament and a metal plate inside the sealed lamp. He subsequently patented a device for measuring this current, but made no attempt to follow up the scientific ramifications of his discovery. Several years later this so-called "Edison effect" intrigued John Ambrose Fleming, an Englishman working on Marconi's research staff. In 1904 he patented a radio detector based on it, taking advantage of the idea that a two-element tube (diode) can convert energy at radio frequencies into electrical currents.

De Forest, too, began experimenting with this device, and thought that he might be able to make a giant leap forward with it. And he did. Using the Fleming idea of an enclosed tube, De Forest placed a mesh or spiral of very fine wire between the filament and the plate of the Fleming valve, enabling the current passing between them to be controlled, thus allowing the valve to be used both as a detector of signals and as an amplifier as well. De Forest called this valve an Audion (it should more accurately have been called a triode vacuum tube), and secured a patent for it in 1907. The invention has been compared to the invention of printing as one of the great technological advances in civilization, and there is no doubt that the triode tube is the foundation stone of modern electronics.

The years following De Forest's invention of the Audion tube are confused and cloudy ones in the history of wireless technology. De Forest never managed to advance the art of his little tube or even fully realize this great potential. For example, it was some time before he realized that the heated gas inside the tube was a hindrance rather than a help, and that a vacuum tube was more

There was no greater gadfly and promoter of radio in its first two experimental decades than Lee H. De Forest, inventor of the Audion tube, which in a refined version made commercial radiotelephony possible. (Photo courtesy New Jersey Historical Society.)

effective for transmission of radio signals. Similarly — and this was even more strange — it took him a number of years to realize that several Audions would amplify sound better than one.

De Forest's claim to being the Father of Radio is probably best supported by his ceaseless and fanatical support of all aspects of radio technology in the early years, his many patents for all sorts of devices, and his never-ending struggle to dramatize to the world that the radio could really talk. When Fessenden made the radio talk, nobody listened, but when De Forest made the radio talk people did listen — if not right away, certainly in time, after endless demonstrations, exhibits and promotions in America and around the world.

In his autobiography, *Father of Radio*, De Forest immodestly claims to have begun regular radio broadcasting in 1907 from his laboratory in the Parker Building in New York City. Of course the broadcasting he did was strictly experimental, sporadic, intermittent, and not what we mean today by broadcasting. But as a prophet of broadcasting and as a publicist of the art he had no equal.

In 1908 he married a pianist who lived in the apartment next to his in New York; they went on a honeymoon to Europe, where De Forest got an idea for one of his best promotions. He set up a transmitter at the foot of the Eiffel Tower and, using an aerial suspended from the tower, gave a demonstration consisting of a program of gramophone records. This was a spectacular success reported in the news everywhere, one listener actually picking up the broadcast in Marseilles, 500 miles away.[2]

Back home De Forest did everything he could to publicize the value of radio, perhaps sometimes to the detriment of his scientific experiments. In 1909, Mrs. Harriet Blatch, his mother-in-law, was invited to speak over the radio, delivering a plea for women's suffrage. De Forest claimed another milestone: the first propaganda broadcast over the radio. Too, De Forest was coming closer to his great dream of "attuning a new Aeolian harp and having it vibrate to the rhapsodies of master musicians played in some far distant auditorium." On January 12, 1910, a fever of excitement spread over the New York area when De Forest broadcast the voice of tenor Enrico Caruso directly from the stage of the Metropolitan Opera House in New York. He accomplished this using two microphones, a 500-watt transmitter located in a room at the top of the opera house and an antenna in the attic suspended from two bamboo fishpoles. Groups of listeners in the New York metropolitan area gathered to hear the broadcast, and although there was interference from other stations and some inevitable "fading" due to the primitive state of the art, the broadcast caused a great deal of stir and admiration.[3]

Everything that De Forest did commanded attention in those years. Yet his career was not one of unbroken success. Throughout his life De Forest was subject to boom and bust. For example, after only a few years of his association with Albert White he found himself euchred out of his interest in the De Forest Wireless Telegraph Company, the name of which was subsequently changed to United Wireless Telegraph Company. The Wall Street scalawags, including White, pushed De Forest aside with only a token payment, although they foolishly left him with his patent for the Audion, which White and his associates thought to be worthless. Needless to say, De Forest bounced back in a few years, with other bursts of activity and inventiveness.

Soon, however, he would be engulfed in another turmoil that would plague him for years: a cascade of patent infringement suits—suits that had as their wider intention the determination of who really invented radio. Of course there could be no easy resolution of these suits because there really was no answer.

The suits came fast and heavy. For example, after being done out of his company by White, De Forest found the American Telephone & Telegraph Company interested in buying his Audion since they were looking for a way to make coast-to-coast telephony possible. AT&T settled the paltry sum of $50,000 on De Forest at a time when he was hard up—which clearly meant that they stole the invention from him—but they immediately met a roadblock in the form of an infringement suit from the Marconi Company, which claimed that the Audion was really just a variation of the Fleming valve, whose patent they owned. This case was not settled until 1916, when the Supreme Court ruled that when the Audion was used as a detector it infringed the Fleming patent, but that it did not do so as an amplifier. A silly compromise, but about the best that could be expected in those days.

In spite of the fact that De Forest won and lost several large fortunes in the radio field, it would be easy to say that he was unfairly treated by the giant corporations and that his inventions were perpetually being stolen by others. Perhaps so. On the other hand, De Forest himself was adept at playing the high-stakes game and didn't hesitate to lay claim to inventions and developments that weren't really his. A good example of this was the regenerative or feedback circuit, which De Forest claimed for himself, but which was really invented by a young student of electrical engineering at Columbia University, Edwin H. Armstrong (see Chapter Three).[4] What Armstrong did was take De Forest's Audion and feed the output of the detector valve back to the grid circuit, greatly amplifying the strength of the signal received. It was really all a matter of producing oscillations with the Audion, a fact that De Forest strangely missed even though he had experimented endlessly with his Audion and probably should have discovered this effect accidentally.

As soon as De Forest found out about the regenerative circuit he became convinced that it had been a part of his invention all along, which clearly wasn't true. What ensued was one of the biggest and most controversial litigations in American history, for there were soon a number of other players in the drama, all now backed by giant corporations desiring to gain ascendancy in the radio field. There was AT&T with the De Forest patent; there was the American Marconi Company, which had bought up the Armstrong patent; and there was the Telefunken Company with the German Meisner patent for an invention that came out at about the same time as that of Armstrong. General Electric also had an improved Audion, produced by one of its staff researchers, Dr. Irving S. Langmuir, and this development joined the heat of the battle. Langmuir also had discovered something important that De Forest missed: that it was better for the Audion tube to be a vacuum rather than filled with gas. So still another modification was tossed into the patent imbroglio.

(The case was finally resolved by the Supreme Court in 1934. It was resolved in favor of De Forest, although there is no scientist today who believes that De Forest should be credited with the invention of the regenerative circuit — Armstrong clearly had the lead. Alas, even though De Forest finally got his reward, it was now rather meaningless, since the individual patents had all been bought up by the giants, and financial rewards to the original inventors were minimal.)

Happily the worst of the patent wars were ended for practical purposes the year before KDKA began its regular broadcasting in 1920. Quite strangely, the ultimate settlement of the patent wars was a side-effect of World War I, the practical communication requirements of which had convinced the United States government that the various disputes and conflicting patents could not be permitted to interfere with the war effort. In the period before America's involvement in the European war, the American Marconi Company was still the biggest and strongest giant in the radio field. But the company was largely British owned, which was disturbing to American governmental officials, who saw their navy heavily dependent on the manufactures and installations of the company.

On the other hand, Guglielmo Marconi himself perceived that progress in the radio field was highly dependent on the Alexanderson alternator; as early as 1915 he had paid a visit to GE's laboratories in Schenectady, New York, and became convinced that this alternator was the key to reliable transatlantic communication. But GE was not about to turn over its holdings to Marconi, and when the war broke out, GE, as much as American Marconi, had taken a lead in marketing products to the government for use by the navy, the army Signal Corps, and other communication units. In any case the demand soon became so large that all of the major companies in the field—GE, AT&T, Westinghouse and American Marconi—received their share of military orders. On one occasion the Signal Corps placed a single order for 80,000 tubes, which by this time had to be produced according to uniform government specifications. All of the companies were working on the same product, which had the effect of wedding the various companies in a single effort and bringing the various technologies into synchronization.

During the war years there was a regular threat that American ideas and secrets would be stolen by the enemy, and research became top secret. President Woodrow Wilson became convinced that international communication, with oil and shipping, represented the key to the balance of power in foreign relations, and he urged American industry to dominate this field, not letting American inventions or American patents get into foreign hands. When the war was over, with a new wave of isolationism sweeping the land, this technological nationalism did not abate, and there was a continuing pressure to do something about the one foreign apple in the barrel: British-owned American Marconi Corporation.

American Marconi obviously was now in an untenable position. During the war the government had seized all of its land stations, and neither the United States Navy nor the United States government was in any mood to return these installations to a British-owned company. High-level negotiations between government and industry were called for, and most of the talking was done by General Electric's Owen D. Young, one of the most gifted and resourceful negotiators on the American business scene. An outright seizure of American Marconi was of course impossible; the British stockholders would have to be compensated. The obvious solution was to establish a gigantic dummy corporation that could buy out American Marconi, allowing the British to have their share, but at the same time giving even larger chunks to all of the major American companies.

Accordingly, on October 17, 1919, the Radio Corporation of America was born.[5] Much effort was made to give the impression that this new corporation had a quasi-public status: Provision was made for a representative of the government to be on the board of directors. Most importantly, among the articles of incorporation was a provision that only American citizens might be officers or directors, and that not more than 20 percent of the stock could be held by foreigners. Owners of American Marconi were placated by receiving RCA shares in place of American Marconi stock, but the new young giant was mainly beefed up by the interests of the competing companies, all of which stepped forward for a piece of the action. Taking up large blocks of stock were GE, AT&T, the Western Electric Company, and the Westinghouse Electric and Manufacturing Company.

A month after this great paper dragon was crafted, Owen D. Young of GE was elected chairman of the board, and Edward J. Nally of the former American Marconi became president. But because the company almost immediately took over the many installations of the old Marconi Company, it virtually controlled radio telegraphy in the United States.

Chairman Young believed that his first mission was to do something about the patent logjam that had the radio industry paralyzed. Testifying a few years later before the Senate Committee on Internal Commerce, Young recalled the frightful complexity of things in 1919: "It was utterly impossible for anybody to do anything in radio . . . at that time. . . . Nobody had patents enough to make a system. And so there was a complete stalemate." Young, however, found a way to break that stalemate. Over the next few years a series of cross-licensing agreements were made among GE, AT&T, Westinghouse and RCA (the latter now having the patents of the old Marconi Company). The patent pools and licensing agreements broke the logjam and allowed the radio business to move forward.

An auxiliary benefit of these agreements was that they carefully laid down the special areas of interest of the various members of the group. AT&T, of course, was allowed to maintain control over telephonic communication whether by wire or wireless. General Electric and Westinghouse would use RCA patents in the manufacture of equipment, but RCA would get to do the selling of the other firms' equipment. General Electric and Westinghouse could also make transmitters for their own use, but not for sale to others.

One thing that nobody was thinking about in 1919 was radiotelephony. Owen D. Young was too busy thinking about the complexities of patent pooling and of foreign competition. As far as radio operations were concerned, RCA had a virtual monopoly on radiotelegraphy, and that was a more than satisfactory form of revenue. Radiotelephony was still mired in the mud of patent wars, but perhaps it wouldn't matter. There wasn't that much interest in radiotelephony anyway, except perhaps for a few amateurs and dabblers. In any case, commercial broadcasting was not a brisk topic of discussion in the board rooms and offices of the Radio Corporation of America.

There was one exception, and that was in the person of young David Sarnoff, one of the many executives of the American Marconi Company who had moved to RCA. Sarnoff, the boyish wireless operator who had maintained contact from his station in New York with the rescuing vessels at the time of the *Titanic* disaster in 1912, used every opportunity to talk up the idea of radio broadcasting. He had in fact done so while still employed by American

When RCA was founded, it luckily obtained the services of the radio industry's one authentic prophet and organizational genius: the young David Sarnoff, shown here in earlier years as a 16-year-old office boy (1907) for the Marconi Wireless Company. (Photo courtesy RCA.)

Marconi in 1916. In his capacity as assistant traffic manager, he wrote a memo that year to his superiors envisioning a use of radiotelephony that must have seemed foolish and impractical at the time, but that in fact pointed the direction in which the whole industry would have to move. His memo said in part:

> I have in mind a plan of development which would make radio a household utility in the same sense as the piano or the phonograph. The idea is to bring music into the house by wireless.... The receiver can be designed in the form of a simple "Radio Music Box" and arranged for several different wave lengths. . . . The main revenue to be derived will be from the sale of the "Radio Music Boxes" which if manufactured in lots of one hundred thousand or so could yield a handsome profit.... Aside from the profit ... the possibilities for advertising for the company are tremendous; for its name would ultimately be brought into the household and wireless would receive national and universal attention.[6]

Alas, Sarnoff's was a voice crying in the wilderness. He would bring the subject up over and over again to Young and to his other superiors at RCA, but RCA was too big and too busy to be playing around with this puny step-child which seemed to have no clear-cut commercial future. RCA just couldn't be bothered. They had too much else to do. Was there somebody around who did?

Yes, suddenly there was someone interested in radio broadcasting. It was the Westinghouse Electric and Manufacturing Company, which had been the big loser in the radio sweepstakes when the Radio Corporation of America gobbled up all the fruits in 1919. To be sure, Westinghouse was a stockholder in the newly formed radio giant, but that was small consolation for its losses. During World War I, Westinghouse had many government contracts for the manufacture of radio equipment, but these had now dried up. RCA had taken over commercial radiotelegraphy in the United States as a virtual monopoly, so Westinghouse was cut off in this direction also. What was there to do?

For a while it seemed that there might be some opportunities abroad, and immediately after the war Westinghouse sent envoys to European radio companies with the idea of negotiating deals for transoceanic radio since there was seemingly more business than RCA could handle. Alas, Owen D. Young had gotten there first, and had most of the European business sewn up. There seemed to be nowhere for Westinghouse to maneuver.

But Westinghouse had been fortunate in acquiring a few patents that had not already been swallowed up by RCA, one of those belonging to Reginald Fessenden and going back to the primitive days of radio experimentation. Even more important, as things turned out, were the patents of the young Signal Corps veteran Major Edwin H. Armstrong. Armstrong's "feedback" patent was bought by Westinghouse in spite of the dispute with De Forest. Too, Armstrong had come home from the war with something even more important: his "superheterodyne circuit," which accomplished an amplification of sound far superior to the earlier feedback circuit and which would turn out to be a prime ingredient of radio technology in the years ahead. For his two patents Westinghouse offered Armstrong $335,000, payable over a 10-year period, with promise of additional amounts if Armstrong won his feedback patent suit. Westinghouse made the purchase just in time, since GE was also offering money for the same patents, and Armstrong might have been tempted to hold out.

Still, even with these additional patents in hand there was no clear idea of what Westinghouse would do with them. The radio side of the Westinghouse Company was withering on the vine. Production of radio equipment had fallen off sharply and no new customers stepped forward. Westinghouse staged radio demonstrations for railroads that ran tugboats and ferryboats on the Hudson River at New York, with the idea of drumming up business, but this did not meet with success. The scientists who had been assigned to radio work at Westinghouse were eventually given other work. One of the radio leaders at Westinghouse, Frank Conrad, was put to work on electric switches. His assistant, Donald G. Little, was assigned to work on lightning arrestors. Among the newcomers at Westinghouse was Vladimir K. Zworykin, who had been a communication specialist in the czarist army and was a refugee from the new regime in Russia. Zworykin had worked on television experiments in Russia and asked to pursue them at Westinghouse, but Westinghouse saw little hope in that area at the time.

Still, the Westinghouse radio men had not thrown in the towel. They were determined to persist, even if it meant working on their own. And this was particularly true of Frank Conrad, one of the most gifted and resourceful workers in the company's employ. Conrad was another of those self-taught geniuses unblessed by the constraints of formal academic training. He had dropped out of school in the seventh grade, and had worked his way up at Westinghouse from a bench-hand trainee.

But Conrad was a veritable fountain of ideas. Even before the war he was a radio amateur using his garage laboratory, and his wartime contributions were little short of startling. He had designed and tested for the Signal Corps some transmitters and receivers (SCR-69 and SCR-70), and these had been a big success. Much of the testing of the SCR-69 and SCR-70 had been done in Conrad's garage. He came to hold some 200 patents in a number of areas. During the war, in addition to his compact radio receivers and transmitters, he developed a wind-driven generator that could be attached to the wings of airplanes and power their radio transmitters. This resulted, at the end of the war, in the capability of transmitting voice messages from ground to airplanes, a highly prized achievement.

After the war, when Conrad's radio work at Westinghouse fell off sharply, he carried on his experiments in his spare time in his little garage laboratory in suburban Wilkinsburg, just east of Pittsburgh. He was now using vacuum tubes in his amateur operations, and his signal was regularly picked up by a number of other amateurs in the Pittsburgh area. During the early months of 1920 the private Conrad laboratory had become a kind of beehive of radio activity, with enthusiasts and kindred spirits showing up for work and conversation every weekend. Regularly Conrad was sending out his signal, talking to other amateurs, sometimes playing phonograph records, always appealing for information about how good the reception was. Word got out that this radio thing was a lot of fun, and more and more people were swept up in the enthusiasm for what looked like a nifty little hobby.

As time wore on, Conrad's home station (call letters 8XK) more and more took on the appearance of a permanent radio station. Conrad's two sons regularly worked as announcers; the Hamilton Music Store in Wilkinsburg loaned records, for which favor it was mentioned on the air. The music was well enough liked that eventually the Conrads started what seemed to be regular "concerts" on Saturday nights. Even the general public became aware of this burgeoning radio station, and Conrad garnered a certain amount of local notoriety. A newspaper item on May 2, 1920, announced a piano solo by one of the Conrad sons, and the technology of it was explained. A line was to be run from the Conrad home to the garage laboratory, and the sound then "sent out into the ether by the radiophone apparatus located there."

As the months of 1920 passed by, amateur interest increased, and a number of people in the Pittsburgh area were wondering how they might be able to obtain sets of their own. In early September, the Joseph Horne Department Store in Pittsburgh put an ad in the *Pittsburgh Sun* notifying the public that the store had on display a radio set for amateur use that could pick up the Conrad radio programs. Not only was the Horne Company going to display and demonstrate this equipment, they were going to sell it as well: "Amateur Wireless Sets, made by the maker of the set which is in operation in our store, are on sale here, $10.00 up."[7]

Amateur wireless sets on sale! On sale to the general public, not just to the radio ham or buff! The day the ad appeared, Harry P. Davis, vice president at Westinghouse, saw the ad in the newspaper, and it aroused his interest. He was Conrad's superior at Westinghouse, and of course he knew all about Conrad's amateur broadcasts. But the sale of radio sets to the public — here was an idea that nobody had thought of before. Even if Westinghouse had been shoved out of the central core of the radio business as it now stood, perhaps something new could be drummed up. Sets not merely for radio "professionals" but for the general public — all made by Westinghouse, of course.

The day following the Horne advertisement, Davis held a conference with Conrad and other Westinghouse officials raising the possibility of building a bigger and more powerful transmitter at the Westinghouse plant, with the plan of offering radio broadcasting on a regular basis. In subsequent conferences Davis wondered if it would be possible to have a station and a suitable transmitter ready for regular operation in time for the Harding-Cox presidential election on November 2. Yes, it was definitely possible, said Conrad, and accordingly he and Donald Little were assigned to the task.

The immediate objective was to get ready for the election, now only two months away, but the long-term objective was a regular broadcasting service that could be depended on by listeners day after day and week after week. The technical problems would not be hard to overcome with Conrad at the helm; the public relations aspect of the thing was a bit more involved. But everything moved apace. On the roof of one of the buildings at Westinghouse's East Pittsburgh plant a shack and 100-watt transmitter were built. To give additional range, an antenna ran from the roof of the shack to one of the powerhouse smokestacks. On October 16, the Westinghouse Company applied to the United States Department of Commerce for a license to begin a regular broadcasting service. By telephone a few days later Westinghouse received permission to use the amateur call letters 8ZZ in case the formal and written license was not received by November 2. However, on October 27, formal notification arrived, and the station received the call letters KDKA (these were the same as those used in commercial shore stations). The station was authorized to use 360 meters, giving them a clear channel away from amateur use.

Dr. Frank Conrad, the Westinghouse engineer whose experimental work and frequent broadcasts to local radio enthusiasts led to the establishment of station KDKA in Pittsburgh. (Photo courtesy Westinghouse Broadcasting and Cable Co.)

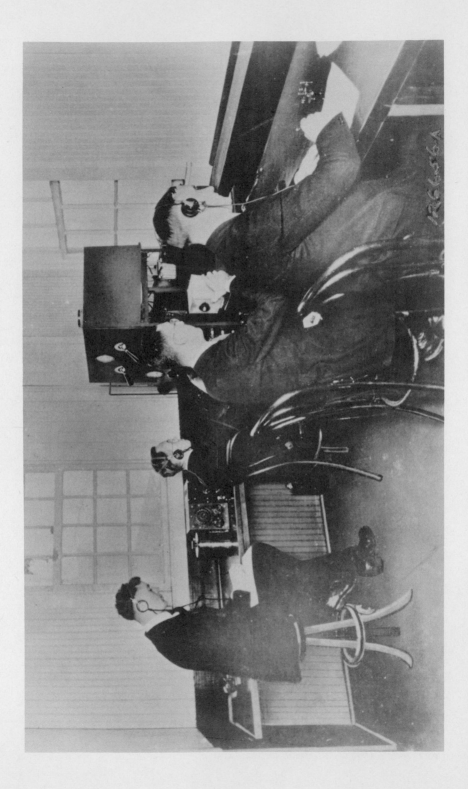

Westinghouse was also beginning production of sets for home use, and these, together with the imminent inauguration of programming, were given ample notice in the local press. As things turned out, the flood of new sets did not begin until well after the election, but Westinghouse was laying plans for selling them. They were also making preparations for the programming that was to go out over the air since if one is going to have regular broadcasting one has to have something to broadcast. Arrangements were made to have the *Pittsburgh Post* telephone the election results to Westinghouse as soon as they became available from the news wire services. Filling up the gaps would be a banjo player and some of those reliable old phonograph records that had been a major part of Conrad's private broadcasts.

The big night came and went without a hitch. To be on the safe side Frank Conrad was standing by at his own transmitter at Wilkinsburg, prepared to send out the returns from there if necessary. But it wasn't necessary. The broadcast on election night began at 8 P. M. Eastern Standard Time and ran until after midnight. Donald Little and John Frazier were in charge of the technical side of the operation, and Leo Rosenberg of Westinghouse's publicity department read the bulletins as they came in.

About the elections there had been little doubt from the beginning—Harding and Coolidge were easy winners over Cox and Roosevelt. There might have been some doubts in the Westinghouse boardroom about the fate of KDKA, but there needn't have been. The evening was a smashing success, and the next day scores of telephone calls from listeners came through the Westinghouse switchboard. There were many more listeners than there were sets, listeners mainly gathering in large numbers at central locations—churches, lodges, the private homes of Westinghouse executives—to be guinea pigs for the experiment. Everyone was delighted.

Historically, the important thing was that KDKA did not simply turn off its power and fold up after the election night special, but, as promised, continued its nightly broadcasts on a regular basis. At first the broadcast time was a single hour—8:30 to 9:30 P.M.—but before long the schedule would be expanded. Quite well aware of the nationwide publicity that had been given to the station, Westinghouse in a matter of weeks replaced the 100-watt transmitter with a 500-watt transmitter. In those days the airwaves were uncluttered and, weather permitting, the signal of the Pittsburgh station could be picked up in Washington, D.C., or out on the prairie of Illinois. KDKA also began experimenting with all the peripheral aspects of the art, constructing the first "radio studio" of record. A national institution had been established.

For the first time a radio station had attempted to appeal to a *mass* audience. KDKA's intent was to sell sets to the general public—not sets by the

The first broadcast of KDKA, Pittsburgh, goes out over the air on Nov. 2, 1920, reporting the Harding-Cox presidential election returns. Pictured here, the first broadcasting staff (left–right): William Thomas, operator; L.H. Rosenberg, announcer; R.S. McClelland and John Frazier handling telephone lines to the newspaper office. (Photo courtesy Westinghouse Broadcasting and Cable Co.)

dozen, but, as things turned out, by the millions. When the year 1920 began the only people who thought about radio thought of it as an art that could be understood and enjoyed only by the expert or the electronics whiz. When the year 1920 was over there were few who failed to see that radio was calling out to everybody. Now it just might be that the radio receiver could be a household utility like the stove, the phonograph and the electric light. The technology of home reception was still primitive, but the institution was there.

2. The Radio Rage

If KDKA was to be the stimulus that would give birth to an entirely new era in wireless history, the evidence of it was neither immediate nor dramatic. A great radio boom was just around the corner, but it did not come, as one might expect, in the months immediately following KDKA's debut — rather it had to wait until early 1922, over a year after that election-night broadcast of 1920. Between November 2, 1920, and December 31, 1921, only nine additional stations were listed in the *Radio Service Bulletin* of the Department of Commerce as being licensed for general broadcasting. But in the first few months of 1922 scores of new stations would seek and receive licenses, and the broadcasting idea would then spread like wildfire around the country.

In retrospect, the rather timid development of 1920–21 is not hard to understand. Westinghouse executives had founded KDKA with the idea that a regular broadcasting station would stimulate the sale of Westinghouse-made radio receivers. But full-scale production of such sets was not yet underway, and the audience for radio broadcasts would of necessity be the same small number of amateurs that had made up the radio audience late in 1920. During 1921 no completely assembled and ready-to-use radio receivers were on the market. Tube sets would be coming in shortly, but in 1921 nearly every set sold to the general public employed the older (and relatively inexpensive) crystal components. Reception on these sets remained difficult and erratic.

Too, broadcasting hadn't really proven itself to be a medium that people couldn't do without. KDKA and soon a few others were broadcasting regularly (although on a very limited schedule), but the quality of programming was primitive and amateurish. Early in 1921 KDKA selected its first regular announcer and program manager, Harold W. Arlin. Arlin used all of his resources to think up new ideas that would appeal to the listening audience, but for many months he had to rely heavily on playing borrowed phonograph records, reading news headlines and community service bulletins, and giving extended explanations of the Arlington time signals. There was not really enough on the radio to make this new medium of communication a wildly popular pastime.

Nonetheless, the broadcasting idea had taken hold. In the wake of the KDKA success, Donald Little was sent around the country to prepare for similar broadcasting stations at other Westinghouse installations in the eastern United States. Three of these began operations in 1921: WJZ in Newark, New

23

Top: *In the early days of radio broadcasting, the engineering department, and even the entire studio, were relegated to some shed or factory loft. Here is WGY's engineer at work in General Electric's Schenectady works in 1922. Bottom: The WGY players. To calm the jitters of performers in the early days, the microphone that made them nervous was often disguised as a lamp, complete with shade. Note also the heavy drapes and thick carpeting used to kill resonance in the studio. (Photos courtesy General Electric.)*

Jersey, WBZ in Springfield, Massachusetts, and KYW in Chicago (atop the Commonwealth Edison Building).

This bustle of activity at Westinghouse did not go unnoticed in the executive offices of the competitor companies. Any and all of the giant companies involved in radio could have thought of the broadcasting concept, but all the competitors had been preoccupied with other things that seemed to be promising big profits. At the Schenectady plant of General Electric, William C. White called for the installation of a station at that plant, and discovered himself and his colleagues amazed at their lack of foresight in thinking up the idea. De Forest Radio and Telegraph Company received a license for general broadcasting (New York station WJX) in 1921, as did the still-skeptical RCA.

Historically, it is interesting to note that RCA had a jump on Westinghouse in the New York area. It did not establish its short-lived station in Roselle Park until the fall of 1921, but just months after the establishment of KDKA, David Sarnoff—who had of course been trying to sell RCA on the broadcasting concept all along—was on the lookout for something big and exciting that might be worth broadcasting and also gain widespread public attention. He found it in the summer of 1921 in one of the most spectacular events of early broadcasting—the heavyweight boxing championship bout between Jack Dempsey and Georges Carpentier. This fight, for which RCA received a one-day license to operate a one-day station (WJY) with a borrowed Navy transmitter, made the radio phenomenon highly newsworthy even before Westinghouse was able to open its first regular station in the New York area. The fight, broadcast by Major J. Andrew White, editor of *Wireless Age* magazine, was said to have been tuned in by as many as 300,000 listeners, some as far away as Florida.

As to WJZ, the new Westinghouse station was licensed on June 1, 1921, but did not begin broadcasting until September (officially, it began its operations on October 1, 1921). The studio and transmitter were located at the Westinghouse meter plant in Newark at the corner of Plane and Orange streets. The location was not, as some later recalled, in a forlorn part of the Newark factory district, but only a few blocks from the downtown business district. It was nonetheless a factory, with a strictly factory-like atmosphere.

This first long-term, regularly broadcasting New York area station had been planned by Westinghouse for over a year, apparently, but little was done with the project for many months. When regular broadcasting began on October 1, it was from a hastily gotten-up studio, and in response to an immediate need, which was to broadcast the World Series between the New York Giants and the New York Yankees. It was an ideal opportunity to cash in on the radio enthusiasm generated by the Dempsey fight three months before. The World Series was broadcast as the station's highly successful debut, although the techniques of transmission were crude and tentative.

As manager for WJZ, Westinghouse had chosen an engineer from its own staff, Charles B. Popenoe, a man with no previous radio experience but apparently full of ideas and anxious to learn. Popenoe had been born in Dayton, Ohio, in 1887, and studied mechanical engineering at the University of Texas,

The First General Broadcasting Stations in the United States

(Stations listed in the Radio Service Bulletin of the Department of Commerce as broadcasting market or weather reports, music, concerts, lectures, etc. and licensed during the years 1920–1921. These ten stations were the only stations listed for 1920–1921. They were joined by scores of others in the first few months of 1922.)

Station	Owner	Location	Date of Listing
KDKA	Westinghouse Electric and Manufacturing Co.	East Pittsburgh, Pa.	Nov. 1920
WJZ	Westinghouse Electric and Manufacturing Co.	Newark, N.J.	July 1920
WRR	City of Dallas, Texas	Dallas, Texas	Sept. 1921
WBZ	Westinghouse Electric and Manufacturing Co.	Springfield, Mass.	Oct. 1921
WDY	Radio Corporation of America	Roselle Park, N.J.	Oct. 1921
WCJ	A.C. Gilbert Co.	New Haven, Conn.	Oct. 1921
WJX	De Forest Radio and Telegraph Co.	New York, N.Y.	Nov. 1921
KQV	Doubleday-Hill Electric Co.	Pittsburgh, Pa.	Nov. 1921
KQL	Arno A. Kluge	Los Angeles, Calif.	Nov. 1921
KYW	Westinghouse Electric and Manufacturing Co.	Chicago, Ill.	Dec. 1921

where he graduated in the class of 1912. Trained for construction engineering, Popenoe took his first job with the Department of Public Works in his home state of Ohio, a job he kept until World War I broke out. During the war he served as an army engineer, rising to the rank of captain, but did not see service abroad. He joined the Westinghouse Company in 1919, handling a number of different assignments until he became manager of WJZ when it was founded in 1921.[1]

As station manager Popenoe reported directly to the plant manager, H.E. Miller. To assist him in running the station he was assigned an engineer, George Blitziotis, a Belgian who had once worked for Marconi, and Thomas H.

Cowan, who became announcer and general factotum. Cowan, a native New Jerseyan, was also a Westinghouse employee with virtually no experience or knowledge of radio, summarily requisitioned to develop this new field of radio announcing. Like Popenoe, he started knowing nothing about broadcasting, but he would soon know everything there was to know.

The studios and other facilities were every bit as primitive in Newark as they had been at Pittsburgh. In a memoir of the early days of radio, Popenoe described the facilities at Newark:

> It was now decided to establish a studio, and half of the ladies' rest room of the Newark works was set aside for the purpose, making a space some thirty feet long by fifteen feet wide. Microphones were installed, the necessary wiring from these instruments to the roof, a control panel placed in order to keep announcers and operators in direct communication, and the room draped in dark red material not only to add to its appearance, but to subdue any echo noticeable. A few pieces of furniture were secured and a piano rented of the Griffith Piano Company of Newark.[2]

Filling the broadcast day at WJZ was something of a problem, as it had been at KDKA. In the beginning the station only broadcast in the evening, unless of course there was some eminently attractive daytime event like the World Series. Announcer Cowan, who had once worked for Thomas Edison in his laboratory in West Orange, New Jersey, borrowed a phonograph from that device's celebrated inventor and played records to fill up the gaps. Occasionally a speaker or singer would be invited or somebody would play a few songs on the piano. A typical Sunday schedule from WJZ's Newark days indicates the sparseness of the programming:

7:55–8:05 — Two test records on Edison phonograph.
8:10–8:15 — *Newark Sunday Call* news read by Thomas Cowan.
8:15–8:18 — Stand by 3 minutes.
All quiet.
8:20 — Sacred selections on Edison phonograph.
8:35 — Sacred selections on Edison phonograph.
8:50 — Stand by 3 minutes. KZN and WNY.
8:55 — Sacred selections on Edison phonograph.
9:15 — End of concert.
WJZ signing off.
9:50 — Explain Arlington time signals.
9:55–10:00 — NAA time signals.
10:05 — Weather forecast.
10:10 — WJZ signing off.
10:25 — Played an Edison record for Walter 2B2H, a local manager, the gentleman who installed Westinghouse receivers.[3]

Programming was not to remain this lean for long, however. Announcer Cowan proved to be very resourceful in rounding up talent and bringing to Newark entertainers who would sound good on the radio. Most of them had to come out from New York, which was none too pleasant. Newark was a mere ten miles away, but it was a trip by Hudson Tube or Pennsylvania Railroad across the foul-smelling Jersey Meadows. Nevertheless, as it shortly became evident that the station *was* being listened to in the vast New York metropolitan area, the performers—at least those with a sense of adventure—soon started to come in larger numbers.

After exhausting the generosity of his old employer Thomas Edison, who wasn't too keen on radio because he thought it vastly inferior to his phonograph, Cowan began to solicit record companies and musical organizations in New York. On the first of November, Pathé Records sent a quartette called the Shannon Four, later to be known as the Revelers. Shortly thereafter Pathé sent another act, Billy Jones and Ernie Hare, soon to become the best known song and comedy act in the early days of radio.

Officials of the Aeolian Company in New York became very interested in WJZ and loaned the station a Weber-Duo-Art grand piano and a vocalion for playing records. In November and December 1921 they sent the famous pianist and composer Percy Grainger, and a number of singers, including John Charles Thomas, Johanna Glaski, May Peterson and Marie Sundelius. (Thomas, for one, would remain an important figure in radio music for years, and appeared regularly on musical programs throughout the golden age of radio.)

Very quickly at WJZ, radio programming took on the general mix that it was to have in the years ahead. There were times for orchestral music, times for humorous speeches, times for weather programs. Special programs for women appeared, and also for children (a time for children's bedtime stories was established between 7:00 and 7:30 in those early days). One of the best known of these early children's series was "Man in the Moon," in which Bill McNeary read the stories, most of which were written by Josephine Lawrence of the *Newark Sunday Call*, a lady who later went on to become a highly popular writer of adult fiction.

Religious programming soon became an important feature of radio, and it started at WJZ on Christmas Eve, 1921, when the Rev. George P. Dougherty of the Christ Episcopal Church in suburban Glen Ridge, New Jersey, read a Christmas Eve message to the public. The next month Rev. Dougherty was asked to inaugurate a religious service to be heard every Sunday from 3:00 to 3:45 P.M. Clergymen of all other denominations were invited to participate, and the series became a solid success. Religious broadcasting would assume large dimensions by the end of the twenties, with many religious denominations and even individual churches having their own radio stations.

WJZ's biggest concern, however, during the first year of its operation, was getting performers to come to Newark who would be reliable and regular. One of the most reliable from Cowan's point of view was Vaughn de Leath, the young lady who had earned the title "First Lady of Radio" way back in 1916 when she sang over the airwaves for Lee De Forest. She earned her title once again in 1921–22 when she became a regular on WJZ. Tommy Cowan would sweep by her New York apartment and proclaim, "Come on, you're going to Newark," and Miss De Leath would obligingly take the foul tube ride over to Newark to sing before the mike.

Before WJZ phased out its Newark studio, the station made every effort to lure and pamper singers and stars of Broadway or vaudeville. For a time they provided a limousine to fetch the stars to the studio, posted a uniformed doorman at the door of the factory, tendered champagne and flowers. Tommy Cowan would even greet the stars dressed in a tuxedo, and the studio which had been moved to the first floor for ease of accessibility, was as opulently decked out as was humanly possible in a factory ambience.

Present and future big names did come to Newark late in 1921 and early 1922. Paul Whiteman brought his orchestra. On February 19, 1922, WJZ presented its first Broadway stage show on the air: Ed Wynn's "The Perfect Fool." Wynn's first encounter with the radio microphone was apparently not a happy one, and he disappeared from the radio scene for nearly a decade, finally returning as one of the medium's most popular comedians in the early days of the depression.

Opera by radio came to the New York area for the first time on March 15, 1922, when WJZ broadcast Mozart's comic opera *The Impresario.* This was not a "remote" telephone broadcast from the stage of the Metropolitan Opera House in New York; rather a touring company was hauled in toto to the Westinghouse plant, where they were herded into a 10' × 40' makeshift studio on the second floor for their first exposure to the medium.

A figure whose name was long identified with opera broadcasting appeared at WJZ in those early days in Newark. This was Milton J. Cross, who heard the radio for the first time when he was visiting some friends in the New Jersey city. Cross gathered that WJZ might be looking for talent to perform on the air, and being a trained tenor with some performing experience to his credit, he wrote Tommy Cowan offering to sing over the airwaves. Cowan invited him to visit the studio, but he and Charles Popenoe were even more impressed with his speaking voice than his singing voice, so he was offered an announcing job, which he took with some reluctance. Cross went on to become one of the great radio announcers, for many years the announcer of the Saturday afternoon Metropolitan Opera broadcasts, his devoted listeners probably forgetting that he began his radio career in 1922 singing plaintive songs like "Little Mother of Mine."

When Milton Cross joined WJZ, radio broadcasting was still a primitive, catch-as-catch-can business. Everybody on the payroll was expected to do everything there was to do: give time signals, play records, announce a singer, improvise at the piano, perhaps even double as engineer if the need arose. But things were ready to boom, and before long station WJZ and all connected with it would be in the big time. Before too many months, WJZ opened a studio in New York at the Waldorf Astoria Hotel (then located at Fifth Avenue and 34th Street, the present site of the Empire State Building), this studio being connected to the Newark transmitter by a Western Union wire. By the spring of 1923, the whole WJZ operation was moved to New York, where it was housed at Aeolian Hall at 33 West 42nd Street. By this time, the experimental phase of radio broadcasting was quickly fading into the history books.

Westinghouse's WBZ in Springfield, Massachusetts, and KYW in Chicago also opened in 1921. WBZ actually began broadcasting a few days before WJZ, in September 1921, but received its license later. The choice of Springfield as a location may not be obvious today, but the Springfield plant had been selected as the place where Westinghouse would turn out those newly demanded receivers that were supposed to be the financial base of this new phenomenon called broadcasting.

What went on in Chicago was altogether different. KYW deserves a high place in the annals of radio history because it was, from the start, a specialized radio station. Here were no time signals, no weather bulletins, no phonograph records, no chitchat, none of the usual attributes of a general station. KYW in its first year had but one kind of programming: opera. Programming consisted of broadcasts of the Chicago Civic Opera Company, six days a week, afternoon and evening. The first broadcast in the Chicago area took place on November 11, 1921, and featured the voice of soprano Mary Garden. This program and subsequent broadcasts of the opera were a phenomenal success, and apparently did as much for the radio in Chicago as the Dempsey-Carpentier fight did in New York. As the year 1921 ended, there were plans for as many as a dozen new stations in the Chicago area.

Of course when the 1921–22 opera season was over in Chicago, KYW had to look around for something else, or face the prospect of trailing off into silence. Accordingly a small studio was prepared in the Commonwealth Edison Building (a welcome departure from the usual Westinghouse practice of factory studios), suitably hung with heavy draperies for acoustical purposes. Area Westinghouse salesmen were requisitioned to serve as announcers, and plans were shortly made for more diversified programming. Almost immediately a full range of programming was projected: Western Union was hired to run lines to the baseball stadiums, arrangements were made with the International News Service to provide news bulletins, and the inevitable playing of phonograph records filled in the gaps. But the phenomenal popularity of those early opera broadcasts would not fade from memory, and opera would become an early favorite of radio listening audiences everywhere during the 1920s.

If a dozen new stations were in the planning stage in Chicago as the twenties began, it was clear that broadcasting was about to discover an unwanted and hitherto undreamed of ingredient: competition. All of the stations operating in 1921 were placed sufficiently distant from one another that they could freely beam their signals to their listening audiences without interference. But as the popularity of radio broadcasting spread, interference would become a nagging anxiety. Shortly would come a time when the proliferation of broadcasting stations would seem to present insurmountable problems.

At first there was a spirit of cooperation whenever a second station moved into a given area, but this cooperation eventually evaporated when the going got tough. And at the time, there was no way of keeping competitors from entering the same territory and on the same wavelength. WJZ, for example, was for some time the only station broadcasting regularly in the New York metropolitan area. The headstart it enjoyed continued to make it the dominant station in the area for several years. But when competition arrived it was pretty brisk. It arrived first at the hand of the Radio Corporation of America. Newly named RCA General Manager David Sarnoff, not satisfied with the one-day broadcast in July 1921 that actually preceded WJZ's debut, had been itching to have his own broadcasting station in the New York area long before Westinghouse intruded into this vicinity so far away from its corporate headquarters. WJZ had clearly stolen the march on Sarnoff, but he was undaunted, and before the year 1921 was over he had his own station in operation.

The station was WDY, and it went on the air at Roselle Park, New Jersey, on December 14, 1921. In a way, the station was a successor to the one-day WJY. In fact some of the equipment used for the broadcast of the Dempsey-Carpentier fight back in July was put into use at Roselle Park. The reason for the station's location at Roselle Park is rather curious. This suburban town in Union County, New Jersey, only a few miles from WJZ's transmitter in Newark, was the site of a General Electric plant, and RCA had arranged this station as a cooperative venture with General Electric, which was chafing at the bit and anxious to get into the broadcasting field.

Once again the ambience of the station's studio was that of a factory, poorly located in terms of the entertainment centers of New York. On the other hand, Sarnoff had taken some pains to do the thing right, and the studio was more spacious and pleasing than the factory loft studios Westinghouse had started out with. Swept away was the workshop atmosphere, and instead there were a dignified studio and foyer, decorated with rugs, draperies, and specially appointed furniture. More important, Station WDY hired a manager with extensive radio background. He was Major J. Andrew White, founder and editor of *Wireless Age* magazine, a man who knew everything that was going on in the radio field and had large numbers of contacts with every phase of radio broadcasting and technology. It was he who had broadcast the Dempsey-Carpentier fight for RCA in July. He was also a man with a wide range of acquaintances in theatrical and sporting circles, so it seemed obvious that he could get programming going at WDY in a glorious fashion if anybody could. And he did.

The first program on WDY was broadcast from 9:15 to 10:15 P.M. on December 14, 1921. There were several artists on hand for the occasion: Louis Brean, piano solo; Harry Howard, singer of popular songs; Jack Cook, vaudevillian; and Nat Saunders, comedian. Major White was not necessarily more assiduous in rounding up talent than WJZ's Tommy Cowan, but his theatrical contacts proved invaluable. Comedian Eddie Cantor came over when he was not appearing in the Ziegfeld Follies. There were entertainers on all levels. Friday night became a special event at WDY, especially a program called "Radio Party," which invariably featured one or more big stars from New York. The stars' only payment was a champagne dinner, but of course all were aware that there was a certain amount of benefit accruing to their professional reputations.

In spite of its sprightly programming, the WDY experiment was short-lived, suffering a sudden but painless death before the winter of 1922 was over. The reason for its demise was that RCA reached an agreement with Westinghouse to buy and operate WJZ, which, for all the efforts of WDY, still had the largest listening audience in the New York area. By early 1922, parent companies were deeply concerned about the rising costs of broadcasting and about the still unanswered question of who was going to pay the bill for this new form of communication when it grew to gigantic proportions. The thought doubtless was that a single powerful station in New York would be the most practical solution, and plans were afoot to move WJZ to New York and away from the factory in Newark. WDY went off the air on February 24, 1922, thus giving WJZ a monopoly of the New York metropolitan area listening audience.

Not for long, however. It was now 1922, the year when the desire to own and operate radio stations became a national passion. Stations sprang up everywhere, like mushrooms on a spring lawn. For half of 1921 there had been a single station, KDKA, broadcasting on a regular schedule. Then, at the end of the year, a flurry of others. But according to the *Radio Service Bulletin* of the U.S. Department of Commerce, the numbers of new stations in the first five months of 1922 looked like this:

Month	No. of Stations Licensed
January 1922	26
February 1922	14
March 1922	27
April 1922	88
May 1922	99

All of a sudden everybody wanted to own a broadcasting station and have his message heard over the airwaves. Of the scores of new stations that turned on the power in the first six months of 1922, no single pattern of ownership appeared. Probably the largest numbers were owned by radio stores, electric supply companies, radio dealers and equipment manufacturers. But there were plenty of others, including a substantial number of individuals who had the money to plunk down for a license, but doubtless only a faint idea of what they were going to do with this strange new opportunity. A few distinct trends did become evident, however.

Among the earliest to get on the radio bandwagon were newspapers. Very few of them thought of this new medium as a competitor, but they obviously realized the public relations value of radio station ownership. Among the newspaper-owned stations from early 1922 were KUO, San Francisco (*San Francisco Examiner*); WAAL, Minneapolis (*Minneapolis Tribune*); KWH, Los Angeles (*Los Angeles Examiner*); and WAAB, New Orleans (*New Orleans Times-Picayune*). The very early *Detroit News* station continued in operation, now known as WWJ.

Another category of owners was department stores, many rapidly opening radio departments or radio sections. Among the stores starting stations during these early months were John Wanamaker in New York (WWZ), the Fair Store in Chicago (WGU), Stix-Baer-Fuller in St. Louis (WCK) and Gimbel Brothers in Philadelphia (WIP). One of the most important of the early department store stations was WOR, started by the L. Bamberger Department Store in Newark, obviously an affront to WJZ, still located in the same city. In later years, after it moved to New York, WOR became the anchor station of the Mutual Radio network.

Colleges and universities also saw the educational possibilities of radio, either for instructional purposes or because radio technology was a hot topic in the curriculum. Many of the new educational stations were started to serve a quasi-public function at large land-grant universities, and a good number of these were established in the first few months of 1922: WCM at the University of Texas, Austin; WRM at the University of Illinois, Urbana; WLB at the University of Minnesota, St. Paul. But private universities were also interested, as evidenced by WAAC at Tulane University, New Orleans and WEW at St. Louis University. Even small colleges did not hesitate to enter the hotly competitive field, producing WBAW at Marietta College, Marietta, Ohio; WBAE at the James Bradley Polytechnic Institute, at Peoria, Ill.; and KGY at St. Martin's College, in Lacey, Washington.

Another pattern that persisted over the years was the ownership of radio stations by churches and religious organizations: KJS, of the Bible Institute of Los Angeles; KTW of the First Presbyterian Church of Seattle, Washington; and KOA of the Young Men's Christian Association of Denver, Colorado.

Municipal ownership of radio stations would become commonplace in the 1920s, although the practice declined somewhat in later years. The first such station was WRR in Dallas, Texas, which actually made its appearance late in 1921. The station was run by the Dallas fire and police departments but was licensed for general broadcasting to the public. The city of Chicago established WBU in March 1922.

All of these styles were and are readily understandable, but they hardly exhausted the possibilities, and in those euphoric months of early 1922 radio stations were licensed to some very eccentric and inexplicable owners. There was the Yahrling-Rayner Piano Company of Youngstown, Ohio (WAAY); the Palmer School of Chiropractic, of Davenport, Iowa (WOC); the C.F. Aldrich Marble and Granite Co., of Colorado Springs, Colo. (KHD); the Omaha Grain Exchange (WAAW); and even the Nushawg Poultry Farm of New Lebanon, Ohio (WPI).

Naturally not all of these stations survived. Many of them lacked the resources to do more than greet the sunset with feeble exclamations of their presence. Some died sudden and inglorious deaths; others were later merged or absorbed. But a number of these eccentric pioneer stations still exist. Today we realize with a smile that not all of them could have survived, but in 1922 the future looked so bright that there seemed to be room for every comer.

This veritable cascade of stations was unexpected by both the general public and the Department of Commerce, whose job it was to license them. It quickly became the source of difficulties. By the end of 1922, 690 stations had been licensed, and long before this number was reached many of them were in audible conflict with one another. So unexpected was the radio boom that only one spot on the radio dial had been assigned to general radio stations— "news, lectures, entertainment, etc." All of these stations broadcast at 360 meters (618.6kc). By the middle of 1922 the multiplicity of stations in various geographical locales would make this situation intolerable.

For a while some spirit of cooperation prevailed. For example, with the two powerful stations in the New York area, WOR at Bamberger's Department Store, and WJZ at the Westinghouse plant (both transmitting a few blocks apart in Newark), it was necessary to effect some kind of compromise. It was decided that on one day WOR would have the hours between sunrise and sunset while WJZ would have the evening hours. The next day things would be reversed, and WOR would get the more popular evening hours. Peace treaties of this kind didn't last too long, however, and with more and more stations trying to squeeze onto the air, the government would have to take unto itself a role it then viewed with suspicion: the role of regulator and arbitrator. It did so only following many months of chaos and frustration.

Among the hundreds of stations newly licensed and operative in 1922, one would suddenly attract more than its share of attention and bring an entirely fresh concept to the practice of broadcasting. Not surprisingly, it was another station located in New York City, but this time not a stepchild of the Radio Corporation of America, or of Westinghouse, the original broadcasting pioneers, but instead of the American Telephone & Telegraph Company.

Naturally AT&T had the power and the money to get into the act, but during the pioneer years of 1920 and 1921 it hesitated, not seeing broadcasting as germane to its central mission of the telephone business. Then, finally, it jumped. And when it jumped, it was with the idea of making a quantum leap. It hoped to build the biggest and the best radio station in the country — a radio station that would dwarf all of its predecessors.

The station begun by AT&T was WEAF (for the first few months it was known as WBAY). Unlike other pioneer stations, it was born with a silver spoon in its mouth, for when AT&T decided to try broadcasting it marshaled all of the company's vast resources to the task of providing the best transmission equipment, the best studio and the best all-around facilities in the land. Here was to be no factory loft experiment, no distracting plaything at the back of a radio parts store, no department store sales gimmick, but rather a big-time radio station that would display all of the virtues of radio to the general public — one that would exhibit the most advanced state of the art. It would be more modern and more powerful than any other station then on the air.

AT&T made the decision to enter the broadcasting field at an executive meeting held in New York on January 12, 1922, and the plan was released to the public four days later. Station WBAY, predecessor to WEAF, began broadcasting six months later, on July 25, from the company's long lines building at 24 Walker Street, New York.[4] From the very first, however, this pioneering

By the early 1920s, AT&T was making a bid to dominate the radio field, as evidenced by these impressive-looking towers at 24 Walker Street in New York. The station here, WBAY, with its 500-watt transmitter, was the predecessor of the company's landmark station WEAF. (Photo courtesy AT&T.)

station was to be conceived differently from all of the existing stations. This new broadcasting station would offer marvelous broadcasting facilities but would do no broadcasting itself. WEAF was to be a "toll broadcasting station," open to the general public, or to anybody who wanted to buy time to speak or perform over the air. Just as ordinary citizens could contract with the telephone company to provide two-way phone service, so would WEAF offer anybody who so wanted the opportunity to broadcast a message to the multitudes.

It was not only the analogy with telephone service that appealed to AT&T executives in inaugurating the "toll broadcasting idea"; rather it was the hope that they had discovered the answer to a question that had puzzled all of the early pioneers of broadcasting: How could radio be made commercial, be made to pay? The answer now seemed easy: anyone wanting to broadcast would pay for the privilege—such was the hope—eventually bringing in sufficient revenues to make the service pay for itself. (The charge decided on in 1922 was $50.00 for a fifteen-minute period in the evening and $40.00 for a similar period in the afternoon.)

Although AT&T was not putting out a call for paid advertising, with the passage of time tawdry ads did of course slip in, for such was the only way that the idea could have been made to work. This might have been evident from the beginning since few toll users showed up. Nearly a month of broadcasting went by before a single toll user approached the station asking to purchase air time. Very few others followed, meaning, in essence, that the toll broadcasting idea was a flat and dismal failure.

But the WEAF experiment was not a failure in other ways. Undaunted by the inability to attract toll broadcasters, AT&T willingly supplied programming of its own. It cheerfully decided that since it had gone into broadcasting, even though few were willing to play by its new rules, it would provide the kind of programming that other stations offered at the time. With the new station only a week old, AT&T hired a "program director," Samuel Ross, to do what Tommy Cowan had done for WJZ and Major J. Andrew White for WDY. With much more specific experience in dealing with musicians and performers, and with plenty of staff help in all areas, Ross was quickly able to put together a full programming mix in a matter of a few months. With the station's New York City location, Ross was able to draw many performers to the microphone who would not endure the trek to the factory neighborhood of Newark, so that almost immediately the new station was giving brisk competition to WJZ as the premier radio station in the New York City area.

When the telephone company's station opened, the most obvious marvels seemed to be technical, for the equipment was a veritable museum of the state of the art. The station was equipped with a Western Electric 500-watt transmitter and all of the high-quality pick-up experience that telephone engineers had to offer. Introduced into broadcasting at this time was the condenser microphone that was nearly flawless in its reproduction and created very little noise through its own operation. Another instrument introduced at this time was the "volume indicator," which allowed the operator of the transmitter to control the intensity or level of the audio frequency currents passing through his apparatus. This prevented the transmitter from becoming overloaded and the program from becoming weak or faint.

Other "telephone" miracles contributed mightily to the radio art. With vast experience in sound reproduction, telephone engineers were able to equip the radio station with several microphones harmonized by means of a mixer or fader so that the output of one microphone could fade out while the output of another was increased. In the early radio studios the announcer or technician with a single microphone had been forced into all sorts of acrobatics as performers moved around or turned their heads, or as an orchestra played louder or softer. Multiple microphones and mixers allowed all these problems to be adjusted smoothly in the control room.

On April 10, 1923, WEAF moved to grander and better equipped studios at the AT&T Building at 195 Broadway, where studios took up the better part of the fourth floor in the company's national headquarters. The services of an interior designer were engaged, and the studios were given an air of formality and dignity. There were rugs, draperies; a receptionist greeted visitors and performers. The atmosphere was "homelike," with oil paintings on the wall, easy chairs and other comfortable fittings. There were two commodious studios separated by a control booth, from which the technicians were able to monitor the activities in both studios through a soundproof glass pane. Except for minor details, the modern radio studio was thus born at 195 Broadway.

A mere month after its removal to company headquarters, station WEAF obtained one of its greatest assets in the person of young Graham McNamee, who would shortly become the best known radio announcer in New York, perhaps the best remembered announcer of the 1920s. McNamee's sparkling and lively personality would make WEAF the radio voice of the New York area. But the programming skills of Mr. Samuel Ross were also responsible for turning this once-experimental station into one with the sound and personality that most people even today would associate with the idea of professionalism. In the matter of only a few months the WEAF studios were bustling with orchestras, soloists, distinguished speakers, "gypsies," troubadours, "Happiness Boys," vaudevillians, storytellers, jokesters, song and patter men, and nearly every kind of radio sound that would become familiar in the golden age of radio.

The WEAF experiment obviously turned out to be a salutary one in the history of broadcasting. It did not succeed exactly as planned, and the toll broadcasting idea was quickly supplemented with something else; but it succeeded in showing that radio as a means of mass communication had a solid future.[5] Those hundreds of stations popping up all over the country in 1922 proved that radio was infectious, that some great and happy potential was there. The telephone company proved that listeners would flock to the radio in droves—not anymore in hundreds, or thousands, but in millions.

3. Up from the Crystal Set

Making radio into a household utility was an achievement of the 1920s. This achievement did not come about overnight, or because of one single technological advance; rather the technology needed to make radio come alive was the work of many forward steps over the period of a number of years. In spite of the big splash made by KDKA in 1920, and even the vast proliferation of broadcasting stations in 1922, broadcasting as an amusement for the masses crept forward with unusual slowness. For a long time the amateurs with their fractious crystal sets remained the only audience.

Still, these thousands of amateur enthusiasts were vital to the growth of radio broadcasting. Without their help there would have been no impetus to make the improvements on the other end: to upgrade and refine transmitting equipment, microphones, studio acoustics, and to establish broadcasting stations that operated on a regular basis. When KDKA began its regular programming in the fall of 1920 it was fully understood that the audience would be made up almost exclusively of knowledgeable amateurs, many of whom had been communicating with one another for years, many of whom were members of radio clubs and subscribers to radio magazines and trade journals. The hope was that the number of these radio enthusiasts would grow rapidly, but in 1920 there was little expectation that casual listeners with no expertise in radio would be drawn into the listening audience.

Radio amateurs or enthusiasts had been regularly active in the United States at least since 1910, and doubtless there were many listeners to KDKA in 1920 who had been experimenting with homespun radio equipment since before 1910. Radio receiving parts and equipment had been available for retail sale for a long time in the United States, and a small but nonetheless vigorous manufacturing industry had grown up long before the formation of the Radio Corporation of America, and long before Westinghouse talked of building sets for the multitudes.

In the early days New York City became the home base of both manufacturing and the retail trade in radio components. The city was already clearly the leader in the industry in 1901, when Lee De Forest first became active in the city. As early as 1906 wireless equipment was on sale in New York by Hugo Gernsback, who formed the Electro Importing Company specifically to make and sell parts and sets to the amateur. In the years that followed, Gernsback's crowded radio shop, crouching under the old Eighth Avenue El at Fulton

Street in lower Manhattan, sought to be a clearinghouse for information as much as a junk collector's heaven.

Because not all radio enthusiasts lived in New York, retail sale by mail shortly became the best way of reaching thousands of customers. Before World War I, the Electric Supply Company and John First (with a line called Firso) were active in selling by mail from New York. But New York did not enjoy a monopoly on this market. J.J. Duck and his brother William B. Duck of Toledo, Ohio, were among the first to put out a mail-order parts catalogue, which was warmly received by countless amateurs. F.D. Pitts of Boston issued a radio parts catalogue that offered written testimonials as to the reliability of his equipment. The National Radio Supply Company of Washington, D.C., sold both amateur and commercial receiving and transmitting equipment by mail. Pacific Laboratories was selling Audiotron and Moorhead tubes by mail in 1916. The De Forest Radio Telephone and Telegraph Company, the successor to numerous earlier De Forest firms that had been battered out of existence by infringement litigation and financial storms, made a big effort to reach the amateur by mail in the years following World War I. In Pittsburgh, where a hardy band of amateurs would be on hand to hear Frank Conrad's experimental broadcasts after the war, the Merker-Flocker Electric Company had been in business selling to the amateur since 1914.

The amateur spirit in radio was also urged along by clubs, societies and organizations of both local and national scope. For example, the American Radio Relay League helped to link enthusiasts in all parts of the country. Magazine and book publishers were also active in spreading the gospel — with Doubleday, Street and Smith, and *Scientific American* making a serious effort to publish things of interest to radio enthusiasts. Some of the equipment dealers also linked amateurs by means of magazines, newsletters and circulars.

By the time that World War I came along, a whole generation of American boys had already grown up on the excitement and secret mysteries of radio. The *Boy Scout Manual* contained information about radio equipment and urged boys to make their own sets. The popular heroes of boys' fiction of the 1910 period — the Motor Boys, the Rover Boys, Tom Swift and others — introduced radio adventures of one sort or another into their plots to accompany all of the usual staples of boys' adventure fiction in those still-innocent times — dirigibles, submarines, electric rifles, flying boats, giant telescopes. Sometimes whole books were built around radio adventures, as in one of Tom Swift's exploits in 1911: *Tom Swift and His Wireless Message*, or *The Castaways of Earthquake Island*.

Some of the thousands of American boys who were bitten by the wireless bug in the early days followed the pursuit into their adult years. Some intensified their interest, others fell by the wayside, failing to get response from their primitive and awkward equipment. One lad who didn't fall by the wayside was the youthful Edwin H. Armstrong, who began fiddling around with the simple equipment of 1905, at which time he was a mere stripling of 15. Like many another boy of the time, Armstrong became a radio fanatic who had to be dragged away to bed from his attic laboratory in his family's suburban New York home. But unlike most other boys, Armstrong never deviated from his fanatical pursuits. Even as an engineering student at Columbia University he gave his top priority to finding ways to improve the primitive equipment of the day. By 1908 he had come into possession of a Fleming tube, and a year or so later of a De Forest Audion tube, which he instinctively knew held promise if only it could be improved. And in the summer of 1912 Armstrong discovered the feedback principle that would indeed make the Audion speak.

Young Armstrong knew he had something, and he displayed to his father and his friends what loud and clear signals he was getting with his device. Armstrong pleaded with his father and his uncle for money to take out a patent on this circuit, but his elders were reluctant to lay out money for patenting the fruits of a boy's tinkerings. After all, every other boy on the block was playing around with radio equipment; some were getting sounds clearer and louder than others; there couldn't really be that much difference between one of these improvements and another. Nobody could have suspected that Armstrong was on the verge of an illustrious career in the radio field. His inability to take out a patent on his feedback circuit in 1912 caused him later grief and long years of litigation with Lee De Forest, but it took no luster from the achievement of this classic American tinkerer and lone-wolf inventor.

Armstrong may be the stellar example of the radio-crazed youth in the pre–World War I period, but there were thousands of others who pursued the same goals at a somewhat lesser velocity. Any boy worth his salt and having in his hand a copy of *Popular Mechanics* or *Scientific American* could at the very least attempt to put together a crystal detector that might, with a little luck, pick up sounds from the air.

In 1920 the vast majority of receiving sets owned by amateurs were of the crystal variety. By this time the commercial companies had much more sophisticated equipment at their fingertips, but most of this equipment was priced way beyond the means of the typical adolescent boy. Anyway, the typical boy enjoyed the challenge of being able to assemble a receiving set of old junk found around the house—parts from old alarm clocks, worn-out fishing tackle or rusty door fasteners. What appealed to the youthful imagination was that with a few scientific principles well applied you could get the same result with very different contraptions. Uniformity of design was scorned: The ideal was to put together some apparatus that looked miraculous and was all your own.

Many boys by 1920 were proud to say that they had made a crystal set from scratch. It wasn't very difficult, and the parts weren't very expensive. Everything you needed would cost about $6.00—actually only $2.00 for the set itself, and another $4.00 for a pair of commercial earphones.

You could start out with nothing more complicated than a Quaker Oats box. To this box you would apply a coat of shellac. Then you would carefully wind a copper wire around the box and shellac that. Now you already had a copper coil, the heart of the device. The coil would then usually be attached to two wooden coil heads at either end. The next step was to affix brass slider

The crystal set shown in this 1922 photo would be a relic of the past before the decade was over. (Photo courtesy NBC.)

tracks along the length of the coil with a small slide (or slider) to run along the track. These sliders would then be used to tune the different stations (if there were any). One end of the coil would be connected to the aerial, the other end connected to your earphones. The wooden coil head also had a binding post for a ground wire.

One other little piece of magic was needed to make this contraption work: the glistening piece of galena crystal with a cat's whisker (or feeler) that also had to be hooked into the apparatus. If the cat's whisker hit the right spot on the crystal—by no means certain—you had a chance of getting some kind of reception; if not, you wouldn't get anything at all.

A crystal set of this period also required a good outside aerial and a good ground connection. It was also a help to the owner of one of these simple oatmeal-box sets to have a neighbor with a high-quality regenerative receiver that radiated the station he was listening to, obviously permitting much better reception. On the other hand, if you had a commercially made crystal set, with two circuits and spiderweb coils or other low-loss coils, you could (in theory at least) pick up stations as far as 1,500 miles away. These factory-made crystal sets were out of financial reach of many, costing from $10.00 to $35.00.

By the time the broadcasting era began in 1920, the number of amateurs had not only swelled tremendously, but a great number now had more refined and sophisticated equipment. Many of those young radio fanatics of the 1910 era were older now, secure wage earners perhaps, with the money to invest in better receiving equipment. Many of them had a number of years of radio experience behind them. This was made very clear early in 1920 when AT&T, in earnest preparation for its own broadcasting station, began a series of experimental transmissions from two stations, 2XJ at Deal Beach Laboratories, and 2XB at the Bell Labs in New York. When AT&T began these transmissions with the latest and most powerful transmitters, they invited written responses from radio listeners on the quality of the signal and the circumstances of the reception. Some radio companies and laboratories were specifically contacted by AT&T, but dozens of other letters poured in from radio amateurs who had picked up the request for feedback. These letters were kept in the Bell Lab files, and a rich sampling of them was later reprinted in William Peck Banning's book *Commercial Broadcasting Pioneer: The WEAF Experiment*. Some of the responses revealed how widespread the bacillus of "radio-itis" had become by 1920, but they are strong testimonial to the considerable knowledge and sophistication of the radio enthusiasts at the time broadcasting began.

Here are three of these testimonials to the enthusiasm and expertise of the 1920 listening audience:

West Haven, Conn., March 8, 1920.

This is to advise you that I very successfully picked up your wireless phone tests at each of the fifteen minute periods on Friday evening March 5th.

The speech was very clear and pure, it being possible to understand every word, even to those not accustomed to wireless. It was possible to understand every word approximately one foot from the receivers.

The apparatus used at my station consists of the following:

Receiving transformer, 800 meters, primary #22, secondary #30; loader #22 wire; straight audion hookup used; auditron detector; B-battery 30 volts; variable condenser shunt across secondary; 600 ohm phones; aerial thirty feet high, approximately 85 ft. in length, two-wires; water pipe ground.

Locust Valley, N.Y., March 8, 1920.

I am an amateur experimenting to some extent with wireless, and while listening in this evening at 11:45 P.M. I overheard your conversation. Then you asked that anyone hearing you would write to the Western Electric Co. Room 721 and owing to interference I could not catch your name.

Perhaps this would be of interest to you. I was using a crystal detector (Radiocite), Murdock Loose Coupler, Variable condenser (.0004M) Murdock Phones (3000 ohms).

New Haven, Conn., March 13, 1920.

Although not a hundred miles from N.Y. I must write to tell how I heard your signals last night. I happened to catch a part of the 10:45 period. At 11:15 when I found you were on a longer wave length than I expected, heard every word beautifully.

Monday night we are having a little company to listen to you and if you can acknowledge by a word or two to me, will be more than delighted.

Received you on a tuning coil only 1¼-inch diameter and 3 inches long, 9 taps on primary and 8 on secondary (tunes from 300 to 2500 meters). Used one and an Audiotron 40-volt "Hi Volt" Storage Battery with self-contained rectifier, which I manufacture. These batteries are for sale by the C.D. Tuska Co. of Hartford, Conn. My aerial is mostly under the roof of an ordinary two-family house. No. 22 cotton wire four strands the length of the house.

I worked with Prof. Fessenden on Roanoke Island and Cape Hatteras in 1901 and 1902, old coherer days; then did nothing more with wireless until about three years ago, since which time I have been more or less associated with Mr. Tuska. All this history just to show you why I am such a bug on wireless.[1]

What these letters prove, and quite eloquently, is that an enthusiastic audience was there in 1920, ready and anxious for radio to have some further consequence and development. On the other hand, they also prove that radio was still a long way from being a reliable household utility. Like the scientists at the Bell Lab, these radio listeners conceived of themselves as "experimenters" in some kind of elite partnership with other experimenters and tinkerers. The equipment had gotten ever so much better in just the last few years, but radio reception was still an art and not a ready-to-the-fingertip utility. Doubtless most of those who responded to the Bell scientists in 1920 were writing about receiving sets on their workbench out in the garage, or down in the basement, or up in the attic. Wives and sisters were warned away from the radio receiver—it was all strictly a man's preserve.

Where, then, did radio have to go at the dawn of the broadcasting age in 1920? A long way, really, even though so much had already been achieved on the laboratory level. The quality of sound was still poor on most home sets. Remaining to be solved was the problem of decent amplification, so that the human voice did not sound like some faraway squeaking or rattling. Static remained a problem of some severity, although the scientists had been working on removing it for a long time. And there were numerous other problems as well: blasting, a loud, horrible sound that occurred when moving from one signal to another; station interference; battery problems that made the radio an unwelcome device in the family living room (the A-C plug-in radio was not to make its appearance for several years). The radio receiver was usually forbidden in the living room because the device was more than likely to leak its noxious and damaging battery fluids onto a carpet. Too, there was as yet an inadequate technology of listening devices—most radio operators had long been accustomed to the headset, but now the time had come to develop a satisfactory loudspeaker so that presumably an entire family might be able to hear amplified sounds as they sat around their hearth on a cold winter's evening. All of these needed improvements were the products of the 1920s, although many could not have been produced without the long years of research that had gone before.

The first and most important steps that had to be taken in the improvement of radiotelephony was the advancement in the art of the De Forest Audion tube. For the Audion (and its various heirs and descendants) was the heart and soul of modern radio. Without it the broadcasting era could never have come about.

It ought to be stressed that tube development was as important in the development of usable transmitters as it was in the advancement of home receivers. In fact the motivation was strongest on this end since there was no sense talking about improving home reception if a high-quality telephonic signal could not emanate from the broadcaster.

For effective transmission, tubes capable of generating large currents had to be developed. This development progressed rapidly after 1913. Following the work of Meissner in Germany and Round in England, AT&T engineers, using a high-voltage tube oscillator, carried on a test conversation between a station at Wilmington, Delaware, and another at Montauk Point, New York, a distance of 300 miles. During these years the telephone company's intense interest in improving vacuum tubes was a result of their desire to improve the telephone wire-line repeater and thus improve the poor quality of long-line transmission. But the experiments around this time also proved to be especially useful to the United States Signal Corps during the war years, and a regular and intense effort continued during the war by numerous manufacturers to improve the power and quality of radio tubes of all kinds.

Every year after AT&T's 1915 experiments, tubes became larger and more sophisticated. The 1915 tubes had a rating of 25 watts. With tubes of that kind, 500 tubes would be needed in a complete radiophone transmitter to radiate a mere 1½ kilowatts of useful power. Two or three years later, during the war, tubes of 250 watts were being used. By 1921, 10-kilowatt tubes (now requiring water cooling) had been produced and were being manufactured. By 1923, 20-kilowatt tubes were being made, and a few years later, 100-kilowatt tubes were available.

For purposes of transmission, this discovery of the usefulness of tubes for sustained oscillation led to improvements in other areas as well. Vacuum tubes could also be used successfully as modulators, and this in turn motivated engineers and scientists to improve the quality of microphones. Again, World War I had a remarkable effect on research in this area because of the strongly felt need to effect voice transmissions between airplanes and ground stations.

By the end of World War I the vacuum tube had also shown itself to be the means of upgrading the radio receiver. It would be the device that would make the manufacture of reliable home sets possible. Edwin Armstrong's 1912 experiments with the De Forest Audion tube had already demonstrated the tube's value in reception. In his feedback circuit, Armstrong proved that part of the received current in the Audion could be fed back through the instrument to reinforce itself many times. In this way received radio signals could be amplified hundreds of times beyond the strength offered by the single vacuum tube itself.

Armstrong kept after this matter of amplification and improvement of sound, and during his war service with the Signal Corps in France in 1918 he made his greatest single contribution to the broadcasting age that was about to dawn: the superheterodyne receiver, which became the basic circuit of most

Edwin H. Armstrong, whose experiments with the De Forest Audion tube eventually put radio sets into the hands of the general public. His Radiola Superheterodyne revolutionized popular radio reception. (Photo courtesy Columbia University.)

radios in the days of commercial radio broadcasting. The superheterodyne receiver was a perfect piece of Yankee ingenuity, developed by Armstrong when conditions of the war forced him to depend upon low-frequency vacuum tubes. Armstrong built an effective fixed-tuned amplifier for the frequency of the French tubes, and then transformed the incoming frequency to an easily amplifiable value by heterodyne action (heterodyne comes from the Greek words *heteros,* meaning other or different, and *dynamis,* power) and rectification.

With this superheterodyne principle at his command, Armstrong designed an eight-tube receiver of unusually high quality. The set included a rectifier tube, a separate heterodyne oscillator, three intermediate-frequency amplifiers, a second detector, and two audio-frequency stages. The first sets were somewhat complicated to operate, but when the war was over, Armstrong, later joined by Harry W. Houck, worked intently on the task of creating a set that could be used by an unsophisticated public and on which only a few controls would be needed. A major part of this set was to be an intermediate-frequency amplifier for a given frequency and for a band of 5,000 cycles above and below that, which would then cut off sharply on either side of the desired band.

By the spring of 1922, having worked through an infinite number of possible and quite distinct uses of the vacuum tube, Armstrong was ready with a receiver that would revolutionize popular radio reception. This set, eventually to be called the Radiola Superheterodyne, consisted of a radio frequency stage (nontuned transformer), a rectifier tube, an oscillator tube, a three-stage, iron-core, intermediate-frequency amplifier for a band of 20,000 to 30,000 cycles, a second detector tube, and two stages of audio amplification.

Even though the quality of reception was unusually high in this set, it was not immediately apparent that it would be the great breakthrough that the radio industry was looking for in the early twenties. To many home crystal set receiver owners of the day, accustomed to paying $10.00 for a complete crystal set, the high initial outlay for the Radiola Superheterodyne seemed to be a dark cloud on the horizon. But those who heard the set knew otherwise. This set, with its vast array of functioning tubes, was obviously going to put home radio reception on the high road.

Such was certainly immediately evident to David Sarnoff of RCA when he heard the set for the first time in 1922. It was also immediately evident to members of the board of directors of RCA, who previously had given a green light for the manufacture of another kind of "improved" receiver that was developed in RCA's own laboratories. On hearing Armstrong's set they promptly cancelled these plans, much to the chagrin of their own engineering staff, as well as their friends and collaborators at Westinghouse and GE, who were all set for large-scale production of a much more primitive instrument.

The story is told that the RCA board was to assemble at Board Chairman Owen D. Young's apartment for a demonstration of the Superheterodyne set, and that most of them were cold to the proposal of converting to this "outsider's" set, about which there had been many secret meetings for months. But Major Armstrong stepped off the elevator carrying the set under his arm in full operation with an opera program in progress. The device, which was battery-operated, required no antenna and could be easily tuned. The RCA board needed no further convincing.

This set, as Armstrong turned it over to RCA (for which he was handsomely paid), was not quite ready for marketing. RCA engineers spent months trying to get the cost of the unit down to a figure that would be tolerated by the public, mostly through the development of low-current dry cell tubes that were not only cheaper but much easier to obtain. By the time that the revolutionary receiver finally got on the market in 1924, the instrument was a very efficient and reasonably priced six-tube receiver. Now it was ready to sell to the multitudes.

While these improvements were being made in the vacuum tube, other scientists and engineers addressed the many other bugs in the system — static, for instance, which had been around since the time of Marconi and continued to be one of the petty nuisances of radio during the early 1920s. The solution to the problem lay mostly in the area of improved antennas, and scientists were working on this around the world—men like H.M. Airy in England; Max Dieckmann, H.G. Moller and M. Bauemler in Germany; H. de Bellecize in France; and Roy A. Weagant, H.H. Beverage, Greenleaf W. Pickard, and E.F.W. Alexanderson in the United States. World War I again provided a strong impetus to improved antenna design. For example, it was the war that gave rise to E.F.W. Alexanderson's "barrage receiver," a bridge type of receiver combined with highly directional aperiodic antennas. Later years saw many refinements in the kinds of antenna sets that could be used for home reception.

Problems of fading, of fluctuation noise and of blasting all eventually found their solutions. Blasting was a listener's headache with the growing number of stations going out over airwaves. This phenomenon occurred when a listener changed the dial from one station to another. Tuned into a station at some distance which accordingly had a rather weak signal, he might later wish to turn to another station closer by, and perhaps with higher power. In doing so he might not think to adjust his volume control, and in hitting the more powerful station he might be blasted off his chair by the increased volume of the next station. By 1923, radio engineers had a solution to this problem—at least in theory. But not until 1928 was a truly successful method of automatic loudspeaker control available to consumers.

Not all of the problems of the early twenties were strictly technical. A good example of this was the problem of station interference. Many old-time radio listeners will recall the frequent disagreeable experience of being obliged to listen to two or three radio programs at the same time. This problem greatly puzzled radio engineers at the time, but most often the problem was due to stations that didn't adhere carefully enough to their assigned frequency. The solution, when it came, was thus both a technical solution and one of governmental regulation.

Too, not every advance in radio technology during the twenties was an achievement of radio engineering. There was the development and improvement of the loudspeaker, an essential part of most radios after the mid–1920s. Those who sought to improve the quality of sound reproduction not only had to know the basics of radio transmission, they also had to know something about acoustics, about the human ear, perhaps about aesthetics as well. It might well have been possible to have merely amplified radio sounds sufficiently to make them fill a room while not making them tolerable to the human ear. Vast new technical areas had to be opened up.

Early loudspeakers were usually nothing more than horns with arms or a base to accept the familiar headset receiver. Many of the early listeners to KDKA doubtless fashioned their own crude loudspeakers by placing their headset in a wooden bowl or cardboard box to increase the volume and distribute the sound. Of course in the early twenties loudspeakers didn't need to be very elaborate anyway, since broadcasting stations were transmitting signals that were heard as 200 to 2,500 cycles/sec audio. When the broadcast quality improved, the loudspeakers would have to be improved also.

The loudspeaker was not completely new in 1921, since it had been used on phonograph sets for some 25 years. But after all these years the quality of sound reproduction on the phonograph was not good: the output was usually thought to be "tinny" in character. Most people in the radio industry in 1921 knew that first-time radio listeners were so startled by the miracle of radio that they accepted any sound they heard as remarkable; but it was obvious that the sound quality available in the phonographic field would have to be greatly upgraded for radio.

Engineers conversant with acoustics made careful determinations of the frequency range of the human voice and of musical instruments such as the piano and the organ. In the early loudspeakers nearly all of the lower tones tended to be distorted. The fundamental frequency range of a piano was 27 to 4,096 vibrations per second. None of the early loudspeakers could handle frequencies lower than 256 (middle C on the piano) without distortion, and this problem had to be solved. At the same time there were increasing demands for amplification of sound and a rapidly increasing volume of air to be set in motion by the loudspeaker's diaphragm. Almost immediately, though, engineers began investigating the characteristics of transformers used in audio-frequency stages of amplification, and more efficient transformers were designed and produced — transformers that passed on to the loudspeaker low tones in faithful outline. Improvements were also made in coupling, in bypass condensors, in the impedance and resistance units used in amplification.

The loudspeakers of the early 1920s were largely the work of Irving Wolff and Abraham Ringel, and most of this work was incorporated in the more advanced instruments marketed by the Radio Corporation of America. Shortly thereafter, C.W. Hewlett designed an induction type of loudspeaker specifically for large rooms and auditoriums. Laboratory investigations carried on at Western Electric by C.L. Farrand, C.W. Rice and others found ways to use large diaphragms to advantage, which resulted in the introduction of more efficient cone-type loudspeakers, a further departure from the mere telephone headset modification.

Generally speaking, loudspeaker development was the work of the experimental laboratories of the large companies that dominated the radio industry in the 1920s. Magnavox brought out a speaker with a six-volt field that gave much-enhanced volume. Western Electric's cone-type speakers came in three sizes: 18, 24 and 36 inches, and they could be hung on the wall. Prices ran from $35.00 up to $60.00 — not paltry sums in those days. Other giants of the field making effective loudspeakers in the twenties included Atwater Kent, Baldwin, Crosley, Stromberg-Carlson and Thorola. Western Electric, Magnavox and RCA led the pack in technical advances. Magnetic speakers were greatly improved in the mid-twenties. In 1926 RCA hit the market with its 104-Dynamic Radiola with voice coil. This represented the top of the line in its day.

With advances like these in loudspeaker technology, and with a sophisticated receiving set like Armstrong's Radiola Superheterodyne, the era of modern broadcasting was a mere jot away. With the price of tube radios coming down rapidly, mostly due to mass production, there were only a few technical wrinkles to iron out before the radio receiving apparatus could take its place among respected home appliances.

One persisting problem was the battery (Armstrong's Radiola was still battery-operated). Nearly all batteries in use in the twenties were potentially destructive and noxious. One type used in early wireless sets was the Lalande cell, which used caustic soda for the electrolyte; there were plates of cupric oxide and zinc. Another early type in common use was the plunger battery. This used an acid solution and carbon plates. To turn the cell on, a zinc electrode was plunged into the solution. By the early 1920s, rechargeable storage batteries, mostly of the lead-acid type, were available; these had longer life, but didn't overcome the old problems.

During the infant days of broadcasting, dry cells came into wide use, especially what were called the "B" and "C" batteries. But there were still the old fears of fluid leaking onto carpets, and fumes would sometimes give the living room a bad aroma. Too, when the terminals got corroded, the audio reception was greatly impaired. Most importantly, perhaps, storage batteries were relatively expensive for this era when there wasn't that much to listen to on the radio. They also needed frequent recharging, which added appreciably to the cost. Battery charging stations would pick up a battery and charge it for $1.00. B-type dry batteries for a 90-volt set cost about $10.00; they lasted only about three months and cost about $5.00 a month for upkeep in a typical five-tube set.

Beginning about 1922, made-up power packs called B-eliminators began to appear, and these eliminated the dry-cell B battery, using home current when it was available. But they were considered very expensive indeed, costing about $125. Their best feature was that they needed little attention.

The biggest step forward, however, was the total elimination of the battery. This didn't happen until 1925, when the A-C radio tube became available. For the next two years these tubes did not come into widespread use because of their high cost. But at RCA and elsewhere, herculean labors were going on to make a cheap and practical A-C tube. When this tube was finally placed on the market in 1927, the radio at last became a home appliance that could be plugged into the wall — just like the table lamp and the electric clock.

The easy availability of A-C radios led to the proliferation of large console sets for the living room.[2] Console sets were often constructed of the finest woods and were specifically and obviously designed as furniture, sometimes with baroque flights of fancy. As such they became a necessary part of any middle-class living room. Most of the manufacturers of radio receivers began supplying consoles and had their own furniture departments and designers. Among the leaders in this field were RCA, Magnavox, Zenith, Atwater Kent, Stromberg-Carlson and Philco. Console sets quickly came to dominate the radio receiver market in the late 1920s and would continue to do so until the depression brought about a demand for cheap table models and portables.

The presence of these handsomely designed and usually large and heavy pieces of furniture also brought about, almost by accident, a reconciliation of two old enemies: the radio and the phonograph. For a long time the radio and phonograph industries would have nothing to do with one another, but by the mid-1920s, things began to change. With plug-in electrical radios coming on the scene, and with the large console cabinets being in production everywhere, the possibility emerged that these two one-time enemies might learn to live in peace and harmony.

With bigger and better loudspeakers becoming available, the phonograph companies were anxious to make use of this new technology. In 1925, the Victor Talking Machine Company of Camden, New Jersey, the leader in the field, contracted with a French firm to supply them with a loudspeaker of French design said to be more sophisticated than any on the United States market, and at the same time made a secret agreement[3] with the Radio Corporation to supply radio sets to go into consoles made by the phonograph manufacturer. As part of the agreement they promised not to go into the business of making radios themselves, and promised that their recording artists would be allowed to appear on radio programs.

By 1929 this spirit of cooperation would no longer be necessary, for early that year the Victor Talking Machine Company was acquired by the Radio Corporation of America. At long last came the logical and obvious marriage between these two great rivals. It has been a long and prosperous marriage.

Other innovations of the 1920s have persisted as well. One was the car radio, which made its appearance in 1928, although there were only a very few in circulation until the early depression years. The first car radio was designed by William Lear, today best known as the designer and manufacturer of the small jet airplane known as the Learjet. In the fall of 1928 Lear visited Paul Galvin, a battery manufacturer in Chicago, and placed on his desk the first car radio ever built. Would Galvin be interested in making them? Yes, he would.

Car radios doubtless could have been made several years before. Indeed, as early as 1922, with his usual prescience and foresight, David Sarnoff had predicted that radio would shortly spread to automobiles and other forms of transportation. On May 14 of that year Sarnoff wrote in the *New York Herald Tribune*: "It is reasonable to expect radio's application to automobiles, and in some cases to individuals." We don't know whether Sarnoff could have predicted the age when "individuals" would skim their way down the streets on skateboards listening to the local rock station through earphones, but shortly after his 1922 prediction he was boosting the radio idea for trains, airplanes, steamships and even motorboats.

Still, when William Lear came up with his car radio in 1928 most people were scoffers. There was an almost universal feeling that car radios would be legislated out of existence for safety reasons. Nonetheless, Galvin moved ahead and began production. In the following year, 1929, Galvin and Lear were en route to a radio manufacturer's conference in Atlantic City when they came up with a name for their product—Motorola. The Galvin Manufacturing Company became Motorola, and production of car radio proceeded apace. Early models were awkward and bulky. Most of them operated from separate B batteries under the floorboard. They were subject to a great deal of ignition interference, and reception was generally poor. Antennas were run under the running gear to the rear shock absorbers.

After World War II the technology of car radios improved rapidly, and sales increased accordingly. By 1946, 9 million cars had radios; by 1979 110 million American cars had radios—95 percent of cars in operation as of that year.

Obviously many of radio's progeny were crude and primitive in the 1920s. On the other hand, nearly every radio convenience that we enjoy today was available at least in a primitive form before the decade was over. A great many advances would be made in the next several decades of course, but the pace of things would never be able to rival the hectic growth of the twenties. When the decade began, radio was little more than a trinket; when it was over, radio was offering most of the services and applications that it offers today.

4. The Rise of the Radio Announcer

Those who watch television in this last quarter of the twentieth century cannot possibly imagine what an important individual the radio announcer once was. He was a genuine American hero who touched the lives of people everywhere. To keep his job he had to have style and verve and personality. There are announcers in television too, but mostly they are disembodied spirits, "voice-over" functionaries, their personalities and voices very professional, very competent — but altogether undistinguishable. Post-network radio has its announcers, its talk-show hosts, its disc jockeys who carry on the old art with some degree of personal identification, but somehow or other the once-splendid institution of the radio announcer has departed the scene — a sad loss.

The radio announcer was the first personification of the mass media in America, and, as such, he came to play an important role in American life. He was a popular figure of the national culture, a link between the city and the country, the East and the West, the highbrow and the lowbrow, the rich and the poor. He was hired because he spoke well, because he pronounced words with some precision and with aesthetic effect; accordingly, his influence on the American language was both profound and lasting. One radio announcer with splendid diction could have a more beneficial effect on the national literacy than ten thousand schoolmarms with their drills and chalkboard grammar lessons. If the average American speaks his language as clearly and distinctly and uniformly as the average Englishman — and there is every reason to suspect that he does — that facility is probably due in no small measure to the speech patterns, the happy self-assurance, and the smooth continuity of the old-time radio announcer.

The numbers of radio announcers increased phenomenally in the 1930s, as did their pay and prestige. Advertising had stepped in to fatten up the paychecks. The radio audience continued to grow dramatically in those years, and the craft of announcing moved into the big time. When commercial broadcasting began, the radio announcer *was* radio.

But where did radio announcers come from? In 1920 there was no such animal and there obviously was no training school or apprenticeship program to supply the need when it arose. The first announcers simply fell into their jobs or were tagged for the chore when they hung around the transmitting apparatus for a bit too long. When KDKA went on the air with the election returns in 1920, the announcer was Leo Rosenberg of the Westinghouse

Advertising Department; the poor man had been arbitrarily chosen for the job of reading the election returns over the air. He stayed on for a number of weeks as announcer, working overtime nightly between 8 and 10 P.M. He just read into the microphone whatever he was given. Announcing was for him just one chore among many—like sharpening pencils or picking up proofs at a printer's office.

The first regular radio announcer worthy of the name was Harold W. Arlin, who came into a field in a similarly informal manner. Arlin was a young Westinghouse engineer who had a habit of poking around the primitive roof-top transistor shack and suddenly found himself tapped for the job of regular announcer. Arlin was born in La Harpe, Illinois, and grew up in Carthage, Missouri. He later attended the University of Kansas and earned a degree in electrical engineering in 1917. Upon graduation he enrolled in the Westinghouse graduate student training course and was working in the East Pittsburgh plant when KDKA went on the air for the first time on November 2, 1920. At that time Arlin was working as a time-study supervisor in the firm's manufacturing division, which tended to get him all around the plant. He knew that the company was now operating a little radio station, still thought to be experimental, so one day curiosity got the better of him and he peeked into the studio where Rosenberg was carrying on his nightly chores before the mike. Rosenberg explained to Arlin that the company would like to have a regular announcer (part-time, to be sure, since the station was only broadcasting for a few hours in the evening), and after the two talked for a while, Rosenberg asked Arlin if he'd be interested in the job. It was just before Christmas, and Arlin had been thinking of ways to earn a little money to buy his wife an extra-special Christmas present, so he said that he would.

Company executives listened to Arlin talk over the radio, and thought that his voice projected well, so in the next few weeks he alternated with Rosenberg on the nightly programs. On January 1, 1921, Rosenberg went back to the advertising department and Arlin became the first permanent announcer at KDKA.

At the time the station had nothing resembling a studio. The plant's auditorium was used briefly for the purpose, but the hall was so large that the acoustics were an abomination. Later, a tent was set up on the roof next to the shack that contained the transmitter. This was slightly better acoustically, but was unsatisfactory in any kind of inclement weather. At 8:30 every evening, a freight train passed the plant, and the wail of the whistle became a regular and unwanted feature of whatever programming happened to be in progress. One night Arlin brought a tenor to the roof for one of the nightly broadcasts. When the man opened his mouth to let out a high note, an insect flew in, causing the tenor to utter a string of words unsuitable for audiences of any age, and the engineer wasted no time in cutting off the power.

In the months that followed, and before Westinghouse actually designed and built something like a true radio studio, Harold Arlin *became* radio station KDKA—announcer, program director, news director, disc jockey (the term of course unknown then), sports announcer, advertising man and general

Harold Arlin became radio's first full-time announcer, beginning work at KDKA at Christmas time 1920. The tuxedo was a curious and seemingly unnecessary appurtenance of announcers in the early days of broadcasting. (Photo courtesy Westinghouse Broadcasting and Cable Co.)

factotum. Whatever there was to be done, he did. Mostly he played phonograph records borrowed from the same local department store whose advertising venture had given birth to the station back in the fall of 1920, but occasionally he would tempt some local singer or personality to the inglorious tent for a few minutes before the microphone. Now and then he would bring in remotes from theatres, churches, halls or auditoriums. Arlin also became the first sports announcer in the land when on April 11, 1921, Florent Gibson, a sportswriter for the *Pittsburgh Post*, was prevailed upon to give a blow-by-blow description of a prizefight at Motor Square Garden. But it was Arlin himself who put the description on the air, taking the blow-by-blow from Gibson over a telephone line (which remained the usual practice for a long time thereafter).

When Westinghouse opened WJZ, its first station in the New York Metropolitan area, in the fall of 1921, it was clear that a full-time announcer would be needed there too. Again the man picked for the job was a

Westinghouse employee who happened to be at the right place at the right time. The first regular radio announcer to be heard by the millions of potential listeners in New York was Thomas H. Cowan, familiarly called "Tommy" Cowan by everyone in the business.

Tommy Cowan had grown up in the suburbs of northern New Jersey, and at an early age had gotten a job as an assistant at the laboratory of Thomas Edison in West Orange. During the war he worked for a while in a Hoboken munitions plant, but later he found a job with Westinghouse in Newark—at first nothing to do with radio. But when it came time to find an announcer for station WJZ, Westinghouse once again looked to one of its own for the job. Qualifications? Nobody had the slightest idea in those days of what the qualifications for a radio announcer would be—just someone willing and able to talk over the air. Cowan apparently did know something about music, or told people that he did. At the age of fourteen, while staying with an aunt in New York City, he had worked briefly as a nonsinging child extra at the Metropolitan Opera House.

The WJZ studio—and of course there was no studio—was located in a shack up on the roof at the Westinghouse plant in Newark, New Jersey. One day Tommy was told by his supervisors that he would have to go up on the roof to talk over the radio. To get there he had to climb an iron ladder through a hatchway. On the roof he found engineer George Blitziotis, a transmitter, some tangled wires and a primitive microphone. During September 1921 Cowan was called to the roof several times for preliminary tests, which mostly consisted of giving the station's call letters over the air.

WJZ began formal broadcasting on October 1, 1921. At 8 P.M. on that date, Cowan went on the air from the rooftop shack with the words, "This is WJZ, WJZ, WJZ, the radio telephone station located in Newark, New Jersey. This is announcer Cowan, Newark. Please stand by to tune." WJZ was on the air.

But what to put on the air? That was the question. The job of filling up two and a half hours of air time every evening fell to Tommy Cowan. In the early months a great deal of time could be expended giving the Arlington time signals, weather forecasts, extended sign-ons and sign-offs, but shortly Cowan discovered, like Harold Arlin, that the best way to take up time was to play phonograph records. He thus became the second disc jockey in the business.

Getting enough records to play wasn't easy. In desperation, the day before the station went on the air, Cowan went out to West Orange on the streetcar to see if he could borrow a phonograph and a few phonograph records from the instrument's inventor, Thomas Alva Edison. He found Edison had a sign on his door that said, "I will not talk radio to anyone." (Edison may have been miffed at the sudden popularity of radio, which he regarded as a kind of illegitimate child of his invention, the incandescent lamp.) Nonetheless, Edison welcomed his former employee and loaned him a phonograph and a few records. Unfortunately the phonograph turned out to be too big to get through the hatchway of the roof and had to be hauled up on the outside of the building by a hoist.

A few days after the start of broadcasting, Thomas Edison called on the phone and asked Westinghouse to stop using his invention to play music over the radio. "If the phonograph sounded like that in any room, nobody would ever buy it." So the Edison phonograph was returned, and Westinghouse went out and bought its own phonograph and began acquiring its own stock of records.

Eventually Cowan began to bring talent over from New York to appear over the radio. It wasn't easy at first convincing singers to perform to make the trek by the Hudson tube from New York to Newark, but Cowan was a genial and persuasive man. To accommodate the arriving talent, Westinghouse had to fabricate some sort of studio: Opera singers couldn't be expected to climb an iron ladder to the roof. So a studio was set up by partitioning what had been a ladies' cloakroom. Ugly, thick cloth was draped on the walls to absorb sounds; this Cowan dyed red. At an auction down on Halsey Street he bought two old Oriental rugs for the floor. It was hoped that all these coverings would kill the resonance. In time an upright piano was provided, and Westinghouse engineers regularly experimented with the microphones — indeed, with every aspect of sound transmission.

When he wasn't on the air in the evening, Tommy Cowan spent his days in New York looking for performers willing to go on the air in Newark. When actors and actresses started hearing that this new medium of communication was not merely a toy or a joke, and that fan letters from as far away as the Mississippi River were coming in, they started coming. Many performers were in for a jolt when they got quick and copious praise for performances that they thought of as a kind of lark. Eddie Janis was one of these. Cowan recruited him right in downtown Newark, where he was doing a vaudeville act with his wife. Janis sang some songs and played the violin over the air, and no sooner had he returned to the theatre for the final performance of the evening when he was startled to find a telegram from the manager of the Keith Theatre in Cincinnati, Ohio, congratulating him on his performance. Maybe there was something to this new medium of radio after all!

Many of Cowan's recruits became stars of radio in the next few years. One was Vaughn de Leath, already a veteran, since she had been Lee De Forest's first radio girl back in 1916. A rotund and jovial soprano who adopted a crooning style so as not to blow out the tubes in the transmitter, De Leath came over to Newark almost any time Cowan wanted her. He might show up at her apartment on 38th Street in New York at the drop of a hat and say, "Come on, we're going to Newark."

Some of Cowan's performers were sent by the various recording studios whose records he was playing on the air. Pathé Records sent over a quartette known as the Shannon Four, later to become the Revelers. Pathé was also responsible for sending an act that was to become one of the most popular in the first decade of radio: Billy Jones and Ernie Hare, later to be known as the "Happiness Boys."

Before long Cowan and WJZ didn't have to plead; artists and performers began to enjoy making the uncomfortable trip to the Westinghouse factory in

Newark, knowing what it did for their reputations. And Westinghouse eventually did a little more to make them welcome. Moving out of the cloakroom, the company finally decided to furnish a studio with a little class. A large room was found on the ground floor of the building and provided with thick carpets and drapes and a better piano. The station rented limousines to meet the stars at the tubes or ferry, bought flowers for their guests, hung pictures of them on the studio walls. Cowan was provided with a tuxedo, although this was one little touch that couldn't have meant the slightest difference to the listening audience. But it was a sure sign that things were moving up.

Tommy Cowan did not go on to make a permanent career as a radio announcer, although it would be hard to find a figure of more importance in the early days of radio. Cowan did stay in radio, however, eventually becoming studio manager of station WNYC in New York. But the golden voices of radio were just around the corner — one of the first of them being a young man that Cowan had hauled over from New York for what was supposed to have been a single appearance. He was Milton J. Cross, whose mellifluous voice would become known to millions of Americans in the years ahead. Like so many of the first radio announcers, Cross fell into announcing by chance, although here at last was somebody with the voice and professionalism to make it to the top.

Milton Cross grew up in New York City, in the slums of Hell's Kitchen. How he shuffled off the strong New York accent and acquired one of the most polished speaking voices of all time is something of a mystery. But Cross managed to obtain a musical education and by the age of 25 was regularly singing professionally in church choirs, perhaps with the hope of making it in opera. When radio found him, he was taking a course from the famous Dr. Frank Damrosch at the Institute of Musical Art.

Cross had never heard of the radio, or certainly had no idea that people were actually singing over it, when one day he went to visit some friends in Newark who had a crystal set and was told that the little device could actually pick up sounds from the air. He was astounded when he put on the earphones and heard a Newark commissioner telling people to drive carefully on the holidays. A few days later Cross wrote a letter to Tommy Cowan, and Cowan invited him to visit and sing over the air. Cross made out just fine as a singer, but what really impressed Cowan was his speaking voice, and his perfect pronunciation of musical terms, foreign phrases and the like. Cowan explained that the station was looking for an assistant announcer, and asked Cross if he'd be interested.

Cross wasn't overwhelmed by the idea. He considered himself a musician. Furthermore, he had been performing for nothing, and he figured that Cowan would expect him to be an announcer for nothing also. When Cowan offered him $40.00 a week for four nights' work, Cross relented; this, after all, could be a big help in furthering his musical education. He took the job, and four times a week traveled to Newark to work as an all-purpose announcer. He did some singing, too (Cross's singing voice was in the tenor range, but his speaking voice was a pleasant and rather deep baritone); he also introduced other musical performers with skill and aplomb, and he played the Ampico organ.

He even read the Sunday funnies and the daily "Uncle Wiggily" stories when Newark author Howard R. Garis did not come in to read them himself.

By the time Milton Cross came to WJZ, Westinghouse had made the decision that announcers should not use their own names on the air (perhaps they would become too popular and ask for big raises). Accordingly, Tommy Cowan had stopped referring to himself as "Announcer Cowan" and called himself ACN (Announcer Cowan Newark). Milton Cross, whose last name also began with a C, could not use the same letters, so he became known as AJN, and this is how he was first known to thousands of listeners.

Station WJZ was now moving into the big time. All that was needed was to get out of the factory section of Newark and into more elegant quarters in New York City itself. So a studio was rented in Manhattan in the Waldorf Astoria Hotel (then located on the present site of the Empire State Building at Fifth Avenue and 34th Street), and a Western Union wire was set up between that studio and the transmitter in Newark. In 1923 the entire station was moved to New York, and when the two NBC networks, the Red and the Blue, were established in 1926, WJZ became the keystone of the Blue Network.

The year 1922 was to be a time of phenomenal growth in radio broadcasting, and it was obvious that it would not be possible for a single station to monopolize the airways of the New York area. Even Newark had a second powerful station, WOR, set up in Bamberger's Department Store on Halsey Street. But New York was getting ready for an even bigger entry in the broadcasting sweepstakes: AT&T's toll-broadcasting station, WEAF.[1] This station would bring startling changes not only to radio technology but to the craft of radio announcing. AT&T began the station with the idea that it would be a revenue-generating operation, not a free offering to the public. And in starting to offer the first radio commercials, WEAF was about to shoot the profession of radio announcer into the highest firmament.

The most famous name associated with WEAF, and probably the best-known announcer of the first decade of radio broadcasting, was Graham McNamee. McNamee, too, got his start almost by accident; however, like Milton Cross, he was superbly prepared for the job.

Graham McNamee was born in Washington, D.C., in 1888, but grew up in the Midwest, in St. Paul, Minnesota. As a high school student he was interested in all sports and participated in most of them (a background that doubtless accounted for his later success in sports announcing). But he was also musically inclined, and by the time he was 18 he had made up his mind to become a singer. Unfortunately, opportunities for making a living as a singer in the Midwest were slight, and McNamee spent a few years drifting. He worked for a while as a clerk on the Rock Island Railroad and as a salesman for the Armour Meat Packing Company.

During most of this time McNamee had been living with his divorced mother, who was not at all pleased that her son had done little to advance his singing career. She insisted that the two move to New York, where musical opportunities would presumably be greater. And in New York, McNamee's career did begin to pick up, although slowly. He sang minor parts in several

Broadway companies and in grand opera. Eventually he gave a solo recital at Aeolian Hall. Still, he was not exactly bursting into the sunlight.

The summer of 1923 was a lean time for McNamee, for engagements of any kind were few and far between. He was selected for jury duty, which would buy a few meals. Jury duty also brought him downtown to the Federal Court House at Foley Square. One day he was let off early from jury duty and found himself wandering along lower Broadway. He passed the AT&T building at 195 Broadway, where there was a sign identifying the studios of station WEAF. McNamee had never heard the radio, but he had been told that radio stations sometimes use live talent, so he decided to forego lunch and visit the studio.

After taking the elevator upstairs, McNamee met Program Manager Samuel L. Ross and made some discreet inquiries about the possibilities of singing over the air. Ross's ears perked up when he heard that McNamee was a singer with an extensive musical background, but what impressed him most was a certain quality of voice that seemed admirably suited to radio. When he also heard that McNamee had played semiprofessional baseball and hockey, he was determined to give the young man an audition.

McNamee passed the audition with flying colors, was hired on the spot, and told to report for work the next day at 6 P.M. McNamee was pleased with the job as a means of tiding himself over until more regular singing jobs were available in the fall, but he had no intention of staying on after the summer was over. He could scarcely have predicted that he was about to embark on a career that would make him one of the most illustrious radio announcers of all time.

Like all his early colleagues, Graham McNamee was hired as an all-purpose announcer and performer. He announced, he talked, he sang; he acted as his own programmer, and when he was given big jobs, such as covering a political convention—which in present-day television would require the services of hundreds of newsmen of every description—he was all on his own. Before long McNamee became known as the best and most colorful sports broadcaster of his day, perhaps of any day. But from the beginning it was his style and personality that won him the hearts of millions.

Graham McNamee had a speaking voice that in every way equalled that of Milton Cross. But McNamee had some special qualities of his own. He developed a breezy and colorful delivery that contrasted with the formality of most of the announcers of the day—a style that worked particularly well in sportscasting, where color and imagination were needed to surmount the many lulls and dead spots. A man of quick response and vivid imagination, McNamee could fill the air with constant and rapid chatter, even during a slow-moving baseball game when nothing was going on between innings. His eye was constantly on the move, and he could describe to the listening audience all sorts of sideline activities with imagination and enthusiasm: straw hats being torn up during a baseball game, a fight between two fans wrestling over a ball in the grandstand, an argument between an umpire and manager, a pitcher working out in the bullpen, the mayor sitting in his box. McNamee's regular line of patter endeared him to millions of listeners.

Top: Graham McNamee, WEAF's top announcer in the mid-1920s, covers a football game. (Photo courtesy AT&T.) Bottom: WJZ's Norman Brokenshire. (Photo courtesy University of Illinois Library.)

Another announcer who quickly became a rival to McNamee as a popular and easily identifiable radio voice was Norman Brokenshire. Brokenshire was to remain a big-name announcer throughout the golden age of radio, although later bouts with alcoholism—seemingly an announcer's malady as much as it had reputedly long been the newspaper reporter's malady—caused him to be one of those vanishing and reappearing voices of radio.[2] For modulation Brokenshire had no equal in the radio field early or late, but in addition to that he had one of those easily recognizable voices that once heard is seldom forgotten and never confused with any other.

Brokenshire was born in Murcheson, Ontario, in 1898, the son of two parents of Scottish descent, his father being an itinerant Salvation Army preacher and later a YMCA secretary. Brokenshire grew up moving around to a number of towns both in eastern Canada and New England, although he liked to think that his voice retained the slightest touch of a mellow Canadian accent. He graduated from Arlington High School in Boston in 1915 and went immediately to work without much of a sense of direction. During his high school years he had already had a diversity of jobs—worked in a shoe factory, operated his own print shop and worked in a lumber camp, where he lost part of a thumb. After high school, when World War I broke out, Brokenshire was an apprentice draftsman at the General Electric plant at Schenectady, New York.

During World War I, Brokenshire served briefly as an infantryman, but the armistice was signed before he saw any active duty. Because of his father's interest in YMCA work, he got a job at the Fort Totten Long Island YMCA, helping out with returning servicemen. A small YMCA scholarship enabled him to attend Syracuse University for two years, although he had to make ends meet by working as a hotel desk clerk. In 1922 he returned to New York City, where he worked for a while doing advertising for a firm that had developed a new welding process.

Like so many of the other early announcers, Brokenshire got into radio by a kind of fluke. One day, after having enjoyed too many beers, he had shipped a company film to the wrong town and was fired. He kept warm memories of the boss who fired him, however, since while he was still on the job the boss had sent him on an errand to 33 West 42nd Street, a door marked "Broadcast Central," which now contained the studios of WJZ and its twin station WJY. Brokenshire was curious and opened the door leading to the broadcast studio, where he was met by a pretty receptionist. He asked her what were the chances of becoming a radio announcer. She told him they were about a thousand to one. Brokenshire went on his way, thinking that this dream was gone forever.

Later, however, after he had lost his job, and was looking through the want ads, he came across a brief ad that read:

Wanted: Announcer for Metropolitan radio station. Must be college graduate and have knowledge music terminology. Apply Broadcast Central, 33 W. 42nd Street, New York City.

Well, here was the same place he had visited, and they were actually advertising for announcers. Perhaps the chances were better than a thousand to one. Even though he knew he wasn't a college graduate, and even though he had no idea what they meant by "knowledge music terminology," he decided to apply. Boldly disregarding the qualifications, he sat down and wrote out an application. Days and weeks passed, and Brokenshire had nearly given up any hope of hearing about the job, when he received a postcard which read: "Please come to 33 West 42nd Street for audition."

That same old address again. He passed by the pretty receptionist, saying, "Remember me? I'm the one you told the chance was one in a thousand. Well, cross your fingers for me." As it turned out there were not a thousand other applicants, but only 73.

At the time Brokenshire had not the slightest idea of what a radio audition was all about. He was asked to read something out of a newspaper, a few prepared announcements each different in nature, a foreign news dispatch "stuffed with foreign names like dates in a pudding," and finally he was asked to do a little ad-libbing. Out of the corner of his eye, Brokenshire noticed a couple of men hovering over some instruments in a glass-enclosed control booth. He was later to find out that they were looking at an oscillograph that monitored the vibrations of the human voice. What the engineers were looking for in those days of still-primitive amplifiers and of carbon microphones was a well-modulated voice.

This test Brokenshire certainly passed; indeed it is unlikely that there was anybody in the whole history of radio with a more perfectly modulated voice than Norman Brokenshire. He could inject warmth and color in his voice without making that little needle waver in the slightest, no matter what kind of material he was required to read.

Brokenshire was called before Station Manager Charles B. Popenoe, who certainly must have been impressed by the testimony of the oscillograph, although he probably didn't reveal it to his applicant. It was 1924, and the stations were starting to take this craft of the announcer a little more seriously. Did he have a college education? Brokenshire bravely responded that he almost did. Knowledge of musical terminology? Frankly Brokenshire didn't have the musical background of a Milton Cross, but he brazenly insisted that he knew all of the musical terms, and could pronounce names like Peter Ilich Tchaikovsky, Sergei Vassilievich Rachmaninoff, Jean Sibelius, and Jascha Heifetz. He was given an issue of the *Musical Courier* to look over, and with the help of a studio employee, he practiced all of the hard names in the issue that Popenoe was asking people to read. Brokenshire apparently passed this test also.

"All right," said Popenoe, "you'll have a radio tryout tonight." He asked Brokenshire to come back at 6 P.M. and read the Dow Jones averages over the air. Alas, in his wild enthusiasm, Brokenshire took off without thinking about the time interval. He took the subway up to the eighties, where his brother Melvin was living in a rooming house. He was so enraptured by his new opportunity that he lost track of the time. When he looked at the clock it was ten minutes to six. No possible way to get back to 33 West 42nd Street in time to go on the air. But luck was with Norman Brokenshire that day. Tommy Cowan, now the station's chief announcer, called Mr. Popenoe and told him that Brokenshire was ready but flustered and nervous, and that he'd put him on the air later. This turned out to be good luck in more ways than one. Brokenshire's first air spot was an introduction of a pianist named Joel Coffey, and this gave him an opportunity to inject a little personality into the act — something that would have been impossible with the Dow Jones averages.

So Brokenshire was hired, and became a regular WJZ announcer, along with Tommy Cowan, Milton Cross and Major J. Andrew White. Being young and brash, he was determined to be more than a reader of prepared scripts. He believed that an announcer should get his individual charm and personality on the air, and he became an ad-libber and show stealer, to the annoyance and admiration of the studio bosses.

Brokenshire, like Graham McNamee, was blessed with the gift of gab — a sterling gift indeed in those early days of radio. While radio had come a long way in three years, programming was still unpredictable and imprecise. If people dropped into the studio, there was a program; if not, the announcer was usually stuck. If the weather was bad, nobody might show up at all. Brokenshire recalled one broadcast day when three separate acts failed to show. For the first he played the ukulele and piano and sang a bit. By the time of the second show he was at his wit's end. Again using his ingenuity and quick thinking, he pried open a window and dangled the microphone out the window. "Ladies and gentlemen," he said, "I give you the sounds of New York." Remarkably, a large number of people wrote in to say that they had enjoyed the city noises.

When Brokenshire began his announcing duties at WJZ the station was still following the policy of having announcers identify themselves with initials rather than names. Brokenshire became AON, just as Tommy Cown had been ACN and Milton Cross had been AJN. But with announcers over at WEAF like Graham McNamee using their own names, and a flood of mail coming in daily for announcers at WJZ, the policy was finally altered to permit announcers there to use their names over the air. Norman Brokenshire was transiently flustered, fearing that he ought to convert his initials AON into something resembling the initials by which he had become known by the public (for a while he thought of calling himself Arthur Owen), but when the big day came, he confidently and dramatically intoned his own name over the airwaves: "How do you do, ladies and gentlemen, how do you do. This . . . is Norman Brokenshire."

In 1924 announcers were not yet considered the stars of radio by studio executives, and announcers' pay was still low. Several months after starting work, Brokenshire was making only $65.00 a week. Ted Husing started at $45.00 a week. All of that would change when the mail started rolling in, and the listening audience came to identify the announcer as their friend and sole personal contact at the radio station.

For a time the studio bosses made concentrated efforts to keep the announcers from getting too big an opinion of themselves, but it was a losing battle. At WJZ Charles Popenoe heard about the hundreds of letters a day that had been arriving addressed to Norman Brokenshire, and he gave the order that the letters, as property of the station, be held up at the office, perhaps read through, and only a small number passed along to Brokenshire. Brokenshire countered this ploy by going to the post office and filling out a change of address form and renting an oversize box to receive his fan mail. Popenoe was surprised when the numbers of letters to Brokenshire dropped off dramatically, doubly so when he noticed his young star announcer walking around the studio with big wads of envelopes stuffed in his pockets.

By the middle twenties it was apparent to all concerned that the occupation of radio announcer was not to be taken lightly. If early announcers like Harold Arlin, Tommy Cowan and Norman Brokenshire just fell into their jobs by accident, serious efforts would soon be made to audition announcers, and to see to it that high standards of diction and pronunciation were maintained. Enough attention had been drawn to the art of radio announcing that in the middle twenties the English Department of New York University decided to run a voice analysis on the various popular announcers and to make a scientific determination of which voices were the most pleasing, which the most perfectly representative of American speech, and so on. (Graham McNamee and Norman Brokenshire were judged at the top by the professors.)

After the establishment of the radio networks—NBC in 1926 and CBS in 1929—the business of hiring and evaluating announcers became even more formalized and standardized. The networks quickly became aware of the cultural and educational significance of radio as a national medium, and efforts were made to see that announcers whose voices went to every corner of the land were exemplary speakers and men of some culture and educational achievement.

By the early 1930s, CBS took the lead in formalizing procedures of this sort by setting up its own school for announcers, and it appointed Professor Frank H. Vizetelly to head it. Vizetelly had been born in London and lived there until he was a young adult, but after coming to the United States had come to respect the virtues of a uniform American pronunciation, and he was determined to set down standards of purely Americanized English for radio announcers. This was in marked contrast to developments in England, where radio had fallen victim to a dreary high-cultural dialect, which sounded affected and phony to the vast majority of Englishmen.

In his work for CBS, Vizetelly made it clear that attempts to import a stilted form of English had no place on American radio. Some radio stations had previously sought to hire former actors and others who offered a forced British accent over the airwaves, but Vizetelly condemned this tendency in favor of a pure and natural style of American English, a style, it should be added, already spoken by the best of the early announcers. In various lectures on the virtues of American speech, Vizetelly made it clear that he was no admirer of "Oxford English," but instead was bent on "spreading the best traditions of American speech, which does not suppress its consonants nor squeeze the life out of its vowels." In one of his lectures he added:

Those who have been there tell us that only an Oxford man can understand a man from Oxford and that neither would want to understand anyone else.... Thank God that we talk to be understood, and that in the aggregate the voices of our announcers are clear, clean-cut, pleasant, and carry with them the additional charm of personal magnetism, which cannot be said of the delivery of the Cockney-bred announcers.[3]

NBC did not immediately follow suit and appoint an academic expert to monitor the speech patterns of its announcers, but eventually it hired Professor James F. Bender, director of the Speech and Hearing Clinic of Queens College, and Bender wrote a handbook of pronunciation for NBC announcers. Bender was quite in agreement with Vizetelly and others that the phony-sounding attempts at English speech should be purged from the American airways. In the introduction to his book he remarked:

While there are those in America who are strongly in favor of imposing Received Standard Pronunciation (i.e. Oxford English) upon American broadcasters—"to hasten the day when all English speaking people will speak alike"—they are not numerous.... The American broadcaster would be well advised to use a pronunciation widely known among phoneticians as General American, the standard presented in this book.[4]

And standard American it became, although probably not alone through the efforts of the academic advisors, who were mostly codifying what was already a fact of life. From the early twenties onward, with the exception of the occasional unemployed English actor who strayed into the radio world, or the misguided cultural enlightener, the American radio industry had already done the job. As early as 1925 no major metropolitan radio station would have hired to stand before a microphone the possessor of a Brooklyn accent, a hillbilly or Tidewater twang or a Boston broad A. Radio was a mass medium and it was the correct but warm and genial American pronunciation that was wanted. Thus American radio came to provide us with the sound of American English at its best, and it would be hard to think of any greater contribution of the radio medium in the first half-century of its existence.

Standards of hiring and general qualifications changed markedly in the radio announcing field after 1930. One interesting difference between the twenties and thirties was the almost complete disappearance of women as announcers after 1930. In the 1920s a fair number of women announcers were working in radio, but during the golden age of the thirties and forties they almost completely disappeared from the scene. (Women announcers have of course made a big comeback in the last several decades.)

Doubtless there were many people who made the argument that women's voices are not as pleasing over the air as men's voices; that the male voice is intrinsically more pleasing, more resonant, more mellow. The sonic superiority of the male voice is debatable, however, and it seems more likely that the disappearance of women from key announcing duties during the thirties was due to the fact that males simply muscled in on what had become a very lucrative profession and taken all the spoils for themselves.

But in the twenties, announcing was not considered a strictly male preserve. While Brokenshire and Cross were performing yeoman service for WJZ in the mid-twenties, Bertha Brainard was a successful full-time announcer for the same station. She performed regular announcing duties of a general sort, and although she never got assigned to the boxing ring or the Polo Grounds, she had her own show, "Broadcasting Broadway" (started as early as 1922), which she began with a dramatic alliteration: "Bertha Brainard broadcasts Broadway." Brainard for a time claimed the honorific "The First Lady of Radio," a title she shared with singer Vaughn De Leath.

Miss Brainard was actually preceded as an announcer at WJZ by Miss Helen Guy, the first woman to be employed as a full-time worker in broadcasting. Miss Guy went on to other chores, however, and became a longtime employee of NBC.

Some radio stations started right out with women announcers. Even before AT&T began operations at WEAF, it had Helen Hahn acting as "hostess" on WBAY. There was station WGU in Chicago, which went on the air in 1922 and soon changed its name to WMAQ. (WGU was owned by the *Chicago Daily News*, and had its first studio in the Fair Store at State and Adams.) Judith Waller was the first announcer, and she carried out her duties in a little corner of the store, which, like so many others in the early twenties, was seeking to sell radio sets to the multitudes. Waller was both announcer and station manager, and she moved with the station when it finally took up more ample quarters in the *Chicago Daily News* building. She was responsible, among other things, for the first broadcast of the Chicago Symphony Orchestra.

Naturally, women announcers did well on women's and children's programs, many of which made their appearance in radio's first decade. Dorothy Gordon, for example, was in charge of the first program for children on WEAF. Marie K. Neff conducted an early Women's Club feature on KDKA. Aleta Smith was an announcer and soprano soloist for WFI in Philadelphia. A certain "Miss Jones" was a very popular announcer and personality on KSD in St. Louis during the twenties.

By the late twenties, many new announcers, male and female, were coming to the medium from every corner of the globe, and even from abroad. (Alois Havrilla, one of the great announcers of the 1930s, was born in Austria-Hungary and grew up in a Slovakian community near Bridgeport, Connecticut, but he managed to speak a variety of American English that was well-nigh perfect.) Nor must it be thought that all the great radio announcers of the future got their start on WEAF or WJZ—the South, the vast Midwest and the West provided stars of the microphone from the very beginning. Few of the coming great announcers grew up in the affluent cities and suburbs of the East; their clarion voices were cultivated nearly everywhere Americans lived and breathed.

Consider Harry von Zell, for example—a Hoosier born and bred. His early years were spent far from the sophisticated dialects of either the East or West Coast. He spent much of his early life in and around Indianapolis and graduated from high school in Sioux City, Iowa. Later he entered the University of California at Los Angeles, where he played football for a year before being sidelined by an injury. For a while he contemplated a career as a singer, but he never considered himself good enough to make the grade. He did, however, as a kind of lark, sing over the radio in the mid-twenties, and it was soon discovered that he had a pretty good speaking voice. In 1926 von Zell heard that Station KMIC in Inglewood was looking for an announcer. He applied for and got the job, and thus he began his long radio career out on the West Coast.

Another transformed Midwesterner was Don Wilson, who was born in Lincoln, Nebraska, in 1900, but spent some time at the University of Colorado, where he was a football star. Like a number of other early radio men, and like a lot of young males in the twenties, Wilson was interested in singing, and got to announcing by the musical back door. Shortly after graduating from college, he joined a singing trio that became quite popular, and the group was eventually sponsored on tour by the Piggly-Wiggly chain of supermarkets—the "Piggly Wiggly Trio," it was called. The group began singing somewhat regularly on KFRC, San Francisco, in 1927, but a year later it transferred to KHJ in Los Angeles. Later on the group broke up and Wilson started doing stints as a radio announcer. Like Harry von Zell, he entered the business on the West Coast. (Don Wilson's longtime association with comedian Jack Benny began in 1934.)

Radio announcing during its heyday was an infectious disease, and very few who were bitten by the bug ever got away. The radio announcer was a much-loved American character, and even the lesser ones built up big followings. Perhaps it is something about America—the diversity of the population, the wide-open spaces, the impersonality of the cities and urban areas, that it takes to heart those who hold it together—entertainers, singers, movie actors, radio and television personalities. Somehow the early radio announcers were closer to Americans than all of these others; they were the country's friends and confidants even though their listeners didn't see them. The announcer was the link between each American and all the others in the world of entertainment, news and culture.

5. A Million Sets Are Sold

The decade of the 1920s, as we remember from our schoolbooks, was a time of unparalleled growth in the American economy. When the twentieth century began, at least half of the wealth of the nation still derived from agricultural pursuits. World War I changed all that with stunning suddenness. During the 1920s, with the possible exception of a brief period in 1920–22 that was witness to a minor economic slump, manufacturing became the business of America. When the decade was over, the United States led all the nations of the world in manufacturing of all sorts—automobiles, refrigerators, chemicals, dyes, clothing, tobacco, dynamos, road-building equipment, and, of course, radio.

The story of the rapid growth in the radio industry in the 1920s is a remarkable one, chiefly because the companies involved in it when World War I came to an end were poor prophets, and nary a one predicted the unprecedented growth that was to follow. Radio manufacturing slumped drastically immediately after the war. Most of the companies that had seen their lucrative war contracts dry up scarcely imagined the kind of radio boom that would shortly sweep the country.

Thus the hand of fate played a big part in the circumstances of radio manufacturing in the years 1920–22. Since the radio industry was not prepared to get into manufacturing in a big way, the industry itself (at least the giants of the industry) was splintered and subdivided in such a way that production of radio receiver sets was not, and would not be, given high priority until market demand came knocking loudly at the door.

The lack of preparedness can be laid at the doorstep of the newly formed giant, the Radio Corporation of America, which on March 1, 1920, took over all of the wireless stations of the American Marconi Company. When RCA was founded it was committed mainly to developing the field of wireless telegraphy, and it conceived its main business to be the sending of commercial messages over land and sea, ship-to-shore communications, ship-to-ship messages in code, and so on. RCA was conceived as and intended to be a communications company. In signing cross-licensing agreements with Westinghouse and General Electric, the business of manufacturing was turned over to those two companies, who already possessed the facilities for manufacturing. Under this agreement, RCA was to become the seller of equipment of its partners, but it was not permitted to manufacture equipment of its own.

68

All this seemed eminently sensible—in 1920. There would be radio receivers and radio transmitters produced in roughly equal numbers, and what was expected was a slow and steady upward curve of growth in the manufacture and sale of this equipment.

When Westinghouse founded its experimental station in the fall of 1920, with the idea that it might sell a lot more home receivers to individuals, executives at the Radio Corporation showed little if any interest—just a kind of mild amusement. It was just playing around, they thought, and little would come of it.

But the great radio boom of 1922 was to shake things up at the boardroom of RCA. It became suddenly obvious that the manufacturing of radio equipment was definitely going to be big business—so big that it would shortly dwarf the kind of ship-to-shore radio telegraphy traffic that heretofore had seemed to be their sole concern. All of a sudden there was a new kind of radio business that had not even been foreseen when RCA was founded in 1919. There was also a need for manufacturing that did not exist a few years earlier— the manufacturing and sale of vacuum tubes for the radio trade, radio parts for homemade sets, and finally complete radio sets themselves, constructed and assembled in the factory for sale to thousands of individual customers.

Of course, RCA did have that one true prophet on its staff in 1920: the young and brash David Sarnoff, who while still a junior executive of the American Marconi Company in 1916 had suggested the idea of a "Radio Music Box" that could be made and sold for mass consumption. Shortly after the founding of RCA, and before Westinghouse took its first fling into broadcasting, Sarnoff was again pressing his idea for the sale of radio sets to the public, which he believed was eager and anxious to buy. On January 31, 1920, Sarnoff sent a memo to RCA President Owen D. Young, again pushing his idea for the sale of radio music boxes. In this memo Sarnoff proved indisputably, although it could not have been known at the time, what a phenomenal prophet he really was. In that memo Sarnoff claimed that if radio music boxes were put into production and offered to the general public, it would be possible to sell 100,000 sets in the first year, with sales of $7,500,000. (In 1922 RCA's annual sales turned out to be $1,000,000.) During the second year, Sarnoff predicted sales of 300,000 radio music boxes with sales of $22,500,000. (RCA's sales in 1923 were $22,500,000, which means that three years previously Sarnoff had hit the figure exactly on the head!) The third year, he claimed, RCA would see sales of 600,000 radio music boxes at a total of $45,000,000; he was off but a jot (and this time on the conservative side): sales were $50,000,000.

The years between 1920 and 1925 must have given a jolt to executives of RCA (Sarnoff excepted), since by slow degrees they were forced into an awareness of the radio boom on which they would have profited mightily had they not been asleep at the switch when it all began. RCA began to move slowly toward the day when it would become a radio manufacturer, but for a few years it had to bide its time as a seller of equipment. Remember how the pooling agreement worked: Westinghouse and General Electric were to be the manufacturers, and RCA was to be the seller. In some ways this worked out pretty well for a time, although as the size of the stakes increased, RCA found itself having to coordinate the activities of the consortium, thus being drawn into research activities and toward an overseeing of both the market and manufacturing process. When Major Edwin Armstrong's amazing superheterodyne Radiola set was ready to be marketed to the public in 1924, it was largely through the efforts of RCA scientists and experimenters.

For several years, though, RCA had to cool its heels while all of its radio receivers were made by Westinghouse or the General Electric Company.[1] And things rolled along nicely at Westinghouse. A catalogue issued from Westinghouse probably in the early 1920s, referring to Frank Conrad's experimental station 8XK, offered an RC receiver, an RA tuning device (component parts) and DA crystal detector and amplifier. A price list issued on August 21, 1921, refers to this same set plus another called "Aeriola, Jr.," equipped with a crystal detector. This would seem to imply that most of the early sets made to greet the expected radio boom were still of the crystal variety.

After Westinghouse entered the cross-licensing agreements with RCA and GE by the spring of 1922, RCA was offering a number of sets for sale to the public, some manufactured by Westinghouse and some by General Electric:

Receiving Apparatus	Manufacturer
AR 1300	General Electric
AA 1400	General Electric
ER 753	General Electric
Aeriola, Jr.	Westinghouse
Aeriola, Sr.	Westinghouse
Aeriola Grand	Westinghouse
RC	Westinghouse
RA and DA	Westinghouse

This gives a good idea of the kind of primitive receiving equipment available at the time for the home radio enthusiast who was not a do-it-yourself expert. Responding, however, to the great radio boom of 1922, with 200 new radio broadcasting stations springing up all over the country, the number of sets available from RCA nearly doubled by the following year, and a keen interest in merchandising had obviously given them much more exuberant and marketable names. According to the RCA price list of May 1, 1923,[2] the following sets were available from the company:

Receiving Apparatus	Manufacturer
Radiola I	General Electric
Radiola II	General Electric

Radiola IV	General Electric
Radiola V	General Electric
Radiola VI	General Electric
Radiola Senior	Westinghouse
Two-stage amplifier, AC	Westinghouse
RS receiver with detector and one-stage amplifier	Westinghouse
RG Radiola Grand	Westinghouse
RT Antenna coupler	Westinghouse
RA tuner	Westinghouse
AR three-stage radio amplifier	Westinghouse
DA detector-amplifier	Westinghouse
AA 1520 three-stage radio amplifier	General Electric
AA 485	Wireless Specialty

The very nifty and attractive name "Radiola" was to remain the sole possession of RCA and its collaborators ever since David Sarnoff had been attracted to the term for his radio box in 1920. The first Radiola, Radiola I, was actually nothing more than a crystal set, but soon the term would be applied to assembled tube-sets, later to Major Armstrong's superheterodyne, and still later to AC plug-in sets and giant consoles. This magical word was RCA's ace-in-the-hole for an entire generation.

None of this means to suggest that the manufacturing of radio sets became the sole province of RCA and its manufacturing allies, for such was not the case. It is true that when RCA was founded, and when it brought Westinghouse into its ken in 1921, every single important radio patent was in its pocket, and the stage was set for a complete monopolistic takeover of the radio industry. But in 1923, when RCA had sales of $22,500,000, nationwide sales of radio equipment totaled $136,000,000, meaning that the Radio Corporation had less than a fifth of national sales. These figures indicate that there was still plenty of room for the small manufacturer. And some of these manufacturers were not so small. Indeed, some of them became pretty gigantic in their own right.

One may wonder how it was that RCA, with all of its patented richness, was not able to gain a nearly complete monopoly over the radio sales business. The answer is that patents on radio equipment just didn't amount to anything in those days. In fact, they hadn't really stood up very well since the appearance of the Audion. Beginning as far back as 1910–12, Lee De Forest's little device was bootlegged, pirated, modified and revamped so many times that patent infringers were always one step ahead of the legal system. It was usually the case that by the time an offender was hauled into court for patent infringement, the state of the art had advanced so far that the old issues were moot.

The same thing would happen in the 1920s when the battle for sale of home sets was joined. So fast and furious were the developments during those years that even the giants were not able to keep up with it all. As soon as they took it upon themsleves to bring to the bar of justice some offender in Philadelphia, Chicago or Cincinnati, the technology involved in the lawsuit was already too crude and primitive to be squabbling over. At the same time, some of these rival companies became exceptionally good customers for RCA tubes and parts, so that RCA's incentive to deal them a real death blow was sharply reduced. Why throw one of your best customers to the mat when he is eagerly sending you orders for millions of dollars worth of parts? The expected war against patent infringers never really got underway, never really had heart behind it. Anyway, these were the 1920s, the great boom years. There was, and would continue to be, business for everyone.

To be sure, in the mid-twenties it looked for a time at least as if RCA would obtain a clear monopoly in at least one area of radio production: the manufacture of vacuum tubes. During 1922 RCA sold 1,583,021 tubes. Many of these went into new sets manufactured by RCA collaborators. On the other hand, it was evident to RCA executives that the many hundreds of little receiver makers were buying RCA tubes and putting them in sets of their own design. RCA took strong actions to stem this tide of wandering tubes, although naturally they weren't completely displeased by the revenues from them. They initiated legal action against firms using RCA tubes in non–RCA sets, and they fired distributors who allowed the tubes to go elsewhere. For a while it seemed that they might be successful in effecting a monopoly.

Still, with some of the older patents wearing out, and with new developments rushing in daily, it became impossible for any one company to secure a monopoly even in a specialized area. RCA had a number of strong competitors in tube manufacturing as the decade wore on: the De Forest Company, Sylvania, Raytheon National Union, Arcturus, Ceco, Ken-Rad, Hytron and others.

Nonetheless, tube-making for sale by RCA was an enormous enterprise, involving numerous plants and many thousands of workers. Most of the tubes during these years were manufactured at the East Pittsburgh Westinghouse plant and at two GE plants, one at Nila Park, Cleveland, Ohio, and the other at the Edison Lamp Works in Harrison, New Jersey. The last named of these plants was eventually bought by RCA, after they had finally broken the agreements which prohibited them from manufacturing. This historic plant, Edison's original lamp works in 1881, converted to making vacuum tubes in World War I, and RCA took it over in the late twenties, intending to push tube production to the limit. And they did. The Harrison installation eventually became the world's largest tube-making plant. By the outbreak of World War II in 1941 it had an annual production of 40,000,000 tubes. At that time it employed 6,000 workers, making more than 300 different kinds of tubes.

Outside the area of tubes, RCA was scarcely ever able to sew up the radio

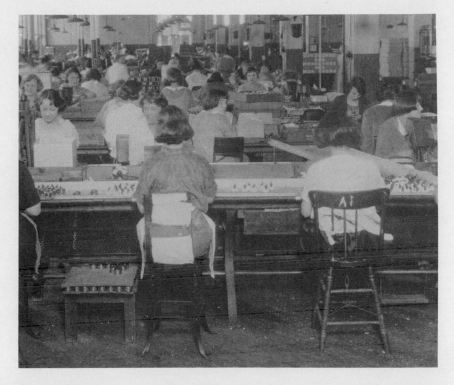

By the mid-twenties, radio manufacturing had clearly become big business. These women, working on mass production lines at General Electric's Schenectady plant, turned out tubes by the thousands. (Photo courtesy General Electric.)

manufacturing business. Some first-rate competitors quickly emerged, and a few of them became large corporations. Even if you added up the sales of the RCA-Westinghouse-GE consortium, the radio manufacturing business remained, as it had been since its inception, a scattered industry, with room in it for plenty of entrepreneurs. Some were fly-by-night operators; others were comers; still others were fanatical scientific types who would look for perfection but never manage to turn a dollar.

Far from being a monopolistic industry, then, as one might expect, the radio manufacturing industry seemed to have a place for every loner and eccentric—at least during the 1920s. By 1924 there were more than 3,000 makers of radio parts in the United States (this before the rage to make completely assembled sets caught on). Consider the example of Newark, New Jersey, home of Westinghouse's first broadcast station in the New York metropolitan area, WJZ, and of that other great early station, WOR. Newark quickly became an important center of the radio manufacturing industry. Not only did it have the Westinghouse plant itself, it had a number of other major companies as well, including Kolster and Splitdorf, the former being one of the largest radio manufacturers in the twenties, the latter devoting itself very early to the manufacture of complete sets. Furthermore, in neighboring Harrison there was the aforementioned RCA installation.

However, in spite of all these giants gathering in the vicinity, the Newark area was a long way from being dominated by the big names. In 1924 Newark alone had 150 radio parts firms, all struggling ambitiously for their share of the ever-growing market.

Certain companies, though, did come to dominate the industry as they do to this day, and some of these names are engraved in radio history. One name that came to the surface in the early twenties was Powel Crosley, Jr., of Cincinnati, Ohio, whose Crosley Manufacturing Company began early production of inexpensive broadcast receivers that he called the "Model T" of radio. Millions of these sets were sold in the twenties at remarkably low prices. Crosley was one of the first on the market with a good regenerative receiver. He also incorporated a popular "book" tuning condenser that had been invented by Hugo Gernsback. The low cost of this condenser helped to endear it to millions. Crosley also involved himself in the broadcasting business as a way of promoting his set, and he founded station WLW in Cincinnati, one of the most powerful American radio stations in the 1920s.

If Powel Crosley's company became the Ford of radio manufacturers, the Atwater Kent Company of Philadelphia became the Buick or Oldsmobile, selling well-made sets to discriminating buyers. Kent had begun his career as an electrical manufacturer, but by 1921 he was marketing a line of high-quality "breadboard" radio components for the home assembler. Kent began making complete sets in 1923, and later made some first-rate console radios. To those who remember the 1920s, the name Atwater Kent remains synonymous with high-quality radio manufacturing. The Kent Company continued in business in Philadelphia until 1936, at which time it succumbed to the deluge of cheaply manufactured sets crowding in to meet the depression demand.

Another Philadelphia manufacturer was Philco (short for the Philadelphia Storage Battery Company), which became a major manufacturer in the 1920s, and which, unlike Atwater Kent, weathered the years. Philco would shortly become a leading supplier of automobile radios.

Out in Chicago another giant was to make an early appearance on the scene. This was the Zenith Radio Corporation, founded in 1923 by Lt. Commander Eugene F. McDonald, U.S.N., retired. Zenith took over the business of the Chicago Radio Laboratory, which had been in existence since 1919, and went on to become one of the world's largest manufacturers of radio sets, a distinction the company carried into the television era.

There were other companies from the twenties that outlasted the pioneering days—companies like Magnavox and Stromberg-Carlson. There were others whose names became household words in the 1920s but who have now faded into the recesses of history, even though a few of them were multimillion-dollar businesses in their day. Their names still mean something to nostalgic radio buffs. In the East, these included the Federal Telephone and Telegraph Company of Buffalo, New York; the Free-Eisemann Radio Corporation of Brooklyn, New York; A.H. Grebe & Co. of New York;

the Mu-Road Laboratories of Asbury Park, New Jersey; the Clapp-Eastham Company of Cambridge, Massachusetts; F.A.D. Andrea, Inc. (manufacturers of FADA), of New York; and the National Company of Malden, Massachusetts (maker of the four-tube "Thrill Box").

Besides the giants, Zenith and Crosley, the Midwest proved to be rich soil for the radio manufacturer. There was the Kodel Manufacturing Company of Cincinnati, Ohio; the Michigan Radio Corporation of Grand Rapids, Michigan; the Thordarson Manufacturing Company of Chicago; and the Pfanstiehl Radio Company of Highland Park, Illinois.

Even the West Coast became a beehive of radio manufacturing activity. Magnavox had its roots there, but there were other leaders, especially the Colin B. Kennedy Company, which, like Magnavox, centered in San Francisco. In Los Angeles there were the Gilfillan Brothers, makers in 1924 of the splendid Gilfillan Neutrodyne.

Interestingly enough, the radio manufacturing scene in the 1920s had room in it for some real old-timers. Lee De Forest, who had seen many of his early radio ventures rudely snatched away, did not roll over and play dead. After 1920 he had to watch the development of radio mostly from the sidelines, while those who had "stolen" his invention made great fortunes for themselves. Nonetheless, there continued to be a De Forest Radio Corporation, successor to other companies of the same name that had been crushed by litigation or poor financial management. During the 1920s De Forest maintained a factory in Passaic, New Jersey, which manufactured all kinds of radio equipment.

De Forest concerned himself with (among other things) the development of talking pictures. Television also became a concern of the De Forest Company during those years. The company tried at first to make something out of a kind of crude television system invented by Charles F. Jenkins that used a mechanical scanner (instead of the video tube employed in today's television). The Jenkins television was actually manufactured and sold by De Forest in the twenties, although it gave a very poor-quality picture.

Though television was an idea whose time had yet to come, radio's day had arrived. It rapidly became a giant — one of the great American industries. The sales figures for radio equipment in the middle years of the 1920s tell the story:

1922	$ 60,000,000
1923	136,000,000
1924	358,000,000
1925	430,000,000
1926	506,000,000
1927	425,600,000
1928	650,550,000
1929	842,548,000[3]

When MARCONI heard the AERIOLA GRAND

"IT comes closest to the dream I had when I first caught the vision of radio's vast possibilities. It brings the world of music, news and education into the home, fresh from the human voice. It solves the problem of loneliness and isolation.

"The Aeriola Grand is at present the supreme achievement in designing and constructing receiving sets for the home—a product of the research systematically conducted by scientists in the laboratories that constitute part of the R C A organization."

In tone quality, in simplicity of manipulation the Aeriola Grand is unrivaled. A child can snap the switch and move the single lever that tunes the Aeriola Grand and floods a room with song and speech from the local broadcasting station.

The Importance of the Symbol R C A

RADIO has taken such hold of the public that it quite naturally has attracted the attention of a host of inventors and manufacturers.

Crude radio apparatus of a kind can be made even by embryonic organizations. But the vitally important inventions that have made radio the possession of every man, woman and child are those developed as the result of costly research conducted in the engineering laboratories of the Radio Corporation of America.

The name-plate of a Radio Set is all-important in the purchase of radio apparatus. If it bears the letters "RCA" the public and the dealer are assured that at the time of its introduction it is the highest expression of the advancing art of radio.

No other organization has manufacturing facilities equal to those of the Radio Corporation of America, and capable of meeting the demands of the public and the dealer.

Before purchasing any Radio Set, be sure to buy the book "Radio Enters the Home" at your dealer—Price 35c or write direct to

Any R C A dealer will be pleased to show you the Aeriola Grand and to let you judge its wonderful tone quality for yourself.

"There's a Radiola for every purse"
—from $18 to $350

Aeriola Grand
with stand
$350

This symbol of quality is your protection

Radio WORLD WIDE WIRELESS Corporation of America

Sales Department   District Office
233 Broadway   10 South LaSalle St.
New York City   Chicago, Ill.

Above and on following page are examples of the kind of advertising that helped swell the sales of radio sets in the 1920s. Above: one of the first ads to appear in mass circulation magazines, 1923. Following page: 1925 ad for a Radiola, a patented name used by RCA in the twenties for many of its sets.

It is doubtful if any other manufacturing industry in the United States witnessed a growth of this rapidity at any point in our history. After three decades, the phonograph industry had managed to place 13,000,000 phonographs in homes. After a quarter of a century, the automobile industry in America had produced slightly more than 19,000,000 automobiles. In half a century, the telephone company had managed to boost the number of subscribers in the United States to 18,000,000 — all this by 1928.[4] In January 1922 there were a mere 60,000 radio sets in use in the United States, probably serving an audience of about 75,000 people. By 1928, however, 7,500,000 homes were equipped with radio sets, with a listening audience of nearly one-third of the population of the United States. The sales figures above show that from 1922 to 1929 there was an increase in sales volume of over 1,400 percent.

Obviously this unique growth was very largely tied to the proliferation of radio broadcasting stations in 1922 and thereafter. On the other hand, that is only one side of the story. The radio manufacturing and distributing industries geared up and met the challenge of the demand as soon as it appeared—even RCA, which a few years earlier had laughed at the idea that individual citizens would want to have radio receiving sets in their homes. Looking back from the perspective of a much calmer and better organized electronics industry in the middle of the twentieth century, it is a great wonder how it all could have been accomplished.

For some reason not altogether clear, the demand for radio was created as much on the retail level as anywhere else. When the great radio boom of 1922 began it seemed as though everybody wanted to get in on the sale of radio equipment. Radio stores popped up everywhere. Department stores all found it necessary to establish a radio department or section, and, as we are already aware, many of them established broadcasting stations right on their premises, sometimes right in the radio sales department itself. But that's only the beginning of the story. During the chaotic days of 1922 and 1923, everybody wanted to sell radio sets, no matter what his original line of business. Florist shops, drug stores, furniture stores, grocery stores, general stores, candy stores, even undertakers and plumbers clamored for franchises. Nearly everybody in any kind of retailing business tried to get in on the act. And because there were so many manufacturers selling their wares, almost anybody who wanted a franchise was able to get one from this manufacturer or that.

Whoever had radio sets for sale in the period between 1922 and 1924 could almost be assured that he would sell out his stock. One could wander down a street in a small town almost anywhere in Middle America and see signs advertising radio equipment. Ofttimes a general store or florist shop would have a radio loudspeaker placed outside blasting away, acting as an advertisement for the equipment on sale inside. It could be that the golden age of radio broadcasting would not arrive until the 1930s, but the 1920s was the golden age of radio technology and gadgetry; the public could not seem to get enough of this marvelous and still magical device.

The large manufacturing companies almost immediately assembled enormous sales forces to distribute their products. By 1923 RCA had 200 distributors or jobbers selling to 15,000 dealers. The jobber became the fulcrum of the sales operation in most of the big companies like RCA, Crosley and Atwater Kent, although other manufacturers—Stromberg-Carlson and Freshman for example—used direct manufacturer-to-dealer distribution.

In spite of the demand that seemed to be springing up so naturally in the early years of the radio boom, the radio manufacturing industry took nothing for granted, and adopted its own aggressive selling techniques to reach out to the general public.

Probably the most widely used advertising technique in the first few years was free newspaper publicity. Since the novelty of radio appealed to everybody, and the newspapers had not yet been threatened by this new medium, most were more than willing to cooperate in featuring news stories

RCA publicity photo shows a Radiola portable, ca. 1926. Radios by this time were available in a variety of sizes and models, adding to their popularity. (Photo courtesy RCA.)

about radio broadcasting in the many fan magazines, such as *QST, Radio News* and *Wireless Age*. By 1924 there were nearly thirty such fan magazines with a combined circulation of over 1,000,000 copies. Advertising in such publications was a surefire way of reaching the hot-blooded radio enthusiast.

Another good way of reaching the enthusiastic amateur was through catalogues, price lists, slick paper brochures, newsletters and house organs. Specialized information of this kind was candy to multitudes who enjoyed being initiates in the arcane art of radio, given every opportunity to assemble the various parts and circuits readily becoming available.

By the middle twenties, every known medium of advertising had been used to sell home radio receivers: direct mail, billboards, newspapers, magazines, trade organs, sales brochures, window displays. Not to be forgotten as a sales tool is radio broadcasting itself. As the restrictions against radio advertising were slowly lifted, receiver manufacturers took to the airwaves and advertised their wares by sponsoring radio programs, some of them highly successful in the twenties. RCA, Atwater Kent, Philco and Crosley all sponsored programs with the perfectly evident and sensible idea of selling their equipment.

Atwater Kent created and sponsored some of the best programming of the decade. The famous "Atwater Kent Radio Hour" made its debut on New York's WEAF on January 22, 1925. Kent also sponsored the "Atwater Kent Radio Artists," and, perhaps most important of all as a trendsetter in excellence, the "WEAF Grand Opera Company," which took to the air late in 1925. These Sunday evening broadcasts became an immediate and smashing success and were channeled to a group of stations (although the NBC network had not yet been established). So it is a splendid truth of history that the radio manufacturers were not interested only in selling sets; they had a vested interest in the quality of broadcasting that reached the general public.

The selling of radio in the 1920s was a herculean effort by any standard of evaluation. On the other hand, when we consider the reluctance of giants like RCA, GE and AT&T to get into the field of broadcasting at the dawn of the decade, there is a certain sense in which we have to admit that the radio sold itself to the American public. This great little contraption was ideally suited to the American continent — a land of great physical distances and frequent isolation. During the 1920s there were literally millions of citizens who got their first radio only a shade after they received electrical power, and when they did so it was because of a felt need for communication with the centers of power, culture and affluence, often thousands of miles away.

When David Sarnoff originally made his prediction about the possible sale of hundreds of thousands of radio music boxes, he was doubtless thinking that these boxes would have widespread appeal because they would be pleasing sources of home entertainment. And they have been, of course. On the other hand, radio became much more — a household utility, yes, but a lifeline that held a nation and society together.

6. The Beckoning Hand
of Advertising

When commercial radio broadcasting began in 1920, there were few who bothered to question how this new means of communication would be financed. Who would pay for programs, radio performers and the like? This question didn't seem to be a momentous one at the time because early stations like KDKA were not very expensive to run. Westinghouse executives were confident that the small expenditures of their own capital would eventually be offset by income from the sale of radio receiver sets to the general public. And if the scale of operations had remained as it was in the early twenties, this might have been a realistic expectation.

But radio grew rapidly and became a popular medium. By the mid-twenties the stations in large metropolitan areas started experiencing demands for better programs and longer program days. Gone were the times when a single announcer could play a few borrowed phonograph records, read headlines from a local newspaper or announce a piano solo by the wife of one of the company's employees. Professional talent would be needed, and eventually this would cost money. To be sure, for a while, some opera star or vaudevillian would consent to go on the air for free, as a caper, or to earn a little publicity, but with the listening audience growing into the hundreds of thousands, and finally the millions, this kind of generosity could no longer be expected.

David Sarnoff of RCA, never daunted by problems that stood in the way of his dream of putting a radio music box in every American home, came up with a proposal for financing that might have worked had circumstances been favorable. Sarnoff immediately saw that the suggestions some had made of persuading listeners to make small contributions were unworkable; collection would be difficult, and eventually people would get tired of paying or being dunned for regular payments. In a letter dated June 17, 1922, Sarnoff made a brilliant and well-reasoned suggestion:

> Let us organize a separate and distinct company, to be known as the Public Service Broadcasing Company, or the American Radio Broadcasting Company, or some similar name. . . .
> Since the proposed company is to pay the cost of broadcasting as well as

81

the cost of its own administrative operations, it is of course necessary to provide it with a source of income sufficient to defray all its expenses.

As a means for providing such income, I tentatively suggest that the Radio Corporation pay over to the Broadcasting Company, two percent of its gross radio sales, that the General Electric and Westinghouse Companies do likewise and that our proposed licensees be required to do the same.[1]

This, of course, was a formalization and codification of an idea that was already implied in the operation of the early experimental stations like KDKA and WJZ, owned by Westinghouse, and WGY, owned by General Electric. It was a good and plausible suggestion that Sarnoff continued to champion and refine over the next several years. Unfortunately it came to naught. While the consortium of RCA, GE and Westinghouse manufactured a large share of radio receiving sets manufactured in the United States, they did not have anything like a real monopoly. Little manufacturing companies were mushrooming up everywhere, and all of them regarded the radio giants as "the enemy." Not a one of them was about to hand over a portion of its profits to some collusive broadcasting entity owned by RCA, GE and Westinghouse for the gain and profit of those monsters. However good the idea may have been, it eventually faded before the realities of the rapidly growing and diversifying radio manufacturing industry.

During the years between 1922 and 1925 there was considerable public discussion in journals of opinion and in all kinds of political forums about possible ways to finance large-scale broadcasting. Persisting during this period was the idea that radio could somehow be sustained by public-spirited citizens. For example, it was widely hoped that a figure like Andrew Carnegie or John D. Rockefeller might step forward and endow some large foundation for the support of broadcasting. But none appeared. Another popular idea called for the establishment of a "common fund ... controlled by an elected board," which would invite donations from the public. Nothing came of that idea, partially for reasons already perceived by David Sarnoff, and partially because skeptics and cynics were not convinced by the allegedly philanthropic nature of this kind of scheme.

Another popular suggestion at this time was that radio be financed by municipalities, and there were numerous early moves in this direction. One example was the city of New York, where two of the city's prominent boosters, Grover Whalen and Rodman Wanamaker, sought to establish a city-owned radio station. The station, when it finally went on the air in 1924 with the call letters WNYC, became a model for a limited number of other municipal stations around the country. On the other hand, outside of the local backers there seemed to be little enthusiasm in radio circles for this kind of approach. Secretary of Commerce Herbert Hoover, an opponent of government-owned radio in any form, was cool to the idea, although he was eventually forced to grant a license to WNYC and other municipal stations. The commercial radio giants were more actively hostile. AT&T at first refused to supply WNYC lines for remote broadcasting, insisting that WEAF was available and at the disposal of the city for public service announcements and programming. But Grover Whalen rightly countered that all of the city's needs could not be met when the commercial stations really got going.

A more likely, and actually more widespread, proposal was that radio be financed in some way by the states. And many states did get into subsidizing radio in the twenties, mostly through the aegis of their land-grant universities, which were natural places for radio trial and experimentation. Interest on state university campuses went back quite a way. Indeed, a few stations, such as 9XM at the University of Wisconsin, predated the KDKA debut. As early as 1917, Professor Earle M. Terry at Wisconsin was sending weather bulletins to nearby farmers, and he had switched to voice transmission of these broadcasts by 1919 or 1920. In the early 1920s, there were a great many college and university radio stations, and they represented during those years a much more potent force in the broadcasting arena than they would in later years.

There was still another strong possibility to be explored, and it was one that surely looked good on paper. In the mid-twenties, *Radio Broadcast* magazine offered a $500.00 prize for the best essay on the topic, "Who Is to Pay for Broadcasting, and How?" The winning essay, which appeared in the March 1925 issue of *Radio Broadcast*, suggested that radio broadcasting be supported by means of a tax—$2.00 per tube or 50 cents for a crystal set—and that the annual proceeds be turned over to a central broadcasting organization.

The idea of supporting broadcasting through taxation was an appealing one, and it took hold briskly elsewhere in the world during the 1920s. Great Britain, the country with the largest number of receivers outside the United States, took the lead. In Britain radio immediately fell under the sway of the government, its radio system being owned and operated by the British Broadcasting Corporation, a public corporation without share capital, organized under a Royal Charter in the national interest.[2] British broadcasting was financed by means of a license fee on sets, which was set at $2.43 (American equivalent) annually.

The idea was obviously a tempting one, and it apparently worked fairly well in England, although it was not without its difficulties. One difficulty was the staggering administrative costs involved. The BBC was operated by the Postmaster General, and an unseemly large portion of the revenues from the license fees disappeared into postal department coffers to meet general expenses of government, with the result that broadcasting per se was not as well funded as it might have been.

Another difficulty of the British system revolved around the means of collection. Owners of sets were supposed to pay their fees at the post office, but many did not. By 1931 it was estimated that there were 400,000 bootleg sets in London alone. Many owners did not pay up in spite of regular coaxing by government officials. Although it was very inefficient, the government had to invest in a fleet of trucks equipped with a radio detecting apparatus. These trucks were sent to various towns and neighborhoods, and the offending owners were hauled into court. The resulting publicity of these cases brought many offenders to heel, but the method was still not altogether satisfactory.

In other European countries a similar tendency to bring radio under government monopoly prevailed in the 1920s. In pre–Hitler Germany revenue was mainly raised by taxation, although the amount charged per set was twice that in Britain. In the 1920s the stations were controlled by the post office as they were in Great Britain, but German radio was far less centralized. Instead of one giant system there were nine districts and a certain amount of local control. Interestingly, too, while the government owned the stations, programming was provided by privately owned companies. Advertising appeared fairly early in Germany, although it was limited to a certain period of the day — between 8 and 9 A.M., or occasionally till noon.

In France broadcasting was poorly developed in the 1920s, but there was a curious mix of private and government ownership. About half of the stations were government owned and half privately owned. The privately owned stations accepted advertising and quickly became prosperous.

Not all of the reasons for nations deciding on private or governmental control of broadcasting were purely economic. Sometimes there were other motives. An excellent example was Canada, which started out in the twenties with a system much like that in the United States, in fact almost exclusively given over to private ownership of radio stations and broadcasting facilities. However, in the early thirties, the Canadian parliament appointed a Commission on Radio Broadcasting, which issued a report in 1932 recommending a drift toward government ownership and operation of stations. Under this proposal advertising would not be completely prohibited, but limited to 5 percent of the entire program time.

But it was not strictly a loathing of commercialism that motivated the Canadians; it was the belief that commercialism brought dominance of programming by their neighbor to the south — the United States. The members of the Canadian commission believed that the majority of programs being heard in Canada came from sources outside the country, and this reception would tend "to mold the minds of the young people in the home to ideals and opinions that are not Canadian." There may have been economic motives underlying this desire for cultural independence, and there is reason to suspect that the Canadian government was annoyed by a rising sale of American products during the dark years of the depression; but most importantly, the impetus which led to the founding of the great Canadian Broadcasing System as a government-subsidized entity was the strongly held belief that only government ownership could secure Canadian programming in the face of powerful radio voices south of the border.

Now there is no reason why some form of governmental or quasi-governmental monopoly couldn't have worked in the United States, with high-quality broadcasting achieved through that end. On the other hand, it is doubtful that purely public broadcasting would have provided for the great diversity of broadcasting that the United States has enjoyed in the last half of the century — and the considerable freedom allowed to it as well. The American way was different from the start, and in large measure this was because the 1920s were a time in which American politics was devoted to free enterprise and to government noninterference. Under the stewardship of men like Secretary of Commerce Herbert Hoover, the United States government was squeamish about regulating radio, to say nothing of owning and operating radio stations. There was never really a strong impetus for radio to be anything but private enterprise.

This did not mean, however, that politicians had determined that radio should be supported by advertising. Quite the opposite. They were appalled by the idea of advertising and made serious efforts to keep it out. Herbert Hoover on numerous occasions made public pronouncements of his fear that the radio airwaves would be polluted by "advertising chatter." In the Washington Radio Conference in 1924 he proclaimed that, "If a speech by the President is to be used as the meat in a sandwich of two patent medicine advertisements, there will be no radio left." The philosophy of the responsible public men in the mid-twenties was that radio should be privately owned and managed, but that selling commercial products should be kept out at all costs.

Nonetheless, in spite of all the good will and public-spirited idealism, advertising did eventually get a foothold in American broadcasting. It crept in slowly during the mid-twenties. For a long time, efforts were made to keep the advertiser's voice in check. But ultimately all efforts to restrict advertising failed, and American commercial radio took the form we identify with it today. But for a few years the advertising interests had to battle their way along.

How, then, did it all happen? Advertising grew out of a concept of radio broadcasting that did not in itself tolerate the idea of advertising in programming, but nonetheless paved the way for commercialism to enter by means of a back door. This concept was enunciated by the American Telephone & Telegraph Company when it established its anchor station in New York, WEAF. WEAF was established as a "toll station," the idea behind it being that people who had something to broadcast would pay for the service, much as they paid for telephones in their homes. It was not commercialism that AT&T had in mind, but public service.

To understand the original and somewhat innocent idea of a toll station today one has to understand how the telephone company conceived of radio. Unlike RCA, GE and Westinghouse, the telephone company got involved in radio as a possible arm of its long-distance phone service. Indeed, when WEAF was started it was a function of AT&T's long-lines department. Having discovered the unreliability of coast-to-coast and other long-distance telephone communication by means of wires stretched out across the countryside, AT&T was very much interested in radio transmission as a way of long-distance communication. (In fact this experimentation did pay off for the telephone company, since most long-distance calls made by telephone today are radio transmissions.) When they established their radio station, the analogy that came to the minds of the telephone executives was an analogy with telephone service.

Accordingly, in 1922, when AT&T was about to open WEAF, a company official explained the mission of the station to the public. "The company will furnish no programs whatsoever over the station. It will provide facilities over which the general public, one and all alike, may use those services." The emphasis would be on the needs of a sender with some message to transmit. AT&T's press memo made the objective perfectly clear. "Just as the company leases its long-distance wire facilities for the use of newspapers, banks, and other concerns, so it will lease its radio telephone facilities and will not provide the matter which is sent from this station."[3]

The stated idea that WEAF would provide no material of its own was particularly shortsighted; AT&T must have realized from the start that few would step forward to pay a toll to broadcast over the radio. As things turned out, the station was in operation for about six months before the first toll broadcaster appeared. In the meantime, the station hired a program manager, announcers and other staff, and essentially operated much like all the other stations then in existence.

Those willing to pay eventually started to trickle in. As far as is known, the first toll broadcast over WEAF took place on August 28, 1922, between 5 and 5:30 P.M., when a program contained a ten-minute message to the public from the Queensboro Corporation to promote the sale of apartments in Jackson Heights, Queens, New York. The promotional message was ingeniously interwoven with a talk about the great American novelist Nathaniel Hawthorne, for whom the Queensboro Corporation had named one of its apartment groups at Jackson Heights.

The speaker, who lauded Hawthorne as America's greatest writer of fiction, cleverly tied the author to the development that bore his name in Queens: "This sort of residential environment strongly influenced Hawthorne. . . . He analyzed with charming keenness the social spirit of those who had thus happily selected their homes, and he painted the people inhabiting those homes with good natured relish."

The Queensboro Corporation paid $50.00 for the broadcast, which was repeated on four additional occasions. They also bought half an hour of evening time at $100.00, bringing in total revenues of $350.00. The following month two other toll users showed up, Tidewater Oil and the American Express Company, each buying a half an hour of evening time. Thus the results for the first two active months of toll broadcasting were $550.00, obviously a mere fraction of the operating cost of the station during that period.

During December 1922 and January 1923 there seems to have been a decided increase of sponsored broadcasts, although still scarcely enough to subsidize the toll booth of the air. Among the sponsors in this period were some whose motives surely must have gone beyond those of the public-spirited citizen. There were, for example, programs paid for by the R.H. Macy Department Store, the James A. Hearn Co., the Greeting Card Association, the American Hard Rubber Company, the Bedford YMCA, the Haynes Automobile Company, the National Surety Company, and the Metropolitan Insurance Company.

Not one of these sponsors made anything like a sales pitch as we know it today, but the identification between sponsor and program subject matter was not exactly what you would call distant. The Greeting Card Association presented a program entitled "The Story of the Christmas Card," which appropriately aired on December 21, 1922. Macy's offered several programs about Santa Claus and other seasonal characters then stalking the halls of the giant store at Herald Square. The Bedford Branch of the YMCA sponsored a religious talk by Rev. S. Parkes Cadman, one of the city's best-known divines. (The program and sponsorship continued on a regular basis for many months.) The Haynes Automobile Company presented the talk "The Story of the Haynes, America's First Car," by the car's inventor, Elwood Haynes.

None of this means to suggest that the sponsored program began to snowball. The truth is, even in the early months of 1923, few businessmen with open checkbooks showed up at AT&T with a strong desire to broadcast something to the general public. In the end, the main impetus to the development of commercial broadcasting came not from the outside, but from a source that was determined to keep advertising messages off the airwaves—the telephone company itself!

The drift toward advertising subsidy was basically a by-product of AT&T's desire to build and run the best and most successful radio station in New York. From the beginning WEAF was committed to beating out WJZ for the best talent and programming available, and this obviously meant big expenditures of money. Mr. W.S. Gifford, Vice President of AT&T, remarked that "there is no reason to do anything at all about broadcasting unless we do it right," and all the efforts of the company around this time were toward making WEAF the leading radio station in New York, if not the nation.

To attract talent and professional performers, WEAF moved out of its original headquarters in the grim and uninviting Walker Street neighborhood and into lavish quarters at the company's new headquarters at 195 Broadway, the building with the endless rows of classical columns. Everything here was modern, sumptuous, and above all expensive. The new studio was amply justified by the assignment of a new wavelength—400 meters—which gave it more air time and less interference. The Department of Commerce seems to have had complete faith in the telephone company's pronouncement that their toll station was an enterprise in the public interest and that it ought to be given clear channel, away from those other stations that were serving only the interest of the owner.

At the same time the telephone company was doing all it could to exploit the technological advantages of its telephone lines. In the fall of 1922 it had broadcast directly from Chicago a football game between Princeton and the University of Chicago, and shortly it would arrange a great many broadcasts produced with high skill from outside locations that always presented difficulties to the competitor stations: a series of organ recitals from the City College of New York, stage shows from Roxy's Capitol Theatre, operas, other football games, and so on. At the same time, in the true spirit of competition, however unfair, AT&T was denying similar hookups to competitor stations, forcing RCA- and GE-owned stations to use the inferior Western Union and postal telegraph lines, which were poorly adapted to voice transmission. AT&T wanted to keep the best of everything for itself.

Eventually the best of everything meant raising more money, and raising more money meant an aggressive selling of the toll idea. WEAF was eventually taken out of the Long Lines Department of AT&T and set up as a new free-standing unit charged with the responsibility of going out and finding customers to use the toll booth of the air. Under the direction of William E. Harkness, WEAF assembled a staff of aggressive promotional men to sell potential users on the advantages of radio broadcasting. One of Mr. Harkness's more successful inspirations was bringing to the station Mr. George F. McClelland, then Secretary of the Association of National Advertisers. McClelland was joined by Harry Smith, George Podeyn and later a group of others, who quickly became evangelists for "sponsored programs" — selling the idea and the service as aggressively as the telephone company sells space in the yellow pages.

In spite of the fact that the young promotional geniuses at WEAF began to sell this new approach to broadcasting, it did not catch on in the advertising industry generally — at least for a while. One reason for this was that competitor radio stations did not immediately pick up on the practice and continued to insist that it was they and not AT&T who were operating in the public interest. Too, although everybody watched carefully the doings at 195 Broadway, the public, the press and the national organs of opinion remained steadfastly opposed to the idea of advertising taking over on the radio.

On February 8, 1923, just as the sales force at WEAF was starting to realize success selling time on the air, *Printers' Ink* magazine ran an editorial entitled "Radio and Objectional Advertising Medium," which expressed the prevailing opinion of the day about what was going on at WEAF. *Printers' Ink* found this drift toward sponsored programs "full of insidious dangers," and it opposed the tendency because it forced listeners to swallow advertising with programming that originally was supposed to be unpolluted and in the public interest. "We are opposed to advertising," said *Printers' Ink*, "for the same reason we are opposed to sky writing. People should not be forced to read advertising unless they are so inclined." The magazine admitted that it had not heard any bald statements or direct sales pitches, but it still believed that any kind of commercial message, however bland or oblique, was "an unwarranted imposition on the public's time."

If the substance of this complaint had been brought to the attention of AT&T in 1923, they would have vigorously answered that they, too, were firmly opposed to advertising, and would have denied that what was going out over the airwaves was advertising in the usual sense. Their rules strictly forbade direct advertising, mentioning of specific products, offering of samples, or any of the other aggressive selling techniques we today associate with radio and television "commercials." Nonetheless, WEAF was slowly and inexorably moving in that direction. By the summer of 1923 there was a decided tendency to make a strong and more or less permanent identification between program and sponsor. Thus Billy Jones' and Ernie Hare's song and patter program came to be known as the "Happiness Boys" because the sponsor was the Happiness Candy Stores.

This kind of tie between sponsor and program became a widespread phenomenon almost immediately. Among the most popular programs of the day were the "Ipana Troubadours," the "Gold Dust Twins," the "Silvertown Cord Orchestra" (sponsored by manufacturers of the Silvertown Cord automobile tires), the "A & P Gypsies," and the "Cliquot Club Eskimos." As early as July 1923 there was a "Lucky Strike Orchestra," indicating that the arm of the sponsor was reaching out far beyond the limited domain set forth by the station.

The sponsor's name and image was slowly allowed to intrude itself everywhere. In the Silvertown Cord program there was not only a "Silvertown Cord Orchestra," but a "silver masked tenor," the idea of which further emphasized the name of the product made by the sponsor. Obvious attention was drawn to Cliquot Club Ginger Ale by beginning the program with some sound effects: the jingling of sleigh bells and the yelping of Eskimo dogs, all to suggest coolness and frostiness. Later the orchestra leader, Harry Rieser, wrote some introductory music for the same program, incorporating the sleighbell motif, and this became the first regular musical "theme" to identify a program—and, in a subliminal way, the sponsor as well.

The pressures from the sponsors were intense even in 1923, so that the WEAF managers had to be eternally vigilant against allowing blatant advertising to creep in. A vacuum cleaner manufacturer was not allowed to use the rather imaginative line "Sweep no more my lady," for fear that listeners might take offense at the corruption of Stephen Foster's famous line from "My Old Kentucky Home." Interestingly enough, too, the first program sponsored by a toothpaste was held up for a number of weeks while one of the station's time salesmen and the station management argued over the propriety of even mentioning such a personal and perhaps unseemly subject as toothpaste.

As late as 1925 there was still strong public opposition to radio advertising, and in Washington, a congressman was laying plans to introduce a bill in Congress to abolish all radio advertising. Unfortunately, conditions were rapidly developing that would make all such efforts futile if not ridiculous. By the mid-twenties the Coolidge era was in full swing; business was in the saddle, and the advertising agency, long a despised poor relation of the business world, came into nationwide prominence. For a long time the advertising agencies themselves paid little if any attention to radio, and mostly warned their clients against entanglements with this brash and undependable medium. But eventually even the most reluctant of the admen were turning their eyes to radio as a vehicle for selling.

The coming of the first great network, the National Broadcasting Company, in 1926, was a powerful impetus to the advertising agencies, who now saw rich sugarplums dancing before them. With a single announcement able to reach millions of people over a large network of local stations, commercial announcements became enormously attractive to manufacturers of every conceivable kind of product. The network also gave rise to better and more expensive programming, and this, in turn, gave rise to a voracious appetite for still greater funds, so that the impetus toward further dominance by advertising was a self-perpetuating cycle. Bigger and better programming required greater and greater funding, with only one hand now left to provide it: advertising.

To be sure, until the very end of the twenties, a great deal of lip service continued to be paid to the glowing ideal that "direct" advertising should not be permitted on the air. But there was evidence of direct advertising even as radio executives insisted that it didn't exist. In 1928, Merlin Aylesworth, NBC president, appeared before a Senate committee and was asked whether there was direct advertising over his network. His response was "No. . . . These clients neither describe their products or name its price, but simply depend on the good-will that results from their contribution of good programs."

This, of course, was a philosophy that might have aptly described the situation in 1923 or 1924, when station WEAF was still a stepchild of AT&T, but now that that station was the keystone of the NBC red network, the description was somewhat stretched, if not a downright lie. By this time advertisers most certainly did describe their products even if they did not actually mention prices.

For years the magic word was "direct" advertising—the grand unholy of holies that everybody wanted to stand clear of. Unfortunately, what was meant by the term came to be more and more narrowly defined until it really meant very little. In 1930 Merlin Aylesworth again appeared before a Senate committee. Again he was asked about his stand on advertising. He was still against direct advertising. But when asked exactly what he meant by that his answer was: "I mean, stating prices." So after seven years the notion of "direct advertising" had shrunken down to the point where it meant nothing more than the stating of prices. Anything else was presumably fair game. Advertising, apparently, had arrived to stay.

7. The Wavelength Wars

The rapid growth of broadcasting in the early 1920s brought many problems in its wake. One that took years to straighten out was the problem of maintaining harmony in the atmosphere, of regulating the broadcasting stations so that all could be heard and stations did not interfere with each other.

When the decade of the twenties began, the only regulation of radio broadcasting was that provided by the Radio Act of 1912, an act that went into effect at a time when there was no hint of an uncontrolled expansion of broadcasting—no expectation that radio transmitters might one day interfere with one another. The Radio Act of 1912 gave to the Secretary of Commerce and Labor (after 1913 the Secretary of Commerce) the power to issue station licenses to United States citizens and to specify the wavelengths that could be used. Later legal rulings provided that the Secretary of Commerce would have no general regulative powers—indeed, it was doubtful whether he even had the power to reject applications for licenses. All that was really provided in the Act of 1912 was a registration procedure, much like the registration procedures for owning ships or automobiles. It was presumed that anybody who had a reason or a desire to own a radio station ought to be awarded a license.

The Department of Commerce shortly set aside certain wavelengths for government use. All other stations were assigned the frequency of 360 meters—an odd circumstance which simply ignored the many available wavelengths. But for years this single wavelength seemed to present no problems. There were very few transmitters, and these were mostly of very low power—from 10 to 50 watts. A great many stations could conceivably be operated around the country with little interference as long as this low power was used. Unfortunately, when stations as powerful as KDKA and WJZ were on the air, it would not be possible to have several stations in the same vicinity broadcasting on the same wavelength. As early as 1922, cities like New York and Chicago would have stations competing for a share of the listening audience, so that a single wavelength for general-purpose broadcasting would not be feasible in these locations.

In the fall of 1922, the Department of Commerce tried to help out a bit by adding an additional frequency for what were called Class B stations. Class B stations were the largest stations with the greatest power, presumably broadcasting high-class programming of widespread public interest. Class B stations were allowed to use the 400-meter wavelength, while all of the others were kept to 360 meters. By the end of 1922 there were several dozen stations operating on the 360-meter wavelength (i.e. the 833-kilocycle frequency), and about a dozen others operating on 400 meters (750 kilocycles).

The only trouble with this arrangement was that dozens of new stations were being licensed each month, and it became apparent almost immediately that this small flexibility would be of very little help. In some places there would be two powerful Class B stations very close to one another. Consider the case of WJZ and WOR, both serving the New York metropolitan area from transmitters that were only a few blocks apart in Newark, New Jersey. Obviously they could not be simultaneously sending their signals at 400 meters without chaos. Accordingly, in the early months of this dual operation, the respective managements of the two stations agreed to divide up the hours of the week. If WOR was broadcasting on Monday evening, WJZ would take Tuesday, and so on. But it was not very satisfactory or agreeable for any station to have to limit its hours of programming just at a time when the demand for services and programming was growing at a phenomenal rate. More importantly, not all station managers were as cooperative as those at WOR and WJZ. To solve the problem, many of the newer stations began to cheat. Instead of sticking to the prescribed wavelength, they adjusted their transmitters so as not to suffer interference. At first they might move ever so slightly, but as more and more strong stations were clustered in a particular area, they began to drift from 360 meters down as low as 280, or as high as 420. In fact it was this very tendency to wander that had caused the Department of Commerce to introduce the Class B designation and permit some broadcasting on 400 meters.

The remedy provided by the Department of Commerce proved to be no more effective than using a Band-Aid to stem the flood of a broken dam. Obviously something would soon have to be done to keep radio stations from stepping on each other's toes and from creating bedlam in the airwaves. The "something" would eventually have to be government regulation, although the word "regulation" was a naughty one in the 1920s, with the government hoping to avoid stepping into an arena that manifestly belonged to private enterprise.

Called forth to solve these new problems of radio was the Honorable Herbert Hoover, the Stanford-trained engineer who was now the Secretary of Commerce in the Harding administration. If any man was up to the task it was Hoover, who a few years before had attained international fame for his superlative management of the war relief program. Where radio was concerned, Hoover had very few tools at his disposal, since the Radio Act of 1912 gave him only the most limited powers and virtually no provisions of enforcement. Furthermore, this was the era of laissez-faire, of business ascendancy, and there was little impetus either from the government or from the broadcasters to give government a club to wield over radio station operators. Hoover's powers, such as they were in 1922, were mostly powers of persuasion, and these he deftly attempted to exercise.

The most popular solution to matters of this kind back in the twenties was to call a "conference" on the subject, all of the interested parties being invited to attend. The first such conference was held in 1922, but there were others in 1923, 1924 and 1925. In 1922 only 22 broadcasters attended the sessions, but by 1925 the confusion in the airwaves had grown to such proportion that over 400 eager and anxious broadcasters attended.

During the first two conferences the expectation continued to be that the problems of interference could be solved by simple agreements. Some handshake pacts were actually reached with minor beneficial results. Unfortunately, at this early time, it wasn't always enough to come to theoretical agreements about wavelengths, broadcasting hours and the like. Many of the transmitters being used at that time were so crude that they were incapable of holding precisely to their assigned frequency. Also, most of those early transmitters were portable, and owners thoughtlessly moved them from place to place, resulting in further disorder. Accordingly, owners of stations who believed themselves to be interfered with took matters in their own hands and changed their own frequency, location and hours of broadcasting, further adding to the confusion and eventually to a warlike atmosphere with every man for himself. Radio shortly came to resemble conditions of the now dying American frontier, with its cattle rustlers and desperados.

The conferences didn't really do much good, although they fostered a superficial impression of cooperation. Mostly what happened was that the larger and more responsible stations urged swift passage of legislation to deal with the wave pirates and jumpers. Constitutionally, Secretary Hoover was opposed to taking that route, but by 1924 he, too, was convinced that eventually Congress would have to act to bolster Department of Commerce authority. That year he observed that the radio industry was "probably the only industry of the United States that is unanimously in favor of having itself regulated."

Congress, however, was ill-disposed to act, at least in 1924, although by this time it was obvious to everyone in the know that a more complete set of radio laws was inevitable. In the absence of specific legislation, Herbert Hoover took it to be his mandate — a mandate he believed to come from his "conferences" — to act as an arbiter of disputes, a czar of broadcasting. Clearly there was no legal authority for it, but everybody who was rational knew that something needed to be done, so it came to be generally accepted that Hoover's administrative enactments following the resolutions of the radio conferences had the force and effect of law.

With a growing staff of radio experts and inspectors, Hoover began to make *de facto* administrative law. The 1924 Radio Conference had urged cutting down on the large number of stations clustered at 360 meters. Hoover began to act on this recommendation, although he knew he had no specific legal authority to do so. Similarly, the RCA-GE-Westinghouse consortium urged that there be permitted, strategically located around the country, a certain limited number of "superpower" stations. This made good sense to Hoover, so he authorized some of the prestige stations, like WJZ and WGY, to experiment with 50,000 watts.

Hoover also began arbitrarily to assign spots on the dial to stations, mostly on the basis of their wattage. High-power stations of 500 watts or more were

given favorable spots; low-power stations of, say, 250 watts were given
undesirable pockets and time-sharing assignments. This action brought plenty
of protests from station owners, who believed that Hoover was currying favor
with big-money interests and neglecting perfectly good local radio stations that
deserved to be heard. Sometimes two stations got into a disagreement on time
sharing, and then Hoover would arbitrarily step in and impose a schedule.
Usually this would stick, but there were plenty of beefs.

Naturally, with an inability to deny licenses in the mid-twenties, there
were many more stations in operation than there would be a few years later—
many more than we have today. It seemed that everybody was operating a radio
station, and the radio men at the Department of Commerce were taxed to the
limit to find air space for every college, church, radio store or grain dealership
that wanted to have a radio station. Large maps of the air space were laid out
on the floor at Commerce, and experts worked over them with little pieces of
colored paper as if constructing a Byzantine mosaic.

And of course they were not dealing with a mosaic of scientific precision.
The vast majority of broadcasters remained little more than semiamateurs, and
getting them to understand the regulations was hard enough; getting them to
comply was almost impossible. Out in Los Angeles, the soon-to-be-notorious
female evangelist Aimee Semple McPherson ran a little radio station from her
temple. Her zealous followers had bought her a transmitter, obtained a
license, and then turned the lady loose to do with the station whatever she
would. Knowing not the first thing about radio, Sister Aimee wandered all
over the dial, broadcasting on whatever wavelength suited her fancy. She was
given a succession of warnings, which she ignored, whereupon Secretary
Hoover ordered his men to seal the station. With this action in the offing, Sister
Aimee wired Hoover:

> Please order your minions of Satan to leave my station alone. You cannot
> expect the almighty to abide by your wave length nonsense. When I offer
> my prayers to Him I must fit into His wave reception. Open this station at
> once.[1]

A compromise was eventually reached in this case: Sister Aimee was persuaded
to engage the services of a competent radio engineer, and the station was
reopened.

But many owners of small stations believed that Hoover was high-handed,
and legal counsel advised many of them that the secretary was making law by
administrative fiat. It was inevitable that sooner or later Hoover's powers would
be tested, and this began in 1925 when Eugene F. McDonald of Zenith Radio
decided to test Hoover's dictums in the courts. McDonald owned a relatively
new radio station in Chicago, WJAZ, which the Department of Commerce had
allotted only two hours a week on a frequency shared with the General Electric
station in Denver, KOA. Without asking permission, McDonald moved
WJAZ to a clear channel. The Department of Commerce brought suit, which
it had to do if it was to maintain its authority. Indeed, it had little choice, since

the channel chosen by McDonald had been given to Canada in a mutual international pact.

Fully aware of the inadequacy of the law, Hoover welcomed the WJAZ violation as a test case. He might have been less well disposed toward a court trial if he had foreseen the result. The court found in favor of WJAZ, correctly noting that the Radio Act of 1912 gave the Secretary of Commerce no such powers as those he had been so freely exercising. The Attorney General advised Hoover that pressing the case on appeal would be fruitless, adding, "It is apparent that the present legislation is inadequate to cover the art of broadcasting which has been almost entirely developed since the 1912 Act."

So now all hell broke loose. From the middle of 1926, when Commerce Department control broke down, there were wave jumpers and pirates everywhere. And in spite of the chaos in the air, new stations continued to apply for licenses every month. A report of the Department of Commerce in December 1926 revealed that since July 1 of that year there were 102 new stations (approximately five new stations a week), bringing the nationwide total to 620. By the end of 1926 it was impossible in most geographical areas to receive a consistent broadcast signal. In large metropolitan areas things became completely intolerable. At this time New York had 38 stations; Chicago, 40. Listeners usually weren't getting anything but babble and conflicting sounds. Sales of radio sets dropped off drastically, and for a time it appeared that all the great hopes for the future of broadcasting were to be dashed to the ground.

Finally, Congress came to the rescue. It was now clear to every intelligent person in the country that something had to be done, and swiftly, if radio was to continue its usefulness as a medium of communication. After turning a deaf ear on Secretary Hoover's recommendations for three years, and after having failed to act on as many as nine previous radio bills, Congress was finally facing up to the extremity of the situation. In his message to Congress in December 1926, President Calvin Coolidge urged passage of this important legislation, noting that "the whole service of this most important function has drifted into such chaos as seems likely, if not remedied, to destroy its great value. I most urgently recommend that this legislation should be speedily enacted."

The long years of squabbling over radio legislation ended suddenly on February 28, 1927, when the Senate adopted the conference report on the Radio Control Bill, and without the slightest change in terminology, sent the act forward to President Coolidge, who immediately signed it. The act called for a Federal Radio Commission to oversee all aspects of broadcasting, with the Secretary of Commerce acting in an administrative capacity.

What was most significant about the legislation, however, was not its specific provisions, but its underlying philosophy. Most importantly, the act rescinded the assumption of the 1912 law that any individual was free to use the ether any way he saw fit. The Radio Act of 1927 proclaimed that the radio waves and channels belong to the people and should be operated in the common interest. No one has the right to "own" a frequency or channel. Thus, by implication, radio frequencies belong to all the people, and all the people (not only owners of transmitters) have a right to expect benefits from them.

So, the act explained, the government must accept basic responsibility for managing the airwaves for the public interest, and it has the implied right to restrict the number of persons using a radio channel. Licensees must expect to meet certain tests, both general and specific.

The government's powers to regulate were generally considered "discretionary," that is, the Federal Radio Commission would have considerable freedom to use its own best judgment in regulating broadcasting, always being directed by "public interest, convenience, and necessity." Of course all of the decisions of the new commission — it was to be called the Federal Radio Commission or FRC — were subject to due process of law and could be appealed in the courts.

Shortly after the Radio Act of 1927 was signed into law, President Coolidge appointed five members of the new Federal Radio Commission, and these five men, all with considerable radio experience, met for the first time on March 16, 1927, using borrowed offices and rapidly improvised facilities and staff. Their task was hardly an easy one since the act had made no provisions for staff, office furniture and the like. (They began with "one desk, two chairs, a table and a packing box.") One thing they did have was a clean slate. By implication, the Act of 1927 revoked the license of each and every radio transmitter in the United States. That included large commercial stations, transoceanic stations, coastal stations, experimental stations, the stations of training schools, colleges and religious organizations, right down to the 14,885 amateur stations of ham radio operators — a total of about 18,000 transmitters.

With this jungle of competing stations on its hands, the members of the commission dug right in, turning their attention to this task of clearing up the chaos in the airwaves. Among their first acts was temporarily setting the period of a broadcast license at 60 days, allowing them to lower the ax on unwanted stations on short notice. They also immediately defined the standard broadcast band as 500 to 1,500kc, and standardized the designation of channels (using frequency rather than wavelength). They also moved to eliminate all portable transmitters.

It was hoped by some that the FRC would move swiftly to chop off hundreds of radio stations that had been stifling the airwaves, but the commission members moved forward prudently and carefully, trying to step on as few toes as possible. Indeed, between 1927 and 1932 the total number of broadcast stations was reduced only from 681 to 604. On the other hand, there was a somewhat drastic cutting back on the number of stations authorized to broadcast at night, when sky interference was a serious and persistent problem. The number of stations allowed to broadcast at night was reduced from 565 to 397.

The commission almost immediately provided free channels for Canadian broadcasters. This action restored the goodwill of Canadians, who had been regularly pestered by American radio during the air piracy period.

The FRC eventually became involved in nearly every aspect of broadcasting. In the late twenties, for example, the number of technical innovations and engineering advances were so many that the commission was obliged to employ on its staff a substantial corps of technically trained individuals to set and enforce high standards of transmission and delivery of service. Very stringent standards were adopted with the intent of reducing interference and improving quality of signal. For example, at one time, stations had been required only to keep within 500 cycles of their assigned frequency; now they had to maintain a tolerance of 50 cycles. The commission also issued a detailed set of "Standards of Good Engineering Practice," and they provided both guidance and surveillance of station engineers and engineering practices.

The commission required stations to maintain logs on both technical operations and on programming. It also established a system of dealing with problems, complaints and the like by using boards of hearing examiners, which held hearings in a quasilegal environment with all parties to any issue or dispute given every opportunity to be heard.

The regulatory operations in Washington were expanded by degrees. In the mid-thirties, further legislation dealing with all media of communication brought about the replacement of the Federal Radio Communication with the Federal Communication Commission (FCC), which functions to this day.

Of course, from the beginning there were scoffers and complainers. Naturally many small stations claimed that the large stations and the networks got the biggest slices of the pie. It was complained, for example, that of 24 clear channels created by the FRC, 21 went to network stations, some authorized to use 50,000 watts. Nearly all stations owned by educational institutions felt themselves very ill-used by the commission. Many got what they considered bad frequencies, and worse, the majority had to accept daytime-only licenses. For example, the University of Arkansas' station, KFMQ, was forced to share time with a local commercial station — with the commercial station getting three quarters of the time, including all the nighttime hours. KFMQ threw in the towel and quit broadcasting.

The same thing happened to many educational stations throughout the late twenties. In the years before the Radio Act of 1927, dozens of educational stations had entered the field every year. Starting around 1928 they began to drop off like flies: 23 stations gave up in 1928 alone.[2] Many of the educational stations had begun operation with the idea of offering nighttime adult education courses, but, cheated of this time slot, many of them saw no purpose in continuing.

However, there is every indication that the FRC acted in what it believed was the greatest good for the greatest number when it carved up the airspace in the late 1920s. And by and large, government regulation of the airwaves has continued to be successful and salubrious in the United States. The regulation has seldom been heavy handed or arbitrary, and most citizens are satisfied with governmental control of the airwaves. Few of today's young people even suspect there was a time when chaos reigned in broadcasting. Most take order and stability for granted, but they resulted from the firm yet gentle hand of those first radio commissioners back in 1927 who started laying down the rules with only a desk, two chairs, a table and a packing box.

8. The Birth of Radio News

The broadcasting of news on a daily basis as we know it today was not a feature of radio in the 1920s. News was not treated as a separate institution, and the "news department" was unknown at the early radio stations. The establishment of radio news divisions and vast news-gathering facilities had to wait until the late 1930s. Still, from the very beginning of regular radio broadcasting it was obvious to everybody that radio as a medium for the dissemination of news had certain decided advantages over all forms of mass communication then in existence. It is not at all surprising, therefore, that the very first radio broadcast from KDKA was a news broadcast—coverage of the presidential election of November 2, 1920. From this very moment it must have been obvious to radio buffs that for reporting occasions of this sort radio was a "natural."

Throughout most of the 1920s such radio news that existed was oriented around special events. When there was an election, or some dramatic public event, or a heavyweight boxing championship, radio men were sent to report their firsthand impressions, but broadcasts of these events were planned for in advance because it was known, or at least hoped, that the reporting would swell the listening audience. In the early twenties no thought was given to offering a regular news coverage or to competing with daily newspapers. Consequently, newspapers weren't in the slightest bit suspicious of radio. The thought that this new medium would someday be a source of competition never filled newspaper executive offices with consternation.

When the newspapers thought of radio at all, they thought of it as an ally. Radio was a great fill-in. It could take care of things on the off hours, after the last edition of the evening paper had been put to bed, making it a natural for things like election returns. Having this new service might actually have the effect of generating free advertising for the newspaper. On hearing a live broadcast of a prize fight on the radio, thousands might be impelled to seek out the next day's paper with the full coverage, including pictures, in-depth comment, and so on.

It wasn't surprising, then, in the early days of broadcasting, that a great many commercial radio stations were owned by newspapers, none of which saw any conflict of interest or likelihood of competition. The time would come when the alliance between the print news media and radio would wear thin—things even developed into temporary but acrimonious warfare in 1933—but

98

to radio and newspaper people alike, radio news in the early 1920s was seen to be a mere sidelight to the vast system of news gathering and news publishing. Very often newspapers were mildly pleased with the free publicity they received by supplying tidbits of information to radio stations. Shortly after Westinghouse opened KYW in Chicago, it entered into an arrangement with the International News Service to broadcast INS bulletins, agreeing to mention the news service over the air. It all seemed a fair agreement and a fair exchange, and no transfer of funds was involved.

Practically it could not have been otherwise. When radio was in its infancy, the resources for full-scale reporting were not available. Most of the news carried by radio was obtained by telephone wire from some cooperating paper, or later from the wire services to which radio stations were allowed to subscribe. Had more substantial bodies of information been available, it is extremely unlikely that the one or two-man radio studio of 1922 or 1923 could have done anything with it. A mass of late-breaking news would have been an intolerable burden. Even picking up the daily afternoon paper and making up a news broadcast on the basis of it would have taxed the resources of the early announcers. But the exciting single event was something altogether different. Here the radio men were ready and able to move in. And the inroads they made eventually led to the expansion and independence of radio news services in the decade ahead.

Nevertheless, miscellaneous news quickly became an important (although sporadic) ingredient of programming. Occasionally at WJZ, Thomas Cowan would read news bulletins supplied him by the *Newark Sunday Call*. Before long he would be getting help from other announcers, one of whom, Charles Hodges, made a success of himself in the radio news of the next generation.

Among the listeners to WJZ during the first year of its operation was a Brooklyn newspaperman named Hans von Kaltenborn. For many years Kaltenborn had been an editorial writer for the *Brooklyn Eagle*, although he had also won a certain notoriety as a public speaker. He had run *Eagle*-sponsored travel tours of Europe, and for the employees and reporters of his paper he gave a weekly series of current affairs talks in the company auditorium. Kaltenborn had bought his own crystal set in 1921 and had become intrigued by radio, although naturally he never gave the slightest thought to his own possible involvement with it. Kaltenborn, however, would go on to be one of the great radio newsmen in the years ahead, and he was clearly the earliest major figure to be active in the field.

Kaltenborn's first talk over the radio was from station WJZ in Newark in the spring of 1922, but this occasion was little more than a lark. To demonstrate the new medium of radio, Kaltenborn had agreed to address a chamber of commerce group over in Brooklyn that had gathered for the specific purpose of hearing the Kaltenborn voice over the radio rather than from the traditional lecture platform. Kaltenborn was delighted with the result. When he returned to Brooklyn he was told, "We heard you—your voice came in as clear as a bell."

Hans von Kaltenborn was born in Milwaukee of a German-American family in 1878. His father had been a Hessian aristocrat who had left Germany

H.V. Kaltenborn, center, before the mike in 1924. A newspaperman, he would become one of the great radio newsmen in the years that followed. (Photo courtesy New York Historical Society.)

in the 1860s to protest the quickly growing dominance of Germany by Prussia. A great many of his later listeners assumed that Kaltenborn had once had a German accent, but this wasn't exactly true. He did have a clipped manner of delivery and an intonation that suggested an exotic variant of English diction, but the truth is that his boyhood was strictly American. On the other hand, he had attended a bilingual school in Milwaukee, and was very proficient in German, a language that would help to raise him to the forefront of newscasters during the rise of Hitler, especially at the time of the Munich crisis of 1938.

Young Kaltenborn, a gangly youth called "Spiderlegs" by his youthful playmates, decided at a very early age to be a newsman. In 1898 he served in the Spanish-American war, from which he sent home reports to his hometown weekly, the *Merrill Advocate*. He also sent home dispatches to the German-language weekly, the *Lincoln County Anzeiger*. After the war he determined to make a grand tour of Europe to broaden his education. In making his way to Europe, he stopped by New York, and he decided that the city was the most fascinating in the world and that he must return there to make his way in the world. Kaltenborn was fond of quoting the Greek dramatist Euripides, who said that the first prerequisite for happiness was to be born in a famous city. Kaltenborn determined that although he had not been born in New York, he would make it his home.

And he did. After two years wandering around Europe, partly financed by working as a salesman of stereoscopes, Kaltenborn returned to America and applied for jobs on newspapers. For lack of experience in big-time newspaper work, he was not able to find a job with one of the great Manhattan dailies, but he did manage to be taken on by the *Brooklyn Eagle* at $8.00 a week. The *Eagle* was then one of the country's most distinguished papers (Brooklyn had not become a part of New York City until 1898, and the community had always maintained its own separate cultural institutions, of which the *Eagle* was one of the most luminous). The year was 1902, and Kaltenborn was to keep some kind of connection with the *Eagle* for the next thirty years.

There were interruptions, however. After a few years, Kaltenborn took a leave from his job to enroll at Harvard University, where he proved to be a good student with a strong interest in acting and dramatics. When he returned to the *Eagle*, the paper's management showed its appreciation of his formal education by raising his salary to $45.00 a week—no mean salary in those days. The raise allowed him to support in modest style a plump and pretty 20-year-old blonde German wife—a baroness, in fact—that he had met on his travels. And Kaltenborn moved up quickly in the *Eagle* hierarchy, receiving some of the paper's best assignments over the next two decades. Among other things, he served as drama critic, European correspondent and Washington correspondent. During World War I, when all things German were unseemly, Kaltenborn dropped the "von" from his name and became H.V. Kaltenborn.

By the early 1920s Kaltenborn was the *Eagle*'s associate editor and one of the paper's most impressive and authoritative public speakers. Accordingly, when the newly established station WEAF, AT&T's entry in the radio station sweepstakes, was looking for things to fill its broadcast day, programmers asked the *Eagle* if it would be interested in sponsoring a series of talks on current affairs. The *Eagle* sent Kaltenborn. His talks at regular intervals were immediately popular with the public, and thousands of letters poured into the studio.

Popularity wasn't everything in those days, though, and Kaltenborn's association with WEAF sailed into stormy weather. Kaltenborn was merely doing the sort of thing he did at the *Eagle*—editorializing, doing commentaries—but he pulled no punches and would occasionally offer harsh criticisms of public figures. In one of his broadcasts he flayed a local judge, and in another a prominent labor leader. An AT&T vice president kindly explained that the airwaves were perhaps not suitable for such strong opinions and suggested that Kaltenborn "tone down" his material. But Kaltenborn believed that he was a spokesman for the *Brooklyn Eagle*, not the broadcasting station, so he continued broadcasting in his accustomed style.

In another broadcast, Kaltenborn had some harsh words for Secretary of State Charles Evans Hughes. Hughes, listening to the broadcast in his Washington home while entertaining friends, was miffed by this disagreeable comment wafting uninvited through the airwaves and right into his own living room. The following day he called AT&T to complain that such ideas ought not be going out to the general public from a station owned by the quasi-public telephone company. The *Eagle* strongly backed Kaltenborn, and WEAF did not cancel Kaltenborn's programs immediately, but when the series ended it was pointedly not renewed. The *Eagle*, however, did not let the whole matter drop so quickly, and it told its readers why the series went off the air.

Since many listeners rose to Kaltenborn's defense, another station took him on. But shortly trouble began there, too, for much the same reason. "Editorials" were and would continue to be a squeamish issue on radio, as they have been to this day even on television. The ether should be neutral, many would say. But other listeners did not agree, and a short time later Kaltenborn received yet another offer, this time from WOR, then broadcasting from studios in the Bamberger Department Store in downtown Newark. Here Kaltenborn continued his commentaries, and became the first of many wandering voices of radio, his admiring public forced to seek out his voice in different spots of the dial.

WOR, much to the gratification of Kaltenborn and the sponsoring *Eagle*, proved independent and stubborn enough to resist all entreaties to put a lid on the speaker's opinions. Even when Mayor Jimmy Walker of New York threatened that the city would bar WOR from covering municipal events if Kaltenborn did not desist from his comments about Walker's shady doings, WOR was not intimidated, and Kaltenborn stayed, thoroughly enjoying his role as "the stormy petrel of the air."

Still, Kaltenborn did not think of broadcasting as an enduring vocation; in time he gave up his association with WOR and returned to his work with the *Brooklyn Eagle*. It was only in the depths of the depression, after the *Eagle* had declined as a national paper of importance, and after a new ownership expected editors to take a pay cut, that Kaltenborn returned to radio news broadcasting as a full-time career. He was then taken up by the youthful and struggling CBS network in 1932, and stayed with it until the late thirties, when he moved to NBC after another set of difficulties over his tendency to editorialize. But Kaltenborn held on to a prominent role as dean of radio commentators throughout the long years of radio network news.

It is hardly surprising that one area where radio news was able to shine in the 1920s, even when regular news staffs were nearly nonexistent, was political news. In a volatile democracy, politics is exciting, and it was only natural that radio would try to respond to quick-breaking political news whenever it was available. For example, the activities of our major political figures, particularly our presidents, often offered ready-made material for the miracle of electric communication. President Warren G. Harding became the first president to speak over the radio (Woodrow Wilson had used radiotelephony to direct the flight of an airplane over the White House during World War I, but he did not use the medium for public address), and as early as Armistice Day 1921, Harding actually addressed the nation over an elaborate radio-telephone hookup arranged by the telephone company. By the summer of 1923, Harding had spoken over the radio on a number of occasions, and a large coast-to-coast hookup was being planned for him at the time of his sudden death in San Francisco on August 2, 1923.

While Harding's first truly transcontinental broadcast never came off, the death of the first "radio president" made clear for all time the growing dependence of the presidency, if not politics in general, on the swiftness of electronic media. When Harding took ill, the telephone company supplied the initiative, under very difficult circumstances, to bring a telephone circuit to the home of Vice President Coolidge's father in Vermont, so that the vice president could keep in regular touch with the news from the president's bedside. If Americans of the time (including Coolidge's father) did not all believe that the great officeholders of the land should be only an electrical impulse away from the centers of power, the death of Harding and the immediate succession of Coolidge must at least have given some faith in the continuity provided by rapid communication.

Radio's first truly earthshaking confrontation with the political process came in the summer of 1924 when for the first time the presidential nominating conventions were heard live from their respective convention floors. Months before the conventions, the leading figures of the broadcasting industry were making preparations for this coverage. It was clearly the kind of spectacular special event that radio relished, and the stations' best announcers were assigned to the job. Since there were no regular newscasters in those days, it is not surprising that the two mini-networks that planned coverage of the 1924 conventions assigned their ace general announcers and sportscasters to the job. But in spite of the skeletal staffs and the technical immaturities of the day, the coverage of the 1924 political conventions was a smashing success, bringing millions of listeners to fixed places in front of their radio sets—sets which by now were good enough to reproduce all of the significant sounds of a political convention with some fidelity.

In 1924 the appearance of the first truly "national" network was two years away, but network setups had been on trial for at least a year. By 1924 AT&T had had sufficient experience with long-line hookups that by the time of the Democratic Convention in New York as many as eighteen stations were linked together by telephone cables to receive broadcasts provided by station WEAF. The job of broadcasting the convention fell to WEAF's Graham McNamee, assisted by newcomer Phillips Carlin. Hobbled by its bad connections and lack of cooperation from AT&T and the telephone group, General Electric and RCA prepared to mount a vigorous but much less successful coverage using New York's WJZ as anchor. WJZ's premier sportscaster, Major J. Andrew White, was assigned to announce, and he was assisted by the then-inexperienced but golden-voiced Norman Brokenshire.

The broadcasts of the 1924 conventions would not have been as compelling to home listeners had it not been for the long bitter fight staged by the Democratic Party at Madison Square Garden in New York which went on for a grueling 16 days before nominating dark-horse candidate John W. Davis on the 103rd ballot! (The Republican Convention, which came first, and was held in Cleveland, Ohio, on June 10–12, was a mere rehearsal for the big event in New York. As expected, incumbent President Calvin Coolidge was nominated without so much as a whisper of dissent. The Cleveland result was so clearly foreordained, as Will Rogers jocularly remarked, that the whole thing could have been arranged by postcard.)[1]

The ruckus at the Democratic Convention in New York was so prolonged and so fraught with mystery that the event must be accounted one of the great broadcasting triumphs of the 1920s. It was an event, too, which served to set the standards and practices of political broadcasting in the years to come.

The broadcasters were hardly prepared for a convention of this length, but they were as prepared as they could be for normal convention proceedings. The main announcers worked in glass-enclosed boxes at the side of the platform, and their assistants did a certain amount of wandering around to pick up tidbits of information and perhaps a little local color. There were numerous microphones around the hall to pick up speeches from the floor, band music, crowd sounds and the like. WEAF provided a kind of birdcage for Phillips Carlin, suspended high above the floor from the girders of the arena. From this vantage point, Carlin could presumably be quick to make mention of any swiftly developing brouhahas, sign-wavings and shouting matches—of which there were plenty.

How teams as small as McNamee/Carlin and White/Brokenshire managed to endure a 16-day convention in the unrelenting heat of a New York summer must give pause to those endless platoons of television workers who cover political conventions today. But they seem to have gotten along marvelously in spite of their inexperience.

There were snafus, of course. Norman Brokenshire was at the center of at least one of them. Brokenshire mostly acted as White's leg man, picking up scraps of information, news of switches in roll-call votes, and color. Occasionally he would take over the booth from White when White was exhausted or needed a break. One day during the protracted proceedings, Major White betook himself to lunch at the Newspaperman's Club, leaving Brokenshire in charge. During this hiatus, Brokenshire saw a really exciting fight break out near his booth at the front of the convention floor—signs were banged down on delegates' heads, chairs and decorations were destroyed. Eagerly, Brokenshire began describing the donnybrook in a colorful and breathless manner.

It looked like a minor revolution, and perhaps, or so he thought, he might be getting a scoop on the WEAF boys.

In the middle of the fracas, however, Major White returned, and grasped what Brokenshire was doing. He immediately signaled the operator to take the description off the air, at which time a studio organist came on playing Schubert's "Traumerei." White unceremoniously informed Brokenshire, and with every expletive he could think of, that WJZ had procured broadcast rights only after making an agreement that no disorders or physical scrapes would be reported. Brokenshire went to lunch dejected, fearing that his station's permission to broadcast might be taken away and that he would find himself out of a job. None of these eventualities occurred, and Brokenshire later learned that the executives back at the studio were secretly pleased at the vivid accounts of these few eruptive moments.[2]

By and large the convention was more tedious than exciting, and Brokenshire's little indiscretion must have provided welcome respite from the endless succession of ballots in this longest political convention in American history. But the suspense of what was going to happen mounted as the days passed, and soon it seemed that everyone in New York (and in the other cities reached by the networks) was listening to the radio. Traffic policemen in New York, expecting large crowds on the way to Madison Square Garden, were amazed to find an absence of the expected throngs. Many places of business seemed deserted as workers left their offices to listen to the convention on their home radios. It was reported that at the moment anti–Prohibitionist Al Smith's name was being placed in nomination, only five people were counted on lower Broadway in New York. One resourceful New York cab driver placed a receiver in the cab so that his riders could follow the proceedings of the convention as he whizzed around town — this several years before the advent of the car radio.

The campaign that followed between Calvin Coolidge and John W. Davis was uneventful, its outcome a foregoing conclusion. The campaign was not covered by radio as thoroughly as later campaigns would be, but it revealed some truths of earthshaking importance to American history. It revealed for all time that henceforth politics would be an art that would have to pay its due respects to the media of electric mass communication. No presidential candidate hereafter could afford to neglect the potentials and the pitfalls of the microphone or (later) the television camera.

Quite unexpectedly, the presidential campaign of 1924 showed that the frail and often prosaic Coolidge was a better radio speaker than the suave and polished John W. Davis, often said to be one of the finest orators ever to plead cases before the United States Supreme Court. Exactly why Coolidge turned out to be so effective when the silver-tongued Davis was a disappointment is a bit hard to understand. Coolidge made few stump-type speeches, carefully selecting the occasions of his public appearances to those which best fitted his flat and colorless style. Largely Coolidge stuck to solemn public gatherings and made dignified set speeches — no direct appeals to voters, no attempt at the "chatty" style so well used by President Roosevelt in the 1930s. But in the right setting, the Coolidge style was effective, particularly so when heard over the

Politicians very quickly adapted to the radio medium, including President Calvin Coolidge, who contrary to the reports of some historians, had a very good radio delivery. (Photo courtesy Library of Congress.)

radio. This was admitted by Charles Michelson of the *New York World*, a Democrat, who perceived Coolidge's advantage over the more articulate Davis:

> Mr. Coolidge is no orator. There is a wire edge to his voice, due in some degree to the regular nasal twang of the thirty-third degree Yankee and in part of his meticulous enunciation of each syllable; but according to the professors of the new art, he has a perfect radio voice. The twang and shrillness disappear somewhere along the aerial, and he sounds through the ether with exact clearness as well as softness. Mr. Davis, on the contrary, has a voice which to direct audiences has the bell-like quality of resonance that doubles the quality of his delightful rhetoric. Via radio, however, this muffles and fogs to some extent. The radio was perfected just in time for Mr. Coolidge.... Before an audience Davis glows, while the President always looks unhappy whether he is or not. Under these circumstances, the radio must be Mr. Coolidge's salvation.[3]

All this need not suggest that politicians made a conscious effort to adjust themselves to the radio medium or that they went out and had themselves coached to sound like radio personalities, although it is perhaps significant that only eight years later the presidential election of 1932 brought to the fore the greatest radio politician of all time: Franklin D. Roosevelt. Very early in the Roosevelt years it was clear that the depression-era leader was not only skilled at traditional public oratory but also, as he demonstrated in his so-called "fireside chats," a master of intimate personal delivery, of low-keyed persuasiveness that has probably been matched by no subsequent president. But by 1932 this was perhaps altogether fitting and proper. Radio was now clearly *the* way a president spoke to his people.

Politics may well have made exciting news in the mid-twenties, as might a great sporting event, or some disaster, such as the loss of a dirigible like the *Shenandoah*, which broke loose from its mooring mast at Lakehurst, New Jersey, on a stormy night in 1924, as reported vividly to an anxious public over WOR in Newark by station manager Joseph Barnett. Generally speaking, though, there was no such thing as "regular" news programs in these early years, and no trained news staffs on any stations. Special and exciting events might get attention if technical means were available to cover them, but beyond that radio news would not and could not go.

Interestingly enough, there seems to have been more interest in news broadcasting in local stations around the country than there was in the pilot stations of the networks. The very word newscasting seems to have come out of the Midwest. WLW, in Cincinnati, Ohio, one of the country's earliest radio stations, had among its announcers a man named Fred Smith, who had long taken a keen interest in the idea of radio news. In 1928 Smith arranged with *Time* magazine to get an advance copy of the magazine each week, from which he wrote ten-minute daily news segments. Later that year Smith moved to New York, where he did the same sort of program over station WOR. In the newspaper's radio page, the program was supposed to be referred to as News Casting, but through an error or misprint, the C wasn't capitalized, and the word became newscasting—a word in common use till this day, although it seemed a barbarism at the time.

Things started to look up for the concept of radio news after 1929 with the Columbia network in full swing and with super-salesman Bill Paley at the helm. NBC had gotten into the act with the first nightly news program, but they didn't really seem to have their hearts in it, and CBS came close to stealing the show away. Paley, who had to get his struggling, weakly financed network off the ground by hook or by crook, was on the lookout for any new broadcasting idea that would work. He saw no rational reason why a network news program would not be popular and compelling enough to attract sponsors. Accordingly, as the decade of the thirties began, and after a lot of tentative spadework, Paley finally did succeed in establishing a popular, regular, nightly news program.

The sponsor of the first nightly network news show was Funk and Wagnalls, the owners of the *Literary Digest* magazine, a very unlikely sponsor for any sort of program—so unlikely that the more powerful NBC wasn't really keen on the idea. The newscaster was Floyd Gibbons, a picturesque reporter from the rollicking *Chicago Tribune* who had lost his eye in World War I, and in wearing an eyepatch had obtained a certain national recognition. Gibbons had first gone on the air on Christmas Eve of 1925 as a kind of raconteur over the *Tribune*'s station in Chicago, WGN, his contribution being a series of tales about his wartime exploits. He later did some sporadic newscasting and sportscasting.

The decision to hire Gibbons for a series of nightly newscasts in New York, beginning on February 24, 1930, was not an altogether wise choice. Gibbons had a colorful, machine-gun-rapid style of talking—somewhat like that later adopted by Walter Winchell—but it was probably not really the sort of style that was suitable for a comfortable suppertime news show. A bit too frantic and nervous. But the program was put on at 6:45, just before "Amos 'n' Andy," so it immediately attracted a good number of listeners. Maybe, thought CBS, a few sponsors would sit up and take notice if they could put on the right kind of show.

The *Literary Digest* did not particularly like Gibbons, and probably did not think that his manner of delivery was harmonious with their image, so it shortly started looking around for someone else to take over the program. But whether it was the hour, or the man, or the concept of a regular news show, a new idea had taken hold. Gibbons had picked up a following, and was sufficiently well-known in 1930 that a Gibbons impostor wearing an eyepatch was able to travel around the country collecting fees for lectures and other appearances. The impostor did pretty well with his routine until a reporter in Newark noticed that the fake was wearing a patch over his right eye, whereas the real Gibbons wore his on the left. The impostor wound up in jail.

Even though the *Literary Digest* was not wildly enthusiastic about Floyd Gibbons, Bill Paley and his minions at CBS had become convinced that there was money to be made in news broadcasting. They were convinced that with one sponsor or another they would be able to keep up the idea of regular nightly news programs. Paley sent out the word to find another newscaster who would be more pleasing to the sponsor, and Gibbons was told that he would be replaced when his contract ran out.

One of the CBS vice presidents was told to find somebody quickly—but where? It wasn't just that experienced, professional newscasters were few in number; they simply didn't exist. Gibbons had been the first network newscaster. Undaunted, the harried CBS executive recalled an American speaker with a polished delivery he had heard once at the Covent Garden Royal Opera House in London. Perhaps that man could be convinced to take the job. His name was Lowell Thomas. A call was made to Thomas, who was living in suburban Pawling, New York, and he was invited to audition at the CBS studios at Madison and 52nd Street in New York.

When Lowell Thomas arrived at the CBS studios, the sponsors were waiting in another room to listen. But how did one audition a newscaster? President Bill Paley led Thomas into a room and asked him to start talking as soon as he heard a buzzer sound. For 15 minutes, Thomas talked about his world travels and other experiences. He talked of adventures in India, pygmies in Malaya, mysterious ceremonies and tribal rites in Afghanistan. The sponsors pricked up their ears, apparently impressed, not only by Thomas's wide-ranging experiences, but by his speaking voice. Perhaps this was just the voice that was needed to rescue the news from the frantic style of Floyd Gibbons.

But the sponsors hesitated. They wanted to hear Thomas once again, over the air, perhaps side-by-side with Gibbons for comparison. So Thomas was asked back three days later at 6:00 P.M.; Gibbons' time slot was 6:45.

The day before the on-the-air audition, Thomas rented a penthouse suite at the Princeton Club in New York and gathered some friends to help him prepare the newscast. How should fifteen minutes of news be treated? How should it be delivered? Among Thomas's helpers were Ogden Nash, soon to gain recognition as America's foremost writer of light verse, and Dale Carnegie, the well-known expert on public speaking and human psychology.

There was a lot of bickering and confusion until 4:00 P.M., at which time Thomas took leave of this little group of advisors, went out and bought the evening newspapers, and walked over to the CBS studios. There he put together some notes from scratch. At 6:00 he went on the air with the words "Good evening, everybody," following it up with fifteen minutes of news. When he was finished, an obviously delighted Paley entered the studio. Thomas was led downstairs to meet an equally delighted group of sponsors. Lowell Thomas was the man of the hour.

That day began the longest career in radio news, and one of the most enviable careers in the mass media anywhere in the world. Within a few years Lowell Thomas became a solid American institution, known to nearly every household across the land, such as Walter Cronkite was in his later (and shorter) television reign. The measured tones, the mellifluous voice had the ring of objectivity and authority. The voice gave credibility and authenticity to the news, a feeling of fairness and impartiality. Unlike H.V. Kaltenborn, Thomas was never an editorialist or opinion-giver. His tone and manner were always calm, neutral, dispassionate. A contemplative man of experience who had formerly been a college professor, Thomas always had the right mixture of drama and solidity. Born in Ohio in 1892, he was 38 years of age at the beginning of his radio career, and it had been a rich 38 years. The son of a doctor with wanderlust who had left the settled climate of Ohio to set up practice in the Cripple Creek Gold Camp in Colorado, young Thomas's formative years were passed in this tumultuous environment. He sold papers in saloons and gambling halls. He learned to fend for himself and to carry a gun. He walked to Sunday school carrying the Bible through the red light district, where a man was likely to get shot for almost any reason, or no reason.

But Thomas's father was a man of culture who had assembled the best library in this rude and vulgar mining town. He was a tireless teacher and advisor to his son, drilling him regularly on the importance of speaking clearly and distinctly. By the time he was ten, Lowell knew by heart and could recite with fervor hundreds of passages from poets both major and minor. He gained

Radio news as a formal institution and a nightly ritual did not become a reality until the end of the twenties. But here (at right) is the man who would bring radio news into the big time—Lowell Thomas, shown in his barnstorming days with (later) General H.H. (Hap) Arnold. (Photo courtesy Smithsonian Institute.)

a reputation as an orator at Fourth of July picnics, lodges, Sunday school suppers. So often had he been drilled in the principles of forensics that young Lowell reached the easy conclusion that the skill wasn't really all that valuable.

He changed his mind about that, however, when his family moved back to Ohio. Shortly after his arrival in a new school, he was asked to speak before the assembled student body. He had not a friend in the place, yet so expert was his delivery, so self-assured his manner, that he immediately found himself the most popular student in the school. Everyone recognized him and talked to him in the halls. He was even elected captain of the football team! His father, apparently, had been onto something.

A restless, peripatetic individual, Lowell Thomas attended several colleges in his youth: Northern Indiana University, the University of Denver, Princeton, and the University of Chicago. He considered an academic career, and even taught English for a while at Princeton. But he quickly discovered that he was making far more money as a platform speaker than as a full-time college professor, and by his early twenties, he was lecturing regularly at lodges, women's clubs and the like. He traveled to Europe, Alaska, to deepest Africa. In World War I he became a war correspondent and roamed widely to all theatres of the war, most notably Arabia and Palestine, where he met Lawrence of Arabia, whose story he later told in books and lectures.

During the 1920s Thomas was indefatigable on the lecture circuit, telling of his travels with high spirit and gusto. During a long engagement at Covent Garden, where he entertained thousands of prominent Englishmen from King George V to Winston Churchill and George Bernard Shaw, Thomas caught the attention of the radio executive who brought him finally before the microphone; but by this time, Thomas had delivered his exciting travelogues all over the world. In Ceylon there was no roof on his "lecture hall," and monkeys dropped coconuts on his listeners. In Malaya the lights attracted bats as big as eaglets.

After a few years of this ceaseless traveling and lecturing, Thomas was ready for something a little more settled. On the proceeds of his lectures and the first of his books (he was to write about 50 altogether), he and his wife, Frances, bought a large farm called Quaker Hill at Pawling, New York—an estate that clearly required a large and steady income.

In spite of his devotion to the arts of the spoken word, Thomas had never thought much about radio. He owned a crystal set and later more advanced receivers, for the adventure, but he was annoyed when friends arrived at his house expecting to listen to "Amos 'n' Andy" before they sat down to dinner. The thought that shortly he and the news would be coupled with this comedy team at the very apex of "prime time" never occurred to him.

Nonetheless, that is precisely what happened. Lowell Thomas began his near half-century of newscasting on September 29, 1930. *Literary Digest* at first decided to sponsor the program on both NBC and CBS, although after six months they dropped the CBS program—much to the chagrin of Paley and the other CBS executives who had recruited Thomas in the first place. But at the NBC Blue Network, Thomas could be run back-to-back with "Amos 'n' Andy," a surefire way of getting listeners.[4]

Lowell Thomas and radio were made for one another. It was a perfect marriage of style and mood. Thomas's long experience on the lecture circuit, his authoritative manner and fluid self-confidence, and his remarkable voice, all offered this new and still struggling medium a confident authority—proof positive that this was not merely some fly-by-night newsman picking up the dregs that the daily newspapers had dropped.

The nightly news never tied Lowell Thomas down to his office in the studio; if anything, he was able to add fuel to his wanderlust in the years after 1930. He could and would deliver a broadcast from anywhere in the world—from his home at Pawling, from airplanes, from balloons, from mountain tops, from ships at sea, from battlefields, from the depths of mines. During World War II, he broadcast from a tomb in the Philippines in the midst of a battle.

But his approach to the nightly news remained impartial, calm, reassuring. From his simple greeting of "Good evening, everybody," to his unvarying closing, "So long until tomorrow," he read the news, and sometimes imparted a little drama to it, but he was not a commentator or analyst. The "editorial writer" habits of a Kaltenborn never infected him. His political biases were never revealed to the audience, and even some of his closest friends had no idea what political party he favored throughout his long years of broadcasting — an enviable achievement that should perhaps be emulated by the typical newscaster of the television era.

As a radio phenomenon, Lowell Thomas caught on almost immediately. On the other hand, surprisingly, there was no immediate profusion of Lowell Thomas imitators on radio in the early thirties. The time for big-time radio news had not yet arrived. A look at the New York radio schedule for the fall of 1933 shows not a single daily news program on NBC-Red (WEAF). NBC-Blue (WJZ) had Lowell Thomas, CBS had acquired Boake Carter, and WOR had Gabriel Heatter. Morning news, noonday news and late-night news were as yet undreamed of.

So radio news continued to be weak and ineffective competition for the printed word during the early years of the thirties, although the press lords became increasingly uneasy about radio's newsgathering potential. It was only as the decade spent itself, and as the shadows of a European war settled once again, that the radio industry perceived that there was a great mission out there waiting to be discovered, that they could compete in new and spectacular ways with the newspapers. Perhaps news might one day be the crowning jewel of the program day.

9. Sportscasting in the Twenties

No people in the history of the world, not even the ancient Romans, have been more attracted to sporting events and contests than the people of the United States. No doubt the American infatuation with sports and with star athletes has deep roots in the country's history, but to no little extent, the vast development of America's major sports has been a byproduct of the electronic media — radio and television. As the twentieth century draws to a close, and the newspapers are full of stories of how a strike of football players has been waged almost exclusively over issues of television revenues and royalties, Americans are reminded of the vital role that broadcasting has played in making sports into a major national industry and source of wealth.

In early radio, the broadcasting of sports got off to a rather halting and irregular start, but hardly a weak and insignificant one. News related to sports was a regular preoccupation of all of the early broadcasters. Indeed, even before the inauguration of KDKA's licensed broadcasting, Dr. Frank Conrad made the reading of baseball scores one of the features of his home experimental broadcasts. Going back still further, we must not forget the reason for Guglielmo Marconi's first trip to the United States: to broadcast the results of the *America's* Cup race in October 1899.

When KDKA started broadcasting in the fall of 1920, no immediate thought was given to the broadcasting of sporting events, although the first regular announcer, Harold Arlin, did follow the practice of Frank Conrad of occasionally reading scores or other sports information supplied him by the newspapers. Nonetheless, among the features of early programming at KDKA were "remotes," so that it was only a matter of time before the station was motivated to put full-length sporting events on the air. The opportunity arose some five months later when a prize fight was held at the Pittsburgh Motor Square Garden on April 11, 1921. The blow-by-blow description was not given by Arlin himself, but by Florent Gibson, a *Pittsburgh Post* sportswriter. The contenders were Johnny Ray and Johnny Dundee, whose names have now faded into the footnotes of boxing history. The program was a decided success.

It would have been a very fortunate stroke of luck if a precedent had been established of having only experienced and well-qualified sportswriters give the descriptions of live events, but this was the age of the all-purpose announcer, and throughout most of the 1920s announcers were not specialists, nor was anything in radio considered specialized. Until the later twenties when certain general announcers like Graham McNamee and Ted Husing allowed themselves to be considered sportscasters, the business of sportscasting remained one of the assigned chores of anyone whose job it was to stand before the microphone.

If the first sports event on KDKA was reported by a professional sportswriter, numerous subsequent broadcasts were handled by Harold Arlin himself. He personally broadcast the first baseball game to go over the air when he went out to the Forbes Field ballpark on August 5, 1921. Arlin was a baseball fan with a better-than-average knowledge of the game, so he was able to give a smooth and articulate report of this game between the Pittsburgh Pirates and the Philadelphia Phillies. (Pittsburgh won 8 to 5.) That same summer KDKA started building a reputation for sports broadcasting, and advance-notice sports broadcasts greatly increased the listening audience wherever the station was heard. The day before the first baseball broadcast, the station presented by remote a description of the United States Davis Cup tennis matches.

KDKA continued to press its success in the area of sports broadcasting in the fall of 1921, and Arlin also won the distinction for being the first announcer to broadcast a football game. The first home game of the University of Pittsburgh was with West Virginia, luckily a rather slow-moving contest so that Arlin was able to build up some verbal techniques for describing this sport, with which he was somewhat less familiar. The next game, between Pitt and Nebraska, was a little more lively, and Arlin had a few problems with the primitive equipment that was used at the time. After one exciting series of plays he got a bit excited and shouted into the microphone so loudly that the needle was knocked off the modulation meter. The station was off the air for several minutes while the engineer got the needle back on.

Even as Arlin and the Westinghouse managers were discovering the popularity of sportscasting in the spring and summer of 1921, preparations were afoot in the East for the earthshaking sportscast of the Dempsey-Carpentier fight, probably the most widely heralded sporting event of the postwar era. It was to be the first sports event broadcast in the New York metropolitan area, and was especially remarkable since a new broadcasting station had to be started just to put it on the air.

Broadcasting the great event was the brainchild of David Sarnoff. In April of 1921, at the age of 30, Sarnoff had been selected as General Manager of the Radio Corporation of America. He was no longer the "eccentric" promoter of broadcasting that he had been a few years before; the company's directors now recognized him as a genius. But still there was no RCA broadcasting station and no firm plans to have one. Sarnoff had to prove that there were millions out there waiting to listen to the radio. What better way to do it than to put on the air the biggest and most talked-about boxing event of the twentieth century?

The problems to be solved were many and varied, but Sarnoff moved on them all like Grant moving into Richmond. The technical problems alone were enough to discourage anyone. RCA had no radio station; it had no transmitter capable of doing the job; it had no facilities of any kind at Boyle's Thirty Acres in Jersey City, the site of the match, and no indication that it would be allowed to install any; no transmission towers; no announcer or sportscaster with any experience in broadcasting. All that Sarnoff had was the will. Even after Sarnoff had managed to borrow a GE transmitter that was on delivery to the navy, after station WJY was given a one-day license, and after the announcing services of J. Andrew White—a wireless enthusiast who had been an amateur boxer—were obtained, Sarnoff still had an enormous job of salesmanship to do.

Fortunately, there were many who wanted to help. Assistance was given by the American Committee for Devastated France, the native land of Georges Carpentier. Since the borrowed transmitter was the property of the navy, the Navy Club was lined up to help. Its president was former Assistant Secretary of the Navy and vice-presidential candidate Franklin D. Roosevelt. The National Amateur Wireless Association, whose president was Guglielmo Marconi, was asked to take care of the publicity and the arrangement of reception at halls, theatres, lodges, clubhouses and other public places, the purpose being to enlarge the radio audience far beyond the paltry few skilled amateurs who owned their own crystal sets. About one hundred large gatherings were arranged far in advance, most of them charging a small admission fee. (The proceeds were divided equally between the American Committee for Devastated France and the Navy Club.)

Even the telephone company, which had no reason to be sympathetic to the ambitions of RCA, finally cooperated in the endeavor, supplying a private telephone wire between the boxing arena in Jersey City and the transmitter a few blocks away in the Lackawanna Railroad yards in Hoboken.

It was a happy and auspicious start for sportscasting in the New York area. It would not have been, however, if the fight had not ended in the fourth round. Shortly after the count when Carpentier went down, the transmitter blew up in Hoboken. And if he had had to go on much longer at ringside, Major J. Andrew White himself might have fallen victim of heat prostration. Provisions for broadcasting (which in this case amounted to talking over the telephone at ringside) were untried in those days, and Major White, cramped into a tiny spot in front of the ring and wearing a starched white shirt with high collar in the steamy July heat, was several times almost knocked over by the fighters as they came to the ropes.

The fight itself was the moment of truth for Major White, for the moment it began he realized that he had never really given any thought to how to use words to describe a fight as it was going on. For a few seconds he was almost speechless, but then he managed to form a few words, and began to move onward gamely, getting into the spirit of the thing. Several times he wildly gesticulated to his assistant, Harry Walker, who was holding a nice thermos jug of ice water, but Walker misunderstood his gestures, and nary a drop got to White's lips during the fight.

In the fourth round, when Carpentier was on the ropes, White had reason

Major J. Andrew White, a wireless enthusiast and amateur boxer, was pressed into emergency service to broadcast the famous Dempsey-Carpentier fight in 1921. He went on to become an "old reliable" in the formative years of CBS. (Photo courtesy University of Illinois Library.)

to fear that he himself might be knocked out as well. When Carpentier was knocked down and fell against the single rope that separated him from the first row of spectators, there was a strong likelihood that the radio broadcaster, his telephone and his cranium would be smashed by the heavyweight contender. Luckily, when Carpentier came down for the last time he fell in another direction. White calmly described the final count over the air and fell back in his seat, the broadcast over. Seconds later the transmitter in Hoboken blew, and one of the great broadcasts of early radio passed into history.

It was said that 300,000 people listened to the match on the radio, some as far away as Florida. The newspaper coverage given to the radio aspect of the fight was more than sufficient to prove to stuffy board members at RCA and elsewhere that there was a vast potential, and even wild enthusiasm, for this new and dramatic means of communication. American sports has continued to mean much to broadcasting over the years, but never again was it to mean so much so quickly.

Shortly after the great event at Jersey City, RCA opened its own experimental radio station at Roselle Park, New Jersey, WDY, and none other than Major J. Andrew White was put in charge of programming. It is not altogether clear exactly what RCA hoped for this new entry into the broadcasting field. The station was considered experimental by RCA management, although doubtless David Sarnoff, for one, hoped that the station could soon be brought into the sunlight and raised to the stature of the Westinghouse station in Newark, WJZ. One of the reasons things didn't pan out, and the station never seemed to gather much of a listening audience during the winter of 1921–1922, the first months of operation, was that there were no stellar sporting events to allow the station to get a foothold in the New York metropolitan area.

Accordingly, the Board of Directors of RCA, which had recently moved into a closer partnership with Westinghouse because of the latter's experience and expertise in building radio receiving sets, to say nothing of its experience in running broadcasting stations, decided to close WDY and merge its New York efforts with WJZ. Some of the people who had been associated with WDY, including Major White, moved over to WJZ, and for several years thereafter White served as a special announcer for sporting events at WJZ.

WJZ did not actually go on the air for several months after the Dempsey-Carpentier fight, although it had been licensed in the spring of 1921. When it did go on the air, it turned its attention to sports almost immediately. Tommy Cowan, the station's announcer, had been struggling heroically for program ideas to fill up the broadcast day when a sportswriter from the *Newark Sunday Call* by the name of Sandy Hunt suggested that the station broadcast the 1921 World Series, which was to begin in only three days, October 3. The series was to be staged in WJZ's back yard, so to speak, being between two New York teams, the New York Yankees and the New York Giants. And there was not another station anywhere to horn in — KDKA was 300 miles away out in Pittsburgh.

So Cowan and the WJZ staff warmed to the idea of getting their station off to a running start with a broadcast of the Series. But could it be done? To start right out with remotes seemed to be awfully daring, and the memory of the near-disaster at the Dempsey-Carpentier fight was green in everybody's mind. Also, the feat would require the cooperation of the telephone company, which could hardly be taken for granted. The telephone company took a jaundiced view of radio stations, particularly ones operated by its rival, Westinghouse.

Cowan nonetheless boldly approached the telephone company with the request that it provide a wire between the New York stadiums and WJZ in Newark. The telephone company would hear none of it. Later WJZ turned to the idea that had been used by Major White in Jersey City. They would rent a box seat at Yankee Stadium and the Polo Grounds and appeal to the telephone company to install an ordinary telephone in the box. After a great deal of persuasion and hectoring, the telephone company complied. Alas, again, the technology was not then available for a direct amplification of the telephone message over the airwaves, so WJZ had to use the kind of second-person announcing that was used in Jersey City. Sandy Hunt would go to the ball game, representing both his own paper and station WJZ, sit in the box equipped with a telephone line, and relate the plays to Tommy Cowan in Newark. Cowan, in turn, would put the plays on the air in his own words.

Over 30,000 people were on hand at the Polo Grounds to watch the first game of the series on October 3. Doubtless few of them knew that history was being made that day as Sandy Hunt sat in his reserved box seat and calmly described the play-by-play action to Tommy Cowan in Newark. Luck was with both parties since the game was dull and slow-moving, making a reasonably accurate account of what went on not very difficult. For Cowan in Newark, however, the whole thing was torture, as anyone will know who tries to hold a telephone to his ear for several hours. His hand became numb and his ear sore as he intently concentrated on hearing Hunt's words and repeating them into a microphone before him.

There were other problems in this kind of broadcasting. It was a line of communication that moved in one direction. If Cowan lost anything, he couldn't very well ask questions of Hunt at the ballpark, since this kind of dialogue with an unheard party would have been confusing to the listening audience. So Cowan just plodded along as best he could, simply repeating what came to him over the telephone wire. But he had no chance to jot things down, to keep the score, so that when the game was over he had forgotten the score, and thus was in the embarrassing position of wrapping things up without being able to give the final score. (The Giants had won 3–0.)

The Yankees went on to win the World Series 5 games to 3, but after the first game Cowan was made a little more comfortable by using a headphone set to receive the play-by-play from the ballparks. As time went on he got a little more relaxed with this kind of remote transaction. More importantly, the broadcasts were a smashing success. WJZ received more than 4,000 pieces of mail congratulating it on this public service to the many at home who couldn't make it out to the ballpark.

Interestingly enough, re-creations of ball games by an in-station announcer continued to be a feature of radio for many years, especially on smaller stations. By the mid-twenties, big stations like WEAF and WJZ no longer needed to resort to the simple telephone hookup, but it remained popular and cheap for less prosperous broadcasters. Sometimes it worked out fine and sometimes it didn't. Sports announcer Ronald Reagan (who later went on to become President of the United States) had reason to find out about that.

After Reagan graduated from Eureka College in 1932, he got some part-time work on WOC (World of Chiropractic) in Davenport, Iowa, where he began by broadcasting a series of University of Iowa football games. Later, he was offered a job with an NBC station in Des Moines, Iowa, WHO, where he changed his name to "Dutch" Reagan, fearing that the name Ronald would not go over very well with sportsfans. The Des Moines station occasionally went far afield to put big-league ball games on the air, and in 1935 they had Dutch Reagan re-create a Chicago Cubs ball game that came to them over telegraphic wire. Unfortunately there was an interruption in the service in the bottom of the ninth with the score tied. For over six minutes Reagan was stranded at the mike with nothing coming in. He reported a long and fictional stream of foul balls during this period, only to find out on the resumption of service that the batter had popped out! Such were the vicissitudes of re-created ball games.

WJZ continued making regular sportscasts when suitable events were available during 1921–22. When the station moved to New York from the Westinghouse plant in Newark, the staff of announcers gradually increased, and all of them had to take an occasional turn at this or that kind of sporting event—even the cultured and fastidious Milton Cross. But in time specialization came to be the order of the day, with some announcers coming to be associated with this unique field of broadcasting.

Among the coming generation of sports announcers who got their start at WJZ was Edward Britt "Ted" Husing, who would be one of the leaders in the field during the golden years of radio. Another "accidental" announcer, he never had the slightest premonition when he went before the mike that the sporting background he did have would ever be of any professional use to him.

Husing was born in the Bronx, the son of a German-born saloon keeper. (His nickname of Ted was given to him by a childhood sweetheart.) When he was a teenager his father got a job at the Columbia University Club, where Ted helped. He developed a passion for sports and served as a mascot for the school's football, basketball and track teams. He apparently hated school and never had good enough grades to get into college, but he was an omnivorous reader as an adolescent and acquired a large collection of books. Above all he was always a superb talker, and early in life he reached the conclusion that he could talk longer and louder than anyone he knew. One of his youthful fantasies was that he would be ensconced in an office with the word "Commentator" on the door—this at a time when there was no such term as "radio commentator" in the language.

During World War I, Husing had served in the National Guard, and after the war he wandered aimlessly to a number of different jobs. On one occasion he applied for a job as a payroll clerk in a hosiery manufacturing firm that was advertising for a married man. Ted had been going with a woman who had been in the Follies, but he wasn't married. He said he was, however, and got the job. A year later he did get married, and when word of it got to his boss he was fired. He and his wife decided to visit some friends in Florida and look for a job after taking a vacation. While coming back to New York, Husing bought a newspaper in Washington and started to thumb through the want ads. One of them immediately struck his attention:

Radio Announcer—Must be young, married, conscientious, social by nature, college graduate, have knowledge of the terminology of music, and the ability to say the right thing at the right time.

Well, now he was really married—but college graduate? Husing was not about to let that get in his way when his eyes ran down to those last words: "the ability to say the right thing at the right time." That phrase fitted Husing's self image to a "T." So he immediately fired off a telegram, inventing the fiction that he had a B.S. degree from Harvard. When he got home a telegram was awaiting him telling him to report to WJZ, Aeolian Building, 33 W. 42nd Street.

That night he sat up late reading over the names of composers of classical music, and all of the strange-sounding musical terms he could get hold of. The next day he showed up at the studio where 600 competitors were standing in line. The studio's waiting room was a mob scene.

When Husing's turn came to speak before the microphone, he was asked to speak for a few minutes about music and then to ad-lib without notes. He noticed that there were men listening in the control booth, and he began talking. He talked about music for ten minutes (reciting nearly everything he knew), but then he started into the news of the day. When he looked at his watch 35 minutes had gone by. He looked over at the control booth, and saw that the judges had filed out.

Assuming that he had been eliminated at the first cut, Husing went home dejected. But when he arrived home the phone was ringing, and Husing was told that the job was his if he could pass an interview with David Sarnoff, RCA's general manager, the next day. Husing was convinced he had won the audition because he talked longer and more articulately than all of the other applicants. He was, to be sure, a no-fail, nonstop talker. In any case, he was hired as a station announcer at $45.00 a week, and joined the WJZ staff along with Milton Cross, Norman Brokenshire and J. Andrew White.

Husing was assigned general announcing duties at WJZ and did not immediately think about becoming a sportscaster. At this time J. Andrew White was doing all of the sportscasting for the station on a job-by-job basis. Husing listened to the station's sports broadcasts, though, and decided he could do as well or better, so he pestered White to give him a chance. White didn't think that Husing had enough resonance for sportscasting, and recommended that the youngster "break his nose." Wanting to please, Husing did have an operation to widen the antra of his nose, and apparently this did give him more resonance, but no sporting jobs appeared on the horizon. White had a monopoly on them.

Finally, a year after he had joined the staff at WJZ, White told Husing that he would allow him to assist with a broadcast. The event would be the Penn-Cornell football game, broadcast on Thanksgiving Day, 1925. Ted Husing's first brush with sportscasting turned out to be a baptism by fire. When the two announcers arrived in Philadelphia, White told Husing to proceed to the stadium to see that everything was set up properly for the game. White wanted to visit some relatives, and promised that he would show up before the game.

The broadcast was to take place at the top of a grandstand that was still under construction—everything open to the heavens. Shortly after Husing's arrival, a big downpour of rain began, and he and the engineer put up a big tarpaulin for protection. This worked for a time, but finally they got soaked through anyway.

The pregame activity got underway, but White had not showed up. The engineer gave Husing the sign that he was on the air. Husing was shocked and momentarily speechless; he was expecting the Major to do the broadcast. But after a few moments he struggled forward gamely, offering descriptions of the stadium, the playing field, and, of course, the weather.

Seconds before the kickoff, Husing saw White scrambling up the rows of seats below, and with a feeling of indescribable relief he handed the microphone over to the seasoned veteran. Between quarters and at the half, White gave Husing a chance, but Husing realized for the first time that sportscasting was more than a matter of having an interest in sports. When the game was over, White told Husing that he had done very well, but Husing knew now what he would have been up against if he had actually had to describe the game himself, so he returned home determined to study and master the art.

For the next year or so Ted Husing took more and more of the responsibilities for sportscasting at WJZ, but like a great many announcers then and since, he did some jockeying for position, and won his spurs at several different stations while seeking to establish a permanent reputation for himself. He didn't think that WJZ was paying him well enough, so when the *Boston Evening Transcript* opened its station, WBET, Husing joined the staff of that station with the promise that he could broadcast the Braves baseball games. But Husing apparently didn't find Boston very stimulating, for that fall he was back in New York, broadcasting Columbia University football games over WHN, a station owned by the *New York American*. His work at WHN skyrocketed Ted Husing into the forefront of sportscasters, where he remained.

The best-known sports announcer of the 1920s did not come from the staff of WJZ, but from the rapidly growing AT&T stepchild, WEAF. It was, of course, Graham McNamee, who captured the hearts of millions of listeners through his vivid and breathtaking accounts of sporting events of all kinds. Though he had begun as a general announcer and was never officially pigeonholed into the sportscasting category, no announcer in radio's first decade, not even Major White, was better known than McNamee in the sports area. McNamee had been active in sports while in college, so it is not unusual that shortly after he showed up on the roster of announcers at WEAF he began asking the station executives about the possibility of doing some sportscasting. But management wasn't much interested. They had enough to keep McNamee busy at the studio. On only a few occasions during the first few months of his service was he allowed to do one or another minor sporting event. For example, he broadcast a prizefight between Harry Greb and Johnny Wilson shortly after he joined the station.

When the baseball World Series of 1923 approached, McNamee asked for permission to broadcast the games, but the station wanted somebody for the job more clearly identified with sports news, so they hired Bill McGeehan, sports editor of the *New York Herald Tribune*, to handle the play-by-plays. (Quite luckily, the 1923 series, like those of 1921 and 1922, were between two home teams, the Yankees and the Giants, so there were no insurmountable technical difficulties in getting the transmissions from the stadiums to the transmitter.) WEAF finally decided to allow McNamee to accompany McGeehan to the games to fill in between innings and perhaps offer a little commentary and color.

The program sheet of WEAF for that year showed what happened. For the first three games Bill McGeehan was listed as the announcer. The last four games were listed as being announced by Graham McNamee. McGeehan was so flat, so unused to oral description, that the multitudes of people who called or wrote the station asked to hear "that other announcer" who had filled in. McNamee's flair for words, the picturesque quality of his language, was what people were listening to, and everybody wanted to hear more of it. From this time on, all of the major sporting events going out over WEAF were handled by Graham McNamee.

Within a month WEAF added to its staff a partner for McNamee, a man by the name of Phillips Carlin. Carlin had been hanging around the WEAF studios for a long time, but the fact that he had a remarkable speaking voice cut no ice with company executives since he had no musical training or background—considered an absolute essential for announcers in the early days. He was finally hired, however, at the end of 1923, and it was soon discovered that he had many of McNamee's skills as a word painter and enthusiastic conveyor of sporting ambience.[1]

For the next several years McNamee and Carlin worked as a team in broadcasting sporting events and came to be known as the "WEAF twins." They were both capable of doing either play-by-play descriptions or back up, and sometimes they would exchange duties, although McNamee was considered the lead announcer. In any case, very early on they devised a method of working together that has more or less remained standard procedure in sportscasting ever since. The man at the microphone would look for the type of play, describe it, and give an idea of how much ground was won or lost. The other man, usually well supplied with all of the official information, team rosters and the like, would determine the ball carrier and tackler and feed this information to the man doing the play-by-play. The second man would also be charged with providing comment, color and miscellaneous information of any variety. He would also be ready to take charge at the mike if for some reason the chief announcer needed a break.

It would be hard to deny that no announcer of record could report on a game with more excitement and enthusiasm than Graham McNamee. He was never flat and never dull, and he never arrived at a game without getting himself psyched up for it first. Knowing that the easiest habit for a sports announcer to fall into was the habit of blandly calling off the plays, he would literally force himself into a state of excitement or frenzy before every game. When he went on the air he was raring to go, and his always-vigorous personality bubbled over the airwaves.

It was sometimes said of McNamee that he was really not a sports expert and that he was not an aficionado of the various sports he reported. This is true, but he was something probably even better. He could make the spirit of the game come alive in words.

McNamee himself was perfectly aware of the implied conflict in broadcasting any kind of sporting event between technical precision and verbal color and imaginative picturing, and he always preferred the latter. His philosophy was very well explained in a piece he wrote for *Radio Guide*, entitled "I Cover the Arena":

> The Red team is up against its own goal posts. The Blue team is marching steadily down the field reeling off gain after gain. Third down and two yards to go. The ball snaps back, a few bewildering gestures with it to confuse the Red players and then a plunging mass of tangled arms and legs. The ball is nowhere in sight. Is it a touchdown? Or did they just fall short of that last white stripe?
>
> Go ahead, tell 'em about it. Out there at the loudspeakers millions of rabid fans are agonizing over the delay. Can't you almost hear their thoughts screaming in your ears, "Come on, what happened?"
>
> Those are the seconds that are years long for the announcer. You can sense the impatience of the listeners but you can't do anything about it until you see what's happened. Perhaps five or six seconds elapse before you can tell about it. To the announcer it seems like five or six minutes and to the average listener—according to letters—it seems like five or six hours.
>
> But I still think honest enthusiasm and the general picture are what the audience wants. . . . And that is what I intend to give them because that is the way I feel.[2]

And apparently the enthusiasm and the general picture were what the multitudes wanted. Graham McNamee's gifts for the general picture probably made him the most successful and best-loved sports announcer of all times. Thousands upon thousands of letters poured into the studio after his broadcasts, sometimes requiring a whole mail truck to bring it from the post office. McNamee received over 50,000 letters following the 1925 World Series alone. And only a small fraction of these chided him for his peccadillos or faulted him for technical inaccuracy. One letter from the proprietor of a hospital for the elderly was perhaps typical of McNamee's mailbag:

> Your knowledge of the game and your colorful description made a big hit here. . . . I wish you could see these helpless men listening to your voice; some are blind and many are bedridden, but the smile on their faces as the game progressed certainly would repay you, had you any doubts as to the success of your reception.

Of course the era of the expert was just around the corner; soon there would be many others in the field of sportscasting, and perhaps some who could tell what happened in two seconds instead of five seconds. But they did not receive 50,000 letters for their effort. They were just men doing their job well. Graham McNamee imparted to the radio audience the fire and spirit of a true believer, of a man who thought that the whole world hung on the utterance of every word. He thought that that was what the medium of radio needed, and that is what he gave it.

The New York journalist Heywood Broun came as close as any to pinning down McNamee's contribution to early radio when he observed that it was McNamee who gave form and meaning to the new medium of radio.

> Mr. McNamee has justified the whole activity of radio broadcasting. A thing may be a marvelous invention and still as dull as ditch water. It will be that unless it allows the play of personality. A machine amounts to nothing much unless a man can ride. Graham McNamee has been able to take a new medium of expression and through it transmit himself— to give out vividly a sense of movement and of feeling. Of such is the kingdom of art.

Of course sportscasting as an art was rapidly developing everywhere around the country by the mid-twenties. Chicago was always a big sports-minded city, and as early as 1924, WMAQ, then owned by the *Chicago Daily News*, had a desire to get into sportscasting for Midwestern fans. As a sports-caster they hired Harold O. (Hal) Totten, who had played baseball at North-western and served as sports editor of the *Daily Northwestern* and who later joined the *Daily News*. He began by broadcasting the University of Chicago football games, and the following year he became the first announcer to broad-cast Chicago Cubs baseball from Wrigley Field. Totten became a big-name sports announcer in the years ahead. A half-century later WMAQ is still broad-casting baseball—but now the White Sox instead of the Cubs.

Another sportscaster who got his start in Chicago in the early days was Quinlan Augustus (Quin) Ryan who became a sportscaster for WGN after serv-ing as a sportswriter on the *Chicago Tribune*. The *Tribune* had bought the earlier Chicago station WDAP, changed its call letters to WGN (World's Greatest Newspaper) and given it a studio converted from bedrooms in the top floor of the Drake Hotel. Ryan was another wildly enthusiastic radio voice of the McNamee variety, and he covered all manner of Midwestern sporting events: Cubs and White Sox baseball, football of the Illinois teams of North-western and the University of Illinois (he reported the famous game in 1924 when Red Grange scored four touchdowns against Michigan in the first twelve minutes of play), the Indianapolis Speedway, the Kentucky Derby. Although he had spent his early years as a sportswriter, and although he would shortly specialize, Ryan also had to do general announcing during the twenties, as did most of the microphone men in the early days. He read the funny pages on the air to children, using the names "Uncle Walt" and "Uncle Quin."

Bob Elson, who had worked for KWK in St. Louis, became another

Chicago personality when he moved in 1929 to the Windy City's WGN. There his "rising inflection" type of voice and animated personality made him a beloved fixture for many years. Another longtime Chicago sportscaster was Pat Flannagan, who began at WBBM in 1929.

Over in Detroit, at WWJ, Edwin (Pappy) Tyson became the first to broadcast the football games of the University of Michigan. He was another of those who somehow drifted into radio and became an all-purpose announcer. He had a degree in forestry from Pennsylvania State College (now Penn State University), and in 1922 he became announcer and program director at WWJ. In doing sporting events Pappy Tyson teamed up with a man named Lawrence Holland, a former Penn State football player who worked at a Detroit gas station but who had caught the radio bug and hung around the WWJ studio.

When Holland first started hanging around the station there was no thought to putting him on the payroll, but he became a kind of volunteer doorman or bouncer, helping Tyson process the singers or other visitors to the studio. But when Tyson started to do the Michigan games he took Holland along, and here the latter proved his usefulness. Holland knew football and became a big help as a spotter. The two men sat in regular seats in the stadium, Pappy Tyson calling the plays, Holland identifying the players and generally keeping track of details. Holland would list the names of the players on a shortened laundry board and then point to the names of the players for Tyson as the action proceeded. Holland also kept a rolled-up copy of the *Detroit News* in his pocket, and if the spectators in the rows ahead stood up or obstructed the announcer's view, Holland would hit them over the head with it. Some might have taken offense at this assault, but one look at the mammoth Holland would settle them comfortably back in their seats.

Holland eventually got on the payroll, and the two men became a well-known team locally, although Holland had few if any talents for speaking. Curiously enough, Tyson was a little, undistinguished-looking man with a resonant voice; Holland was a giant with no speaking voice that anybody would want to listen to. When pictures of the pair were printed in the papers, it was hard to convince anybody that it was Pappy doing all the talking.

All around the country, different styles and talents entered the field of sportscasting during the last half of the twenties. Some of them went on to make big names for themselves during the golden years of radio. In Atlanta, Georgia, Bill Munday had begun broadcasting Georgia Tech games over WSB, and became very popular locally. When Georgia Tech was selected to play California in the Rose Bowl in 1929, NBC decided to team Munday up with Graham McNamee, and Munday's exaggerated drawl and Southern charm soon made him a national favorite. Elsewhere, there was Don Thompson, who got his start at KPO in San Francisco; there was France Laux at KVOO in Tulsa, Oklahoma; there was Walter (Red) Barber, who began his long and distinguished career in sportscasting at the University of Florida in 1929.

The hazards and difficulties of sportscasting couldn't be better illustrated than by mention of Red Barber's difficult initiation in the sports field during his college days. Barber was not a sports authority in any sense, and he hadn't the slightest inclination toward radio work. While a student at the University of Florida at Gainesville he worked as a janitor–errand boy at the university's faculty club, where he was asked by one of the professors to substitute for him in reading a talk about agriculture over the air while the professor had to be out of town. The station manager, liking Red's voice, asked him to stay on as an announcer. Red didn't want to leave his job at the faculty club, but the station manager made it worth his while, and Red began as a part-time announcer in the spring of 1930.

The following fall the college station decided that it wanted to broadcast the school's home football games. Red was asked to do it. But he was ill-prepared for the chore and began broadcasting the first game without knowing anything about football or about the team's players. The first broadcast was a disaster, and the next few weren't much better. Red quickly learned the lesson that many early sportscasters learned: Charm and personality aren't enough. To talk about sports you have to know something about them. Before the fourth game, Red went out to watch the team practice, made a spotting chart and brushed up on the principles of the game. After his next and better-informed broadcast he received two hundred favorable telegrams, one from the governor of Florida.

After five decades Red Barber continues to be one of the most charming voices in sportscasting. His mild Southern drawl imparts a decided warmth to everything he sends out over the radio. A more erudite sportscaster and raconteur would be hard to find. His stock of learning in the sports field is tremendous. On the other hand, he carries his learning lightly, and his association with radio over the years has given him the common touch. Like McNamee and so many of the other sportscasters from the early days, Barber learned the art of painting pictures with words, of putting the living and breathing essence of the sporting contest into the listeners' homes with verve and enthusiasm. The craft is an admirable one, and nowhere has it flourished so luxuriously as in the United States.

10. Networks

Today every American child knows what a radio or TV network is. A cluster of stations form an alliance to share a major portion of their programming. One or two key stations provide high-quality programs to smaller and less powerful stations that could not afford to provide such programming on their own. In the first few years of radio broadcasting, this concept had not entered the national consciousness. Radio broadcasting emanated from individual radio centers and was beamed into the atmosphere from individual transmitters; this was the accepted definition of broadcasting. Nonetheless, network broadcasting would be in full swing by 1926, so it is apparent that it didn't take long for this very practical and sensible scheme to come into reality.

In a sense the technology was already available for network programming in 1920, at least in a primitive form. And the idea of a network or web already had considerable meaning to one sector of the communications industry: telephonic communications, especially as understood by the American Telephone & Telegraph Company and its subsidiaries and tributaries. Telephone service that had already been in place for some decades made use of the concept of a web or network, and long-lines transmission employed a complicated network of exchanges and substations. When the telephone company began its first experimental radio stations in the New York area in the early twenties, it was with the idea that radio might be of some help to them in solving their very difficult problems of long-distance transmission. Of course, they didn't yet see how great a contribution this telephonic idea could make to broadcasting. But certainly the expertise brought by the telephone company carried with it a kind of prejudice in favor of networking; for what, after all, was the Bell Telephone System itself but a network of individual receiver/transmitters tied into central switching stations? The "network" idea in some sense was thus already implanted in the communication mentality in 1920.

Even before the telephone company touched its hand to radio, there was a push in the direction of a network concept, at least in a very simple form. Shortly after it began regular broadcasting in 1920, KDKA adopted the practice, soon followed by other radio stations, of putting "remote" programs on the air. That is to say, when the station wanted to broadcast a Christmas church service, or an address of an important political candidate or a baseball game or prizefight, it was not feasible to bring these special events to the Westing-

127

house factory, so telephonic wires were set up to connect the place of the event with the transmitter of the broadcasting station. At this very moment a network of sorts was established, there being not only a sender and a receiver, but a third element tied to the central transmitting source.

For the first several years, AT&T seems to have balked at the idea of providing telephone lines for radio stations owned by Westinghouse or RCA, and these competing companies had to arrange for telephone wires from independent companies like Western Union. In spite of the poor qualities of transmission in the beginning, this idea of "remote" broadcasting was so compelling and so appealing that there was little doubt that when the technique was perfected it would be an important part of the radio world.

By 1924 the "pickup" side of networking was in full swing, at least with the leading stations in large cities. At WJZ, for example, shortly after that station moved from Newark to Aeolian Hall in midtown Manhattan, a most elaborate pickup network was established, enabling the Westinghouse-RCA station to cover completely the entire city of New York. With the help of Western Union, and partially using preexisting lines and some occasional new cables, WJZ was able to pick up sounds at will almost anywhere in New York. The system as it then existed made use of the several elevated railway lines that traversed Manhattan Island from north to south. These structures carried the trunk line cables, which in turn had outlet terminal boxes and switchboards at important points. Overhead twisted pair connections could be made from the trunk lines to any point in the city where broadcasting pickups were desirable. With this network of cable lines in place, a single lineman employed by Western Union could set up a link with any spot in the city in the matter of a few hours, so that it was virtually possible for WJZ to pick up an event anywhere in the city on one day's notice. Fortunately, almost the entire hotel and theatre district of the city, close to Aeolian Hall, was already fitted up with trunk cables, so extensive installations were almost never necessary in this neighborhood.

A pickup network was one thing; a distributing network was something altogether different. Here the idea is that two radio stations, linked by a telephone or telegraph wire, transmit the same programming. At first there seemed to be little need or justification for such a thing, but, as usually happened in the early days of radio, a great sports event stepped in to get people's imaginations working. In October 1922, WJZ in Newark and WGY in Schenectady both broadcast the World Series, the two stations being linked by a telegraph wire. The results were rather poor, actually, but the fact that such an idea existed got the ball rolling.

One place where the idea quickly took hold was in the headquarters of the American Telephone and Telegraph Company, where executives were more than a little annoyed that the "radio group" had stolen a march on them. They were also convinced that the cross-licensing agreements of 1920 prevented GE, Westinghouse and RCA from involving themselves in telephonic transmissions, and they were not overjoyed at the use of Western Union lines to connect two entirely separate broadcasting stations. Furthermore, they believed that if anybody should be experimenting in this area it was they themselves, and for this reason, a mere five months after the founding of their station WEAF in New York the telephone company was experimenting with the network idea. Indeed, for some time previously telephone engineers had been assigned to this project of linking radio stations by telephone wires, and by January 1923, when the first publicized experiment took place, the telephone company had gone far beyond the kind of crude transmission that WJZ used for the broadcast of the 1922 World Series.

AT&T's first public test of the network principle occurred on January 4, 1923, when WEAF, then located at 24 Walker Street in New York, fed a program by wire for simultaneous broadcast in Boston by station WNAC, owned by Shepard Stores. The program was three hours long and consisted of a saxophone solo, a number of orchestral selections, cello solos, vocals by contraltos and baritones, and imitations of bird calls, whose notes were said to be perfectly rendered by those listening to the Boston transmission. So well was the program publicized that it was estimated that as many as 100,000 listeners throughout New England and along the Atlantic Seaboard picked up the program.

Months of preparation and no small expenditures had gone into making this experiment a smashing success. Two long-distance circuits were used (one an emergency circuit in case the primary circuit should fail through storm or interference) for this distance of 300 miles. The circuits were equipped at intervals with repeaters or amplifiers and with special filters to equalize the circuits so that the sound was of highest possible quality on the Boston end. This latter was an important technical advance: Telephone long lines were usually adjusted to carry a frequency of 250 to 2,500 cps, but here they were equalized for 100 to 5,000 cps to provide suitable broadcast quality.

The success of the WEAF-WNAC experiment emboldened executives at AT&T, and in press releases following the event they boasted that shortly the whole country would be crisscrossed with radio test laboratories and radio toll stations, all connected with one another. However, this great radio/telephone network did not immediately materialize, the first hookup with Boston being little more than a one-night stand. Telephone engineers knew that if the network idea was to flourish they would need still better cables and transmission lines, suited to transmitting a wider diversity of radio sounds.

The following summer, though, brought AT&T a proposal that they could not turn down: a request from someone who actually wanted to "buy" some of their New York programming. This was an opportunity that could not be lost, since AT&T headquarters was still infatuated by the toll broadcasting idea. Anybody who was willing to pay for WEAF programming ought to be welcomed with open arms, and by the summer of 1923, someone walked into those arms.

The someone was Colonel H.R. Green, a millionaire in South Dartmouth, Massachusetts, who surely must have heard the WEAF-WNAC broadcast a few months before. Green owned a broadcasting station on his estate with the call letters WMAF. Like many other station owners of the early twenties, Green was merely a hobbyist who ran the station to amuse himself and his neighbors, without really having any firm idea of what he would send out over the airwaves. The good colonel tried hard, however; he purchased a great many phonograph records and had his servants play them over the air, and even installed loudspeakers in downtown South Dartmouth and nearby New Bedford so that those who did not own receivers could enjoy this essay into local broadcasting. Alas, the colonel simply didn't have enough material to keep a station broadcasting, and soon his neighbors took him for a nuisance, especially since his station prevented them from getting WEAF and WJZ in New York, which by now had regular programming schedules.

To solve these problems, and to keep his own station, Colonel Green contacted William E. Harkness of WEAF, hinting that he might be willing to pay for a telephone line connection with New York so that his listeners could have the benefit of strong WEAF programming. Harkness could hardly turn down an offer to subscribe to the New York toll broadcasting station because the project fitted so neatly into the original intentions of the telephone company in opening WEAF. On the other hand, Harkness doubted that Colonel Green would really be willing to pay an adequate amount of money for the service — the figure named being $60,000 a year. But the colonel eventually agreed, and the telephone company set up a permanent line. Of course the whole project worked out to the marvelous advantage of both parties. Colonel Green got New York programming, and telephone company engineers got an opportunity to experiment with amplification and equalization.

More importantly, when the connection was made on July 1, 1923, the first radio network in the modern sense was in existence. Of course only two stations were involved, but the revenue-producing possibilities of networking were immediately apparent. Undoubtedly more stations could be added when the advantages became more widely advertised.

Even before the arrangements were made for the permanent connection between New York and South Dartmouth, AT&T had experimented with multiple station hookups for a single important broadcast. Some radio historians give the date of June 7, 1923, as the beginning of network broadcasting, for on that date four stations were linked to broadcast the annual meeting of the National Electric Light Association held in Carnegie Hall, New York. In addition to Station WEAF in New York (which picked up the program from Carnegie Hall, thus strictly making a five-point web), there were the General Electric Station WGY in Schenectady and the Westinghouse Stations KDKA in Pittsburgh and KYW in Chicago. In addition to an address by Julius H. Barnes, president of the chamber of commerce, this network program also featured the singing of Ann Case of the Metropolitan Opera Company.

The press was ecstatic about this multistation broadcast, and one especially eager reporter opined that if the network idea caught on, "it might not be too long before farmers at the four corners of the Union may sit in their own houses and hear the President of the United States." This prophecy came a bit closer to fulfillment only fourteen days later, when WEAF long-lines engineers managed to broadcast a speech by President Harding from the

Coliseum in St. Louis, Missouri. From two microphones in St. Louis, Harding's voice was transmitted to the local audience over station KSD on the roof of the *St. Louis Post Dispatch*[1] and to the New York area over WEAF, by means of a telephone link. This broadcast, it was claimed, perhaps a bit extravagantly, could be heard in every state in the Union. An even more ambitious project to broadcast an address by President Harding direct from San Francisco was thwarted at the end of July; the president fell ill during a trip to Alaska, and later died in a San Francisco hotel room. Even though the great experiment never came off, it was clear by the summer of 1923 that network radio was the wave of the future.

This feverish activity on the part of telephone company engineers naturally did not go unnoticed at the radio group, with executives at Westinghouse, RCA and GE stymied by their inability to use telephone wires for their system — that use had been denied them by the cross-licensing agreements of 1920. Nonetheless, all were convinced of the merit of the network idea, so that the group's key radio station in New York, WJZ, began in the months that followed the telephone triumphs to build a network spun from Aeolian Hall in New York. Obviously there were stations available to the radio group to build such a network. RCA owned station WRC in Washington, D.C.; General Electric owned WGY in Schenectady; Westinghouse still owned KDKA in Pittsburgh, of course. Again using the alternate facilities of the Western Union Company and also the Postal Telegraph Company, the WJZ-based network moved forward. Western Union installed a permanent line between New York and Schenectady, a distance of 160 miles, while the Postal Telegraph Company provided a line between New York and Washington via Philadelphia and Baltimore, a distance of 220 miles. Further plans were then made to extend the network from Philadelphia to Pittsburgh, and from Schenectady through Cleveland to Chicago.

Unfortunately the radio group's network continued to be hobbled by poor-quality transmission lines, and feverish activity in their various laboratories pressed toward some alternate solution to the problem. Strongly considered in the mid-twenties was the possibility of radio-relay circuits, but alas, the microwaves so useful for this purpose today had not been developed at that time. Nonetheless, by the end of 1925, WJZ had succeeded in getting together a network of fourteen stations.

By 1925, then, two rival networks were in full swing, although neither was used extensively for uniform broadcasting as it would be in the years ahead. Individual programs and special events were broadcast over the network, but local stations continued to originate the greater share of their own programs. But the important thing is that the network idea had become firmly implanted in the radio industry at large; it was all just a matter of augmenting the idea on a grand scale. What was needed now, to add to the "super stations" that were being licensed, was a "super network," bigger and more powerful than anything conceived before — a network truly national in scope.

But the two networks of the mid-twenties hated and distrusted one another. There was the WEAF network controlled by AT&T, and there was the

WJZ network, controlled by RCA. Each network had assets and strengths that the other needed, but they were hampered in pooling these interests by those now long-outdated cross-licensing agreements. The rivalry between the two networks was more than simply a matter of healthy business competition, as between two hamburger chains or car rental companies. Conflicting philosophies and conflicting technologies were clearly keeping the radio industry from developing to its full potential.

Obviously, sooner or later, something would have to happen. A terrible clash, perhaps a nasty court battle of some kind. Nobody knew what it would be, but it seemed certain to come. However, quite luckily for the nation, the great pitched battle was averted, and peace finally arbitrated between the telephone group and the radio group. It came about in a most unexpected way. The telephone company, realizing that radio was not its bag, finally backed out of radio, leaving the business of broadcasting fully and completely in the hands of the Radio Corporation of America. And with the now all-powerful and healthy RCA in command, a national network of broadcasting could see the light of day.

The withdrawal of the telephone interests from the radio sphere was not a sudden thing, but the result of secret negotiations over a period of several years. The negotiations were so secret and at such a high level of corporate power that even the managers and executives of the radio stations were unaware of their drift. As with many such movements in this period of radio history, it was David Sarnoff who got the ball rolling, first in a memo to RCA Board Chairman Owen G. Young and later through intermediaries to the telephone company. Sarnoff simply suggested that the two rivals agree to render unto the radio group that which belonged to radio and to the telephone group that which belonged to the telephonic realm. There were growth and income possibilities in this separation of functions, plenty of money for both groups.

The telephone people were initially reluctant. Didn't they have the biggest and most successful network? Didn't they have the best sound reproduction? Hadn't their idea of toll broadcasting proven itself, while David Sarnoff's stubborn resistance to this concept had left him in the cold as eager advertisers appeared at the WEAF offices? Yes, the telephone company was clearly ahead now in the broadcasting wars; no need to back down.

On the other hand, executives at AT&T were not unmindful of the fact that they had never really intended to get into broadcasting in a big way; they had opened WEAF as an experimental station, and if the radio operation grew to much larger proportions, as it was bound to do, the operation would require a substantial diverson from what they regarded as their main line of work. Furthermore, they were quite aware that the radio group, or any other system that took radio as its primary interest, would need to have telephonic relay services of some kind; why should this business be going to competitors? Why not cooperate with these radio interests and win their business?

And so it was. After months of discussions and secret negotiations, the telephone group and the radio group signed a pact of peace—a peace that completely changed the face of radio broadcasting. On July 1, 1926, the two groups signed and put into effect a new division of labor in the field of radio. According to the covenants, AT&T was granted exclusive control over wire telephony and two-way wireless telephony, both foreign and domestic. All wire telegraphy rights went to AT&T also, but RCA kept its valuable rights to wireless telegraphy — long an important segment of its business. In receiving rights to the whole field of telephony, AT&T received control of network relays, whether wire or wireless, and that control has remained a great boon to them right down to the television era. In a service portion of the agreement, RCA was to lease radio-relay facilities from AT&T and cease using Western Union wires for network broadcasting.

And there was more. Western Electric was now barred from competing with the radio group in the manufacture of home receivers, but AT&T in turn surrendered its claims on transmitter manufacture. Henceforth RCA would be able to compete in this important and lucrative manufacturing area.

Finally, AT&T would give up broadcasting, leaving this field completely in the hands of the Radio Corporation of America. According to this agreement, station WEAF was to be sold to RCA for $1 million. Henceforth AT&T agreed to stay out of the broadcasting field, although naturally it was planning to profit mightily by the promise of exclusive rights to long-lines service, which, after all, was their prime field of expertise.

This final agreement was a shock felt most keenly at station WEAF in New York, the telephone company's eminently successful station. Apparently no one at the station was aware that the agreement between the radio group and the telephone group was being finalized, and when the public announcement was made, everybody from the station manager to the lowliest office boy was incredulous. They were being sold to the competition! WEAF had built up the best and strongest talent in radio; it had shown the way to success in toll broadcasting (and later, that is to say, sponsored programming) at a time when David Sarnoff and RCA were turning up their noses at that idea. The two stations were like the Yankees and the Dodgers, each with violent partisans. The idea that the one "team" would actually be taken over by the other was inconceivable. Yet that's the way it was to be.

So now the Radio Corporation of America would find itself with not just one network, but two. There was no easy way of combining the two networks, since both already had their own programming, announcers, popular favorites and the like, and there was money riding on each. One network, with WJZ as its anchor, became known as the Blue Network; the other, with WEAF as its anchor, became the Red Network.[2]

Regular operations in these two networks did not begin immediately. The first order of business was to form a company — a subsidiary of RCA naturally — whose sole and exclusive business would be to manage this thing called network broadcasting. This company came to be known as the National Broadcasting Company, was incorporated under the laws of Delaware on September 9, 1926, and officially began operations on November 1, 1926.[3]

One of the first orders of business was the election of officers. An outsider,

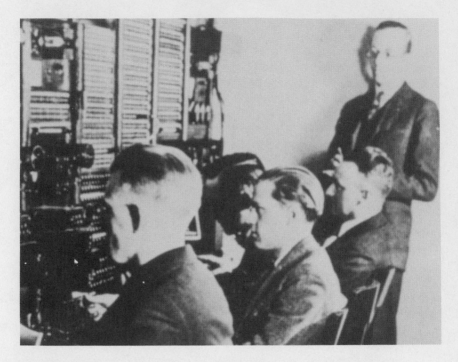

NBC goes on the air, November 15, 1926. Ready to give the signal is Chief Engineer O.B. Hanson, standing at right. The network concept was here to stay. (Photo courtesy NBC.)

Merlin H. Aylesworth, for many years managing director of the National Electric Light Association, was chosen as first president. Aylesworth was doubtless a good choice, since he had no identification with either of the pre–NBC radio networks; indeed, he didn't even own a radio. As vice president and general manager the powers at RCA chose WEAF's super-salesman George F. McClelland, undoubtedly giving a lift to the many employees at WEAF who thought themselves betrayed. Charles B. Popenoe, the very skillful administrator of WJZ, was chosen treasurer, and Lewis MacConnach was elected secretary. Bertha Brainerd of WJZ became the program manager.

Immediate plans were for some kind of gala opening of network broadcasting, and this occurred on November 15, 1926, when a thousand guests gathered at 8:00 P.M. in the ballroom of the old Waldorf Astoria Hotel in New York at 34th Street and Fifth Avenue. Tall and suave Merlin Aylesworth, the new president of NBC, made a gracious five-minute speech in which he estimated that as many as 12 million people might be listening to the program. What followed was a four-hour program, bringing in entertainers from several different network outposts, the distant performers being heard in the Waldorf ballroom over loudspeakers. From New York there was the New York Symphony Orchestra, with Walter Damrosch conducting, as well as the New York

Oratorio Society. From Chicago, with Milton Cross at the microphone, came the voice of famed soprano Mary Garden, who sang several numbers for the popular audience: "Annie Laurie," "Open Thy Blue Eyes," and "My Little Gray Home in the West." From Kansas City, where he was then performing, Will Rogers entertained listeners throughout the network with a monologue, "Fifteen Minutes with a Diplomat," which contained, among other things, a humorous imitation of President Coolidge.

There was the Edwin Franko Goldman Band (quite appropriate in view of Goldman's longtime faith in radio music); there was a light opera company under the baton of Cesare Sodero; there were the orchestras of Vincent Lopez, Ben Bernie and B.A. Rolfe. In general the whole program was a marvelous success (despite a few minor moments of interference, for the interference difficulties had at this point not been completely ironed out), and the invited dignitaries in New York as well as the millions of listeners around the country[4] agreed that the program was a triumph for radio.

This gala premiere was not strictly speaking the beginning of NBC broadcasting on a regular basis. The network programs remained irregular and sporadic for the next several months; a regular broadcasting schedule for the network began in January 1927.

Almost immediately after its formation, the new organization at NBC moved forward rapidly to solve a number of major problems. One was finding a new location for its studios, there now being two major stations in New York to house. Eventually WEAF moved up from the Telephone Building in lower Manhattan, and WJZ abandoned its home at Aeolian Hall. The combined operation was located at 711 Fifth Avenue, which became the home base of NBC until the move to the lavish RCA skyscraper at Radio City in 1933. Eventually, $400,000 was appropriated for the Fifth Avenue facilities, which were completely air conditioned and which featured studios that floated on springs for more perfect soundproofing.

Before the year 1926 was over, NBC had appointed an advisory board of distinguished individuals in a number of fields of endeavor whose purpose was to offer counsel to the network on matters of programming, finance, engineering and social obligations. Within a few more months Walter Damrosch was engaged on a permanent basis as musical counselor to the company. Frank E. Mullen, who ran a successful agricultural program at station KDKA in Pittsburgh, was brought to New York to develop a network farm service. Frank A. Arnold, a former magazine publisher and advertising executive who had taught advertising techniques at Harvard, became director of development. His function was to serve as an "Ambassador at Large to the American Business World." Also a board of consulting engineers was appointed under Dr. Alfred N. Goldsmith, chief consulting engineer of RCA. It included Ernst F.W. Alexanderson of General Electric and Frank Conrad of Westinghouse.

Early in 1927 President Aylesworth and other NBC executives were on the move toward territorial conquest. Neither the Red nor the Blue Network had West Coast outlets, so the "National Broadcasting Company" was national in name only. Aylesworth immediately entered into negotiations with broadcasting stations in Portland, Oregon; Seattle and Spokane, Washington; and Los Angeles and San Francisco, California, with the idea of spreading the web to that part of the country.

The old AT&T concept of "toll broadcasting" faded in name if not in application. NBC and its parent company, RCA, were now clearly convinced of the value of commercial sponsorship of programming, and they saw sponsorship as the key to financing all of the wondrous things that were being planned. No longer would radio depend on performers to donate the time for whatever free publicity might accrue; now they would pay for artists of talent and reputation, and pay well. This would bring higher standards of programming that would match if not exceed the gala opening broadcast.

And yes, as 1927 began, a cascade of fine programs was slated to go out over the network—some of them new, some of them old-time favorites upgraded and restyled. Classical music programs were to be given generous assignments—they were to fare much better on the networks in the twenties than thereafter. There were "The Maxwell House Hour," "The Ampico Hour," "The Cities Service Orchestra," and broadcasts of the Chicago Civic Opera (regular broadcasts of the Metropolitan Opera in New York were not to begin until 1932). There were lighter musical shows like "The Stetson Parade" and "The Wrigley Review," and some of the continuing and ever-popular variety shows: "The Cliquot Club Eskimos," "The Ipana Troubadours" and "The Eveready Hour." A great many more shows were shortly in the planning stage. The commercial aspect was to be muted, played down, dignified, but it was to be there. And of course, as the next few months showed, the commercial approach would not only pay for radio, it would turn this young medium into solid gold.

So there it was! The National Broadcasting Company. Founded solid as a rock, with every technological skill and financial advantage that money could buy, it was the network to end all others. Perhaps it should have been obvious to all onlookers that the radio system was now in place just like the nationwide telephone system was in place. Obviously, no other radio network or system was needed, and none could be tolerated. If there had been any question about monopoly or restraint of trade, it could be pointed out that there were not one but two NBC networks, the Blue and the Red; the two would be played against one another in a spirit of happy competition. There were also, of course, many independent stations outside the network, and these would continue to flourish and provide another kind of competition.

Yet even before the decade of the 1920s ended, another soon-to-be-powerful network was established, although scarcely anybody at the time saw hopeful prospects for it. It was a puny little thing and almost died aborning.

This fresh competition came about by a curious set of circumstances. In the middle of 1926 a well-known concert manager by the name of Arthur Judson, on hearing rumors of the imminent founding of NBC, approached David Sarnoff of RCA with the idea of establishing a bureau of some kind to supply top-flight artists to NBC. Sarnoff asked Judson to draw up a plan for such a bureau, and was generally impressed with Judson's ideas. Of course Sarnoff was well aware that with the network in place there would be a compelling need for new infusions of talent, and Judson, a man of vast experience, seemed to be the man for the job. Sarnoff hinted that he might hire Judson when network broadcasting got underway.

Hearing plans for two NBC networks announced in the fall of 1926, and having heard nothing further from Sarnoff, Judson returned to Sarnoff's office asking what had happened to his plan for a talent and programming bureau. Sarnoff now made it clear that he had scuttled the idea and was planning to employ his own program officers. Judson was shocked by this treachery and let it be known that he would give serious thought to establishing a rival network of his own.

Sarnoff merely laughed at Judson's threat, pointing out that even if Judson could raise the capital, he couldn't establish a rival network because he couldn't acquire the necessary telephone lines. By the recent agreement with AT&T, RCA had received a monopoly on the use of telephone lines for radio purposes. Judson stormed out of Sarnoff's office, determined to establish some kind of broadcasting network that would rival the NBC monopoly.

In a matter of months, Judson had put the framework of his new network together, incorporating it on January 27, 1927, under the name United Independent Broadcasters. In this endeavor Judson was joined by promoter George A. Coates and by a man with vast experience in the radio field — Major J. Andrew White, whose star as a sportscaster had been somewhat eclipsed of late by such giants as Ted Husing and Graham McNamee. White would turn out to be very helpful in getting operations underway, and Coates the promoter went on the road to find stations to join the network, and incidentally perhaps to raise funds from some of the individual station owners. Before long twelve stations came into the new network. Generous terms were being offered to the stations joining — which perhaps accounts for the number willing to join — although the terms would be extremely costly to Judson and Coates, who as yet had found few sponsors for their network programming.

Desperately looking for funds to tide things over, Judson approached the Columbia Phonograph Company and agreed that in exchange for some financial backing the network would be called (at least over the air) the Columbia Phonograph Broadcasting System. With this help, and a few more stations coming on before the end of 1927, the Columbia Phonograph Broadcasting System made its debut on September 18, 1927. A gala affair was arranged to celebrate the event, although it was much less ambitious than that staged a year earlier by the rich young infant NBC. Judson had put together a 22-piece orchestra, and there was a performance of the Deems Taylor–Edna St. Vincent Millay opera *The King's Henchman*. But the affair was too costly, and with not enough money coming in, Judson and his group went broke.

It would seem, then, that this new network would die at birth. The United Independent Broadcasters group was unable to meet the small payroll that it had, and bankruptcy appeared certain. The Columbia Phonograph Record Company, among others, was appealed to for further help, but it turned a deaf ear. With the phonograph industry now having severe problems of its own, this source of help was withdrawn. The link between these two companies was cut, and later the radio network changed to the Columbia Broadcasting System, dropping the reference to phonographs.

Desperately the independent group sought other sources of funds, although for weeks it was touch and go. But Isaac and Leon Levy, owners of one of the member stations, WCAU in Philadelphia, heard of the trouble and offered to help. Together the Levys, a lawyer and a dentist, lacked the resources to bail out the network, but they sought the help of a friend, Jerome H. Loucheim, a wealthy contractor. The Levys and Loucheim managed to come up with $135,000 to keep the new network running for the time being. However, the new network was to eat up huge amounts of cash before turning a profit. More and more money was needed, and Loucheim had to buy more stock to keep everything afloat. For a while there were some discussions with Paramount Studios, which had expressed an interest in some kind of talent outlet, but with Columbia floundering so badly, Paramount's boss, Adolph Zukor, rejected the idea. Loucheim had no wish to run the network himself, and on several occasions he asked Leon Levy to go to New York to assume the presidency of CBS. Levy, however, preferred Philadelphia. As the months of 1928 wore on it appeared that this new enterprise was certain to reach the end of the line.

But before the final death scene, rescue came from a rather unexpected source — not from the canyons of Wall Street, but from a young family friend of the Philadelphia group. The young man's name was William S. Paley, whose father, Samuel Paley, owned the Congress Cigar Company of Philadelphia. At the time Paley was only 26 years old, but he had had considerable amount of managerial experience in the family business. As a mere teenager he had managed the Philadelphia factory in his father's absence, although later he dropped out as an executive to attend the Wharton School of the University of Pennsylvania. Shortly thereafter, William again was given strong responsibilities in the family business, being almost completely in charge one summer when his father and uncle were in Europe. Paley knew the Levy Brothers and their station WCAU, and being somewhat fascinated by the idea of radio, he agreed to sponsor a radio show. The cost was a mere $50 per hour, and the program was called "The La Palina Hour," named for one of the company's popular brands of cigars.

Shortly, however, the elder Paleys returned, and William's uncle found the expenditure on looking through the books. "What kind of foolishness is this?" he demanded. "Cancel it right now." William immediately obeyed instructions. But the whole family had almost immediate reason to regret the decision. In his autobiography, Paley recalls that several weeks later his father took him to lunch and admitted: "Hundreds of thousands of dollars we've been spending on newspapers and magazines and no one has ever said anything to me about those ads, but now people are asking me 'What happened to "the La Palina Hour"?'"[5] Paley's uncle, too, admitted that he had been wrong, and that there was something to this idea of radio. Later on, when Loucheim approached the Paleys to suggest that they might be interested in buying the independent network in New York, the idea began to seethe in young William's brain and he asked his father to let him buy out the Loucheim and Levy interest in CBS.

The elder Paleys at first tried to dissuade William from venturing into this unknown area, but at the same time they knew that the lad needed a challenge and a career of his own, so they relented. The youngster put up about $400,000 of his own money, and his father another $100,000 to buy 50 percent of the stock of United Independent Broadcasters (its off-air corporate name). On September 26, 1928, just two days short of his twenty-seventh birthday, William S. Paley became president of this struggling radio network.

Paley quickly moved from Philadelphia to New York and took command of the company's operations from an office high above the Paramount Movie Theatre. He was, of course, well aware that he was taking over a mere paper empire. All he had really bought with his half million was hope and prospects. The offices of UIB were all located on one floor of the Paramount Building — a narrow floor at that, high up in the tower. There were about a dozen employees, directed by Major J. Andrew White, the only person on the premises with an extensive background in radio.

Paley knew that he had his work cut out for him. The company's finances were in a shambles; there were not enough sponsors; there were not enough stations to offer any kind of effective competition to NBC; many of the employees in the home office seemed to be misdirected or unsuitable. Everything pointed to one single truth: UIB was too small to mount effective competition to the big and powerful force of the National Broadcasting System with its two thriving networks. Shortly after taking over as president, Paley talked a friend into arranging a meeting with Merlin Aylesworth, President of NBC. The friend returned shamefacedly and reported that Mr. Aylesworth wouldn't meet Paley since this would extend some kind of diplomatic recognition to the struggling network. NBC's position was that this "other" network didn't really exist.

A few of Paley's early headaches were settled with some ease. The inability to get long-line telephone service became a thing of the past when the Federal Trade Commission frowned on the monopolistic agreement made between AT&T and RCA. (AT&T was naturally not as averse to supplying lines to competitor radio networks as RCA.) Other problems required herculean effort. Selling programs to advertisers was the name of the game, and here NBC met its match, for in spite of his youth and lack of connections, William S. Paley proved to be one of the great promoters in radio history. Paley was also a superlative financier, and in the years ahead he turned out to be every bit as deft at management as his rival, David Sarnoff.

Before the year 1928 was over, Paley had briskly scurried around the country to sign up more affiliates. At the same time he recognized that the network needed an anchor station of its own, and set out to buy one in New York. Both WABC (now WCBS) and WOR were available, but Paley bought the less well-known WABC because it was cheaper. With WABC came a transmitter and a studio on top of Steinway Hall in New York.

In the first year or so of the Paley regime, it was clear that there was a desperate need for new infusions of capital. With Paley's shrewd management turning things around, some affluent outsiders started taking an interest in buying into the company. Paley was approached by William Fox of Twentieth Century–Fox, who offered to buy a half-interest in the young network. His terms being very ungenerous, Paley turned them down, but the dealings with Fox once again sparked the attention of Adolph Zukor of Paramount, who had rejected offers to become involved with CBS under its old management. Eventually Zukor purchased a half-interest in CBS to the tune of $5 million. This was on June 13, 1929, a mere nine months after Paley himself had purchased the network, giving an idea of the phenomenal growth of this upstart network in the early months of 1929.

Things were going so well for CBS in 1929 that it was able to move to a lavish set of offices and studios at 485 Madison Avenue on September 18, 1929. Away from the four rooms in the Paramount Tower, CBS had now grown to four floors in a modern building, equipped with isolated and air conditioned studios.[6] Around this time, too, the network was rapidly expanding beyond that small group of original stations. On the West Coast CBS had been almost nonexistent, but Paley shortly bought into an already formed and healthy network with strong stations in San Francisco and Los Angeles—the Don Lee Network, owned by a West Coast millionaire of that name who had built his first fortune by owning all the Cadillac dealerships in the state of California (this at a time when General Motors still granted wholesale dealer territories). Paley sold Don Lee on the idea of becoming a CBS affiliate, and an entire roster of West Coast stations came over to CBS at a single bound.

Because he was Number Two, always trailing NBC, Paley knew that he had to be an aggressive salesman of programming, and this turned out to be his métier. If an advertiser or his agency had an idea for a program Paley endeavored to get him and the program together, even if the idea seemed outlandish or unrealizable. Too, Paley was himself bristling with program ideas, and he would sell these ideas to sponsors even if the artists had not yet signed on the dotted line. For example, in the fall of 1928, Paley got the idea that it would be great to have a program with Paul Whiteman. Whiteman had appeared many times on radio since the early twenties, but always sporadically, never on a regular basis. Paley took the idea to Lennan and Mitchell, the advertising agency for P. Lorrilard & Company, the makers of Old Gold cigarettes. "Get Paul Whiteman and you have a deal," said the sponsors.

Paley hadn't the slightest idea how he would talk Paul Whiteman into doing a regular radio program. He had never even met the man. But he set out for Chicago, where Whiteman was performing at the Drake Hotel. At first Whiteman tried to laugh the whole idea off, but Paley stayed on until well after midnight, talking about the magic of radio and the vastly greater audiences it reached than nightclubs or hotel ballrooms. Whiteman finally signed a contract. Beginning on Tuesday, February 9, 1929, Paul Whiteman began his regular broadcast, the "Old Gold Program," on CBS.

One of the most annoying things that happened—and Paley had to endure grave disappointments many times in the early years—was that he might think up a spectacular program idea and sell a potential performer or advertiser on it, only to find the idea stolen away by NBC, which still had the reputation as the leading network. Paley had heard Rudy Vallee, then an obscure nightclub performer, and wanted to sign him for CBS. He suggested the idea to Standard Brands, but Standard Brands turned around and took the program to NBC. Similarly, Paley had to overcome great resistance to putting New York's Metropolitan Opera on the air on a regular basis. Otto Kahn, the Met's chairman, was unalterably opposed to radio, and believed that radio wasn't up to the challenge of faithfully rendering music from the opera stage. Paley wore him down; Kahn became convinced and was ready to sign an agreement with CBS. But NBC stole the march and convinced Kahn that NBC was the "prestige network" and that opera really ought to be heard there. NBC got the opera.

Nevertheless, in the first few years of his leadership, Paley had much to be proud of. He discovered and put on the air Bing Crosby, Kate Smith, Morton Downey, the Mills Brothers, the Boswell Sisters, and many others who became spectacular stars of radio in the 1930s. Occasionally Paley was able to steal a show away from NBC, though generally speaking NBC continued to have the most persuasive voice in radio programming until 1948, when CBS clearly became the dominant of the two. But throughout the 1930s and early 1940s CBS became progressively stronger in all areas, and it was probably clear by the late 1930s that these two networks were twin giants at the top of the heap.

No other major radio networks emerged in the 1920s, and when the two remaining major networks arrived on the scene, both lacked the resources to compete with the two giants. The Mutual Broadcasting System was formed in 1934, with New York's WOR as its anchor station. The American Broadcasting System came into existence in 1943 when the FCC forced the National Broadcasting Company to sell one of its networks. Thus the old NBC Blue Network was sold to Edward Noble, the Lifesaver king, and that year became the American Broadcasting Company. MBS and ABC mounted vigorous but not entirely effective competition to the two industry leaders, NBC and CBS.

The network idea has had its detractors over the years, and on occasion groups and interests have arisen to point out the ills and monopolistic tendencies wrapped up in the network concept. There was a strong impetus in the late 1930s to break the power of the giants and their grip on the airwaves. On the other hand, there has always been vigorous competition in radio, and if competition is the best evidence of a healthy business environment, the electronic media of radio and television have proven to be eminently healthy. If there were any questions in the mid-twenties as to how radio would be financed, and whether it could indeed last and become more than a fad, the network idea gave the answer. Because of networking, radio came to stay.

11. The Educational Stations

During that hopeful and exuberant year of 1922, when it appeared that everyone in the land wanted to have a radio broadcasting station, several clear trends emerged in the pattern of ownership of these stations. One trend that became something of an epidemic was the trend toward ownership of radio stations by educational institutions — colleges, universities, chiropractic schools, Bible institutes, sometimes even high schools or radio training schools.

Needless to say, not all of these stations survived to strong and vigorous maturity. Many died for lack of immediate financial support; many others were eventually lopped off in the late twenties when the Federal Radio Commission was obliged to deal with the problem of the overcrowded airwaves. Others, usually the most affluent and well-run stations, survived, but often on a time-sharing basis, or with disagreeable frequency assignments, or limited to daytime-only programming. But in the early twenties, many educators saw great possibilities for radio as a medium of instruction, and for a while it almost seemed that no educational institution worthy of the name could be without a radio station of its own.

By the mid-twenties the radio spectrum was crowded with education-based stations whose mission was either experimental, which is to say devoted to teaching students the principles of radio engineering or broadcasting techniques, or broadly educational, that is, devoted to the actual process of teaching over the airwaves. By the end of the spring of 1922, about 20 educational stations had been licensed, and by the end of the same year, 74 institutions had applied for and received broadcasting licenses. Between late 1921, when the first educational station was licensed,[1] and 1936, a total of 202 broadcast licenses had been granted to educational institutions. The vast majority of these stations did not survive, but the figures give some idea of the early faith in the educational uses of radio.

What was it that brought this stampede to open educational stations? In the beginning the impetus mostly came from small groups of hams or radio enthusiasts who may have been tinkering with radio on campus, sometimes in connection with courses in physics or electrical engineering. Very often a particular professor had a strong professional interest in radio and gathered groups of like-minded students around him. Quite typically a college or university might take over the work of a radio club or transmitter that had been used for local broadcasting by some faculty member, finally seeking a license in the name of the institution.[2]

As time went on, colleges or training institutes without strong interest or background in radio work might decide that it was time to have a radio station simply because neighboring colleges had them. And also, as time went on, educators and subject-matter specialists far removed from radio technology began to believe that radio could be used for instructional purposes, as a conduit for instructional information such as weather reports, agricultural information, or even entertainment. Sometimes colleges would use their radio stations to recruit students or otherwise serve some public relations function. Some colleges and universities inaugurated full-scale courses in subjects that students could take for credit, but from the beginning there were severe limitations on the use of radio for strictly formal education, so that the stations tended to drift away from this and toward either general information programming or entertainment.

The most successful educational stations from the beginning, and the ones most likely to endure, were in large public institutions and land-grant universities like Ohio State, Illinois, Wisconsin, Purdue, Penn State, Kansas State, Colorado and Arizona. These larger state schools invariably had the technical expertise and wherewithal to maintain a broadcasting service at a fairly high level. Public funds were available, and radio was given high priority for their use, especially since these universities were considered to have a public service function. Very often such stations were considered essential for the spread of agricultural information, including crop and weather reports, home economics, and child rearing. Frequently they were used for the dissemination of information about state agencies and ancillary services. Many of the large educational stations which had firm and healthy growth in the twenties survived; a good number are still going strong today.

On the other hand, many educational stations were weaklings from the beginning, and some should never have been established or granted licenses. They sprouted up like weeds in the glorious first growth of radio broadcasting, but most did not have what it took to endure. The usual reasons for the failure of these stations were either a lack of funds or a lack of continuing interest in radio — often because the institution in question was simply too small or inappropriate in style. Consider the case of the respectable liberal arts school Antioch College in Yellow Springs, Ohio. The station (WRAV) was licensed by the federal government in January 1923, assigned a frequency of 360 meters (834kc), and allowed to operate on an "unlimited basis" with a power of 200 watts. The station continued in operation until 1927, its frequency being changed on several occasions. But the college did not have the funds to provide regular high-quality broadcasting, and when the Federal Radio Commission started instituting more stringent requirements for transmitters and Antioch was not able to improve its transmission and programming, it was decided to let the station lapse. The station's license expired on December 31, 1927, and was not renewed.

Not too many miles away, tiny church-related Ashland College had an even more dismal history. An alumnus of the college, Robert A. Fox, was granted a license to operate a 15-watt station in 1926. Apparently Mr. Fox originally intended to operate the station himself, but when he discovered that he lacked the financial backing he donated his transmitter and other equipment to his alma mater. Ashland College hoped to operate the station (WLBP) as an educational station, and applied for a license from the FRC. Feeling that the equipment and program possibilities were inadequate, the FRC denied the license. The voice of Ashland College never went into the airwaves.

Sometimes stations at small colleges enjoyed a happier birth and better nourishment but still failed. A good example was station WEBW at Beloit College, Beloit, Wisconsin. Charles H. Morse, a member of the board of trustees of the college and of the firm of Fairbanks, Morse, & Co., agreed to donate equipment to Beloit for a radio station, and the station was granted a license on October 9, 1924, operating at 283 meters with a power of 500 watts. Programming started immediately, and the college community did everything it could to keep things going. At first WEBW had an unlimited assignment, and doubtless it wasn't easy for the small college to fill up an entire broadcast day and evening, but in time there were entertainment features, music, religious services, debates, student performances of diverse sorts, descriptions of athletic events; indeed everything that one might expect in such an environment. The station never attempted to offer actual courses over the airwaves, but among the regular features of the station were 20-minute talks by members of the faculty in their areas of specialization. Altogether, WEBW was a pretty good little station.

Unfortunately, in 1928, when the FRC was seeking to prune out the vast undergrowth of small stations cluttering up the airwaves, Beloit College was summoned and asked to demonstrate that operation of the station was in "the public interest, convenience or necessity." The situation at Beloit being not all that bad, the license renewal was not refused, but the station was placed on the 600kc frequency shared with Canada and ordered to shut down every day at 4:30 P.M. so that the Canadian stations would not have nighttime interference.

Thus WEBW became a daytime-only radio station, much to the disappointment of the little Wisconsin college. The 4:30 P.M. Sunday vespers service, which they considered one of their most important missions, would have to be cut off. The college protested its limited license but to no avail.

Nonetheless, the station at Beloit struggled along with moderate success until 1930, when further technical requirements for upgrading of the station made it appear that running the radio station was getting beyond the college's resources. As a result, the station was sold to the Wisconsin State Journal Company in Madison, and a license was granted to this company on April 16, 1930. Beloit followed Antioch and Ashland colleges into silence.

Some stations at smaller colleges and universities survived in good health because of a peculiar set of circumstances. An example of this was station WCAD in Canton, New York, owned by St. Lawrence University. Much of upper New York State is rural, and there is not a single large city near Canton, so that there was very little impetus to start a commercial station in that vicinity. With the cooperation of New York State, General Electric (which allowed St. Lawrence to rebroadcast some of its programs from WGY in Schenectady) and some neighboring institutions of higher learning such as the Clarkson College of Technology and the New York State Normal School, WCAD became a gathering point of radio broadcasting for a large geographical region. The station offered regular weather information, agricultural programming, speakers from the faculties of the participating educational institutions, and enjoyed other programming contributed by the State of New York, farm bureaus, 4-H organizations, and numerous other cooperating organizations. Without this strong interest of public and private supporters and all of the cross-fertilization, WCAD would surely have gone the way of the stations at Beloit and Antioch, but it survived as a healthy public service institution in its region.

If the majority of early educational stations were to experience an initial euphoria followed by eventual disillusionment or rejection by the powers in Washington, a number of others survived and remained alive and well a half-century or more later. Those that survived either tended to have long traditions of serious radio experimentation, or demonstrated a compelling need for their services, as for example the stations in the giant land-grant universities, which often were allied with well-endowed agricultural experiment stations and perhaps also with large public service educational functions. When state funds were available, and when radio was taken as a superlative instrument of carrying on the educational mission of these public institutions, educational radio broadcasting could be seen, even in the eyes of the commercially minded FRC, as "convenient and necessary."

One educational station with all the requisites for successful and continued operation was Station WHA, owned by the University of Wisconsin at Madison. Various professors and students were experimenting with radio transmission as far back as 1900, giving the station a solid pedigree. A forerunner of the permanent station had been doing a great deal of regular broadcasting as an experimental station during the First World War, and the station was known to many people in southern Wisconsin long before KDKA went on the air in the fall of 1920. Later on the station received strong and enthusiastic support from all sectors of the university community, which was vital to its continuance.

The radio work at Wisconsin seems to have begun when a small group of students and professors began experimenting with spark transmitters. By 1915 the station was broadcasting daily weather reports for local farmers, and in June of that year the university received an experimental license to broadcast. The station operated under the call letters 9XM on wavelengths of 475 and 750 meters. In 1915 9XM was merely a 5-kilowatt spark station, but the radio enthusiasts were becoming interested in making their own tube transmitter (tubes then being unavailable commercially).

In the forefront of radio pioneers at Wisconsin was Professor Earle M. Terry of the Department of Physics, who considerably advanced the experiments of Professor Edward Bennett. Among Terry's assistants before World War I were Malcolm P. Hanson, who later won fame as chief radio engineer on Admiral Richard Byrd's famous expedition to the South Pole; also C.M. Jansky, Jr., and G.R. Greenslade.

The weather reports, even though broadcast in Morse code, became a very popular and respected feature in the vicinity of Madison. But Professor Terry was hoping to move on to radio telephony, and in the absence of commercially available tubes, the little group under Terry began making its own tubes — fabricating these mysterious artifacts from scratch, even to the blowing of the glass. The first ones did not prove suitable for voice transmission, and even when they were perfected, most of the tubes had a short life. Many times Terry's assistants had to stay up all night getting a tube ready for the next day's broadcasts, and often the station was forced off the air by burned-out tubes.

By the time America became involved in World War I, Professor Terry and his followers had successfully broadcast music over the radio. The station became something of a wonder in the Midwest — so much so, in fact, that when many amateur stations were forced off the air during the war by the navy, 9XM was asked to continue its operations. The station also served an important function during the war, broadcasting programs for the Great Lakes Naval Training Station on Lake Michigan. Regular two-way communication was maintained between Madison and the naval station.

As soon as the war was over, Professor Terry quickly stepped up his experiments, which had not really abated during the war, and the station quickly became a key broadcasting center in the Midwest, its signal being picked up as far away as Texas. Weather forecasts continued in Morse code for a while, but occasionally the station would break out in song, sometimes to the astonishment of ham radio operators accustomed to nothing but dots and dashes. Occasionally voice would break through. According to campus tradition, 9XM leaned toward Hawaiian music in those early days since the station sounded twangy anyway.[3]

About four years after the first Wisconsin experiments in radio-telephone transmission — to be precise, on January 13, 1922 — the University of Wisconsin was granted a license to operate a broadcast transmitter on 360 meters (834kc), with power of 4,000 watts. At this time the call letters WHA were assigned, and the station was authorized for "unlimited" broadcasting. Station WHA subsequently received strong support from the university, from the neighboring communities and, perhaps most important of all, from the state legislature, which was also located in Madison, the state's capital.

In spite of its growing excellence, WHA did not miss out on the stormy weather that greeted nearly all of the educational stations in the mid-twenties. Its power was raised and lowered on several occasions, and it was requested to share time with commercial stations for a few years. The station was even entirely deleted for about a month in 1924. Later it returned with a new license, using 500 watts with time sharing. On April 26, 1929, a relative state of tranquility was attained when the station was placed on 940kc for unshared daytime-only broadcasting.

The state of Wisconsin was unequivocally committed to educational radio, and in the late twenties was planning to upgrade WHA and another state-owned station, WLBL, at Stevens Point, originally run by the State Department of Agriculture and Markets. It was felt that these two stations, WHA serving the southern part of the state and WLBL serving the northern part, could adequately blanket at least 80 percent of the state's listening area—which they did quite effectively, drawing also a fair number of listeners from the nearby states of Illinois, Minnesota, Michigan and Iowa.

Wisconsin politicians generally were keen on the idea of educational or public service radio. In 1929, Governor Walter Kohler pushed for increased funding for public service radio, and in the years that followed Governor A.G. Schmedeman (a Democrat) and Philip F. La Follette (a Progressive) showered blessings on the university's radio station. Much of this generosity in the early days may have been due to the nearness of the station to the seat of government, and to the fact that it was regularly used to broadcast the governor's message to the legislature as well as speeches by lawmakers and representatives of governmental agencies. Politicians regarded radio as an excellent way to reach their constituencies spread out over Wisconsin's 50,000 square miles, much of it rural and far from the radio sounds of the city belt.

WHA continued to be operated by the University of Wisconsin, specifically by the Physics Department until the death of Professor Terry in 1929, and thereafter for a time by the Department of Electrical Engineering.[4] But a number of other departments of the university were keenly interested in the broadcasting service, most especially (and not surprisingly) the College of Agriculture. In the mid-twenties a radio committee was established in that college to arrange regular daily broadcasts for agricultural listeners. The same college was also responsible for a very successful "Homemaker's Hour," which kept housewives in touch with the latest developments of the Department of Home Economics. Naturally from its very earliest times WHA was strong on weather bulletins, crop reports, market prices and agricultural news of all sorts.

In the early twenties, many university professors, particularly those in the traditional or classical subject matters, were suspicious of the educational value of the new medium, and many were either repulsed or intimidated by the idea of speaking over the radio. But the faith in the effectiveness of radio was there, and in the early days professors would write out their talks, which were then read over the air by announcers. By 1922 or 1923 these fears were mostly vanquished, and professors would willingly read their own talks or lectures.

WHA pioneered in the use of broadcasting to offer instruction for adults in a number of areas, including music appreciation, typewriting, Spanish, American literature, economics, business letter writing and even aeronautics. Later, during the depression years, the station was famous for the Wisconsin School of the Air, which was aimed specifically at school children, providing them with supplemental educational programs of a kind that would be hard to duplicate in the classroom. As piped into the public schoolrooms in Wisconsin, the School of the Air had in excess of 40,000 listeners by the 1934–35 school year.

Naturally a great part of the programming going out over WHA was entertainment, directed at the college community at Madison. There were concerts by the university band, glee clubs, orchestras and organists, as well as accounts of football games and other athletic contests; there were community-interest programs, and hours set aside for children's programming (Wisconsin history stories and the like). Very little time was devoted to jazz or popular music, but like many stations of its kind, WHA soon developed a strong devotion to the playing of classical music.

By the early depression years WHA had a rather lavish setup on the University of Wisconsin campus. It was ensconced in its own building, Radio Hall, a completely modern broadcasting center consisting of a number of studios clustered around a central control room, a separate dramatics studio, a reception room, offices and workrooms. Radio Hall also enjoyed a large pipe organ, recording equipment of various sorts and an extensive music library. The building became one of the showplaces of the campus. In his book *Education's Own Stations*, S.E. Frost, Jr., declared it was "a much finer broadcasting center than that owned by four out of five broadcasting stations in the United States today."[5] By the mid-thirties the station had a total of five full-time and four part-time employees, with a great deal of additional part-time help supplied by faculty members, students and state employees who served the station without compensation.

From the early twenties, WHA took on the coloring of a diversified educational or public service broadcasting station with a considerable variety of programming—some entertainment, some information, some formal instruction. Elsewhere, in other large public institutions, there was an early hope that radio would be a strict arm of instruction, and it was believed that radio could be used to reach out to farmhouses and remote villages to offer instruction to students who might not be able to attend classes but would like to enjoy the equivalent through the airwaves.

One such station was KSAC of the Kansas State College of Agriculture and Applied Science at Manhattan, Kansas (today Kansas State University), established in 1924. KSAC had had a predecessor station, WTG, whose function was solely to transmit weather reports, but the mission of KSAC from the very beginning was "educational," the college's intention being to offer college courses over the air. Shortly after it took to the airwaves, KSAC began offering a series of ten-week courses conducted by college officials and faculty members. The courses were naturally heavily slanted in the direction of agriculture, and included offerings in livestock, dairy, poultry, crops, agricultural economics, agricultural engineering and home economics. These courses were usually supplemented by mimeographed copies of lectures and other technical information.

The idea was an almost immediate success, as indicated by the enrollments in the courses. During its first year, "The College of the Air," as it was called, received over 11,000 enrollments from forty states and Canada (it is very doubtful that all of the enrollees could actually have received the station in spite of its 500-watt power). However, this purely formal set of courses could not easily fill up an entire broadcast day. Indeed, "The College of the Air" filled only a single hour—between 6:30 to 7:30 P.M. Eventually, therefore, with its "unlimited" license, the Kansas station began to offer other kinds of programming. Some of these programs tended to be strongly educational (or at least informative); others moved slightly toward light fare.

One program that became immediately popular, more popular probably than "The College of the Air," was the "Noon Farm Program." The program consisted of a brief musical introduction to lighten the mood, followed by two seven-minute segments in which the audience was addressed by experts from the Division of Agriculture. Then there was a question segment in which extension agriculture specialists answered questions of pressing interest to farmers—perhaps about insect sprays, livestock diseases and problems of marketing crops or livestock.

Within a year a number of other informal "service programs" were added by the station. Early in the morning there was a "Rural School Program," which consisted of the playing of good music, some musical appreciation talks and a short period of calisthenics. Later in the morning the station ran a program called "The Housewives' Half-Hour," which mostly consisted of information from the Department of Home Economics directed to women and homemakers. A year later the station inaugurated a "Matinee" program, and this tended to offer material of a distinctly more popular nature.

By 1926 KSAC had discontinued issuing mimeographed copies of lectures to all those enrolled in "The College of the Air." Yet the program continued, and added new courses to its roster. The university faculty continued to hold faith in the educational possibilities of radio, but the early ideal of running a purely educational station was elbowed out by the expansion of other, very popular, program segments of a more informal and low-keyed nature.

Nonetheless, KSAC did not give up its strong emphasis on topical information. It did not move in the direction of the commercial stations of the day, but continued to be dominated by an informational and didactic approach. The schedule for 1927–28 gives an idea of the kind of broadcasting offered at that time, and clearly there was nothing that would have been morally offensive to the educationist:

Rural School Program	9:00–9:25 A.M.
Housewives' Musical Program	9:25–9:55 A.M.
Housewives' Half-Hour	9:55–10:25 A.M.
News Service (Saturdays also)	12:20–12:35 P.M.
Noon Farm Program	12:35–1:20 P.M.
Music Appreciation	4:00–4:30 P.M.
College of the Air	7:00–8:00 P.M.
Boys' and Girls' 4-H Program	6:30–7:00 P.M. Monday, Wednesday, Friday
Organ Recital	6:30–7:00 P.M. Tuesday
One-Act Play	6:30–7:00 P.M. Thursday
Radio Fans' Program	12:35 P.M. (time unlimited) Saturday
College Organizations' Program	7:30–8:30 P.M. Saturday[6]

In the late twenties KSAC had to undergo the usual indignities of time sharing and limited hours, but it emerged in the thirties as a strong and useful station, still strongly dedicated to informational programming, but with an elaborate program mix.

Although most radio stations in the larger institutions of higher learning — at least those that survived — eventually followed somewhat uniform paths, their early development was dictated by the circumstances of their gestation and birth. Some evolved out of mere tinkering by science students, only to be taken over later by this or that kind of programming influence — agricultural interests, perhaps, or the demands of state and local governments, or the whims of benefactors. By the late twenties, most of them were lacking in the clout of the large commercial stations, but the better ones were clearly justified by their high level of programming, and sometimes, too, by their usefulness in advancing the science of radio technology. Very often the educational stations, because they were able to tap the talent of scientists and engineers, made important contributions to the technology of radio in the early days.

A good example of a station which contributed much technically in the twenties was station WRM at Urbana, Illinois, a station owned and operated by the University of Illinois. The university was endowed with an illustrious Department of Electrical Engineering, and early radio work was closely tied to work in that department. The university's license dated to 1922, at which time it was granted permission to operate a radio transmitter on 360 meters (834kc), with 400 watts of power, from 7:00 to 10:00 P.M. daily, although several months later the station received an "unlimited" license. The transmitter was built by the Electrical Engineering Department and located on the engineering campus.

Within two years a more advanced transmitter was under construction, and on October 28, 1924, the station was shifted to 1,100kc, where it broadcast at 500 watts. With this new equipment, the Department of Electrical Engineering began experimenting with noncontinuous carrier transmission in which no carrier wave was radiated when there was silence at the studio microphone. The university patented this noncontinuous carrier transmission, although power amplifier tubes were in their infancy at the time. It is important, though, that the university's laboratories could move forward in areas that might not be of immediate commercial interest, but which might hope to provide theoretical information or contribute to the state of the art at some future time.

WRM did not receive the same kind of immediate and solid public support enjoyed by WHA in Madison, but in 1926 a Mr. Boetious H. Sullivan made a gift to the university in honor of his father — sufficient funds to build a real radio station. Mr. Sullivan's gift included funds for a 1,000-watt Western Electric transmitter and money to erect a permanent building to house the transmitter, studios and other radio equipment. The building was erected at the south end of Illinois Field on the engineering campus and became known as the Roger C. Sullivan Memorial Station.

While the Illinois station made no immediate effort to reproduce the kinds of programming so successful in Kansas, technical experiments at the station continued to advance the radio art. Perhaps aware of the advantages of having the entire campus tied to the radio station, WRM experimented in improving the quality of remote pickups so that programs could be broadcast not only from the main studio but from six other studios in various locations around campus. There were originating studios in Smith Music Hall, Lincoln Hall, the Band Building, Bradley Hall, the Auditorium and the Electrical Engineering Laboratory. It was further arranged that programs could have been picked up from as many as 27 remote control points. By the late twenties, the University of Illinois station was so well equipped that it was in a better position than any such educational station to put lectures and classes on the air if that had been the wish of the university's administration.

The university continued to experiment and make advances in this area. By the mid-thirties, it had an elaborate buried underground system with eight miles of copper wire, all keyed into a new antenna system and transmitter on the university's south farms. It was also moving forward in an area that was to pay dividends to colleges and universities a few generations later in the television era — the idea that it was possible not only to broadcast *from* the classroom or lecture hall, but *to* it. With a vast system of underground lead-covered telephone lines connecting virtually every important building on the university's large campus, and with the installation of amplifiers in almost all buildings, it became possible, when desirable, to broadcast from a classroom or laboratory to many other places on campus. The use of this kind of elaborate networking declined somewhat in later years, and full realization of its possibilities was never achieved.

In the fall of 1928 the Federal Radio Commission ordered the University of Illinois station into a time-sharing arrangement with two other stations. The station was shifted to 890kc, with authority to use 500 watts of power until local sunset and 250 watts at night. At this time the call letters of the station were changed to WILL, and the station continued with that arrangement until 1935, when it was shifted to 580kc with a daytime-only license. The station was thus the victim of the crowded airwaves at the end of the twenties, like so many other educational stations. But by 1928, the importance of the station, its technical innovations and its programming made it evident that the station was of sufficiently high quality that its continuation was deserved and in the public interest. After 1928, WILL received strong support from the state of Illinois, being the only educational station in that state. It also received funds from student fees, commercial benefactors and federal grants. Because of the technical expertise at the university, the latter were never inconsiderable. During the dark depression and war years of 1934–45, the station received federal grants totalling $409,525.52.[7]

By the 1930s, WILL, like most of its fellow educational stations at large institutions, was being operated as a separate department of the university; it had edged away from its earliest roots in the Electrical Engineering Department as purely technical concerns faded into the background. Its programming was the usual mix encountered at this time: information, informal instruction, with musical programming coming rapidly into ascendancy. In the twenties there was much closer attachment than there is today to student activities — sporting contests, performances of student bands, glee clubs and the like. Like many such stations, WILL also eventually became a training ground for students interested in entering radio as a career — as announcers, engineers, programmers.

Some will say that the educational stations — and in the twenties there were scores of them — failed to live up to their original promise. Clearly that is not the case, although it is true that in the early twenties, when radio licenses were being given out to anybody and everybody, licenses were granted to colleges and universities, high schools and training schools that were in no position to operate them effectively. Most of the tiny stations of this ilk died a swift and probably deserving death in the late twenties. In the 16-year period between 1921 through 1936, 202 licenses were issued to educational institutions, most of them in those optimistic years of the early 1920s. By January 1, 1937, only 38 educational stations were operating, meaning that a total of 164 were either permitted to expire, had been revoked or were transferred to other owners.[8] A poor average, one might say — but many of those that survived were stations of considerable merit and achievement. Many of them continue operating today and remain strong and important influences on society.

The educational stations were nearly all impeded in their development by the severe restrictions placed on them in the late twenties in response to the need for more commercial air time. The time-sharing arrangements and the daytime-only licenses were grievous and unhappy restrictions. Nevertheless, many of the educational stations survived in good health, and in the last few decades many of them have been able to take advantage of FM licenses to broadcast in the evening once again. Also, many of them have recently profited by associations with National Public Radio, which has allowed them to share high-level programming that could not have been provided by any of them individually.

Three things are clear about educational radio. It had a glorious and inspiring beginning. It has always had to struggle for funding in an environment steadfastly devoted to commercialism. But in spite of hardship, the alternative of the educational station will continue to offer something valuable to life in America.

12. Classical Radio Music: The Cultural Windfall

During the first decade of radio more hours of the broadcast day were devoted to music than anything else. To be sure, great sports or political events got more attention and notoriety, but for filling in the long hours of air time — and air time got longer and longer throughout the decade — there was always music to fall back on. It was a perfect age for all the musical arts to flourish.

This state of things was to change drastically during the prime years of network radio between 1930 and 1950. In those years the demands for all other kinds of programming became unrelenting: Afternoons were filled up with soap operas or serial dramas, evenings were filled with drama, comedy and news. During the 1920s most of these variants had not yet gotten a firm foothold, and music was a perfect filler of empty hours. Early announcers were expected to break into song if a speaker or lecturer didn't show up; many would think nothing of sitting at the piano to fill in the gaps with old-time piano favorites.

The public quickly accepted musical programming and liked it. What is more important, though, radio proved to be one of the best friends the art of music ever had, although many purists and professional musicians doubted it at the time. In 1920 the great majority of Americans had never attended an opera or enjoyed a performance by a symphonic orchestra. When the decade was over, millions had enjoyed music of all kinds through the medium of radio, and a cultural miracle occurred: Classical music, which had never played a significant role in American life, became a widespread form of entertainment.

Between 1928 and 1939 the number of major symphony orchestras in the United States increased from ten to seventeen; the total number of orchestras, including those in small and medium-sized cities, increased from 60 to 286. Beliefs by some in the twenties that radio would impede the sale of musical instruments proved to be totally unfounded. Even in the dark depression years, the number of pianos sold in the United States increased at a much greater rate than in any previous period in history. Music courses in the public schools were almost unknown in 1920 — anyone wishing to become a music student had to have a private tutor or attend a music conservatory. But by the late 1930s nearly all schools had music courses in their curricula, and there were some 30,000 school orchestras in the United States and some 20,000 school bands. Clearly the makers of musical instruments need not have worried about the influence of radio.

There were also some fears in the early years of radio that this new dissemination of musical culture would result in a lowering of the quality of musical talent, of orchestras, and professionalism of every kind. But this also proved not to be the case; in fact, from the beginning, many of the most celebrated orchestra conductors of the day were attracted to the vast possibilities of radio as a means of upgrading musical taste. One immediately thinks of Walter Damrosch, Leopold Stokowski and Arturo Toscanini as early advocates of radio music, but there were many others. And whatever doubters there were quickly melted away as the quality of radio acoustics markedly improved and as radio receiving sets appeared in almost every home.

Obviously, when KDKA first went on the air in 1920 the technology of radio broadcasting was hardly adequate to transmit high-quality musical sound, but that would all soon change. Even in 1920, there was a strong belief that radio could be, and should be, an ideal medium for the transmission of music. This idea did not just spring up in 1920 with the beginning of general commercial broadcasting; it had infected some of the founding fathers of radio. Many of these founding fathers were as concerned to get their device to transmit musical sounds as they were to get it to speak. Experiments with the transmission of music began early.

Reginald Aubrey Fessenden, one of the early radio pioneers, was perhaps the first to broadcast music over the air. On Christmas Eve 1906, Fessenden broadcast the sound of a female voice singing a Christmas carol from Brant Rock, Massachusetts, after which Fessenden himself played a violin solo of Gounod's "O, Holy Night." In the following year Lee De Forest was busy at work, passionately, almost fanatically devoted to the idea of getting music disseminated into the airwaves. In his diary he wrote on March 7, 1907:

> My present task (happy one) is to distribute sweet melody broadcast over the city and sea, so that in time even the mariner far out across the silent waves may hear the music of his homeland.[1]

Very shortly De Forest got into a practice that has remained a feature of radio to this very day: the playing of phonograph records into the transmitting apparatus. Soon thereafter, from his laboratory on the top floor of the Parker Building at Fourth Avenue and 19th Street in New York, he was also bringing singers to disseminate live music into the airwaves. A contralto named Miss Van Boos was invited to the Parker Building to sing. Her song, "I Love You Truly," was heard by radio operators at the Brooklyn Navy Yard.

De Forest kept after it, broadcasting single musical programs intermittently during the next several years. A well-publicized triumph occurred early in 1910 when De Forest broadcast the voice of Enrico Caruso directly from the stage of the Metropolitan Opera House in New York, singing the role of Turiddu in

Cavalleria Rusticana. For this broadcast, two microphones were used, one on the stage and the other in the wings. At the top of the opera house was a 500-watt transmitter. De Forest rigged up a temporary bamboo mast on the roof, lashed it to one of the flagpoles there, and ran the lead-in wire down through a ventilator to the transmitter.

Between 1910 and 1920 De Forest (and numerous others) kept the faith, though the problems of poor-quality transmission relegated the broadcast of music to the strictly "experimental" category. But there were other problems as well, and some of them would get worse instead of better in the next few years. In 1916 De Forest had an experimental radio station in New York, 2XG. Here he pressed onward with his musical inclinations, inviting to the microphone Miss Vaughn De Leath, later to be known as the "First Lady of Radio." De Leath's good singing voice and warm, cordial personality drew hundreds of fan letters, perhaps the first of millions to be sent to radio personalities in the decades that followed. But the growing popularity of the station offended some—especially commercial and navy interests. The license of station 2XG was suspended on a flimsy pretext by a government inspector, and when De Forest inquired into the matter, he was told that "there is no room in the ether for entertainment!"[2] This notion may seem preposterous in the light of subsequent history, but there was much confusion in the airwaves in 1916: World War I was in the offing with its pressing military needs, with the result that De Forest's beloved music had to be muffled for the next few years.

But with the war over, and with licenses finally being generously given to general-purpose entertainment radio stations, music once again moved to the forefront of broadcasting. We know, for example, that much of the early fare of KDKA, even in its experimental period when it was still emanating from Frank Conrad's garage, consisted of music. At first there was the inevitable playing of phonograph records and various solos performed by Conrad's family members; later music was provided by members of the Westinghouse company band, solos by employees, and then invited soloists from the community. The acoustic qualities were doubtless poor—but at least it was music, and there was no question that people liked to listen to it.

A very happy set of circumstances arose for radio music late in 1921 when Westinghouse opened its experimental station in Chicago, KYW. With several experimental stations in various stages of inception, Westinghouse was game to try new things, so when KYW went on the air its programming consisted of nothing more nor less than—opera! The new Chicago station was located in the Commonwealth Edison Building, partly on the invitation of the highly cultured, British-born utilities magnate Samuel Insull. Insull loved opera, and he had a soft spot for the very beautiful opera star Mary Garden, who also happened to be the general director of the Chicago Civic Opera Company, into which Insull had poured a good deal of his fortune.

Somehow the idea got established that broadcasting of an opera season on a regularly advertised schedule might attract some attention to the new station, which didn't yet have a real studio or even a program staff. As things turned out, these opera programs proved to be as popular in their own way as the sports spectaculars of WJZ in Newark and the Dempsey-Carpentier fight the previous summer. A strong and immediate pattern of broadcasting was established: KYW sent opera into the airwaves afternoon and evening, six days a week. And apparently people were dying to listen.

The conditions of programming were crude to say the least, and fidelity to the music must have been grievously low—but the novelty of it! Walter Chew Evans, who later became President of the Westinghouse Radio Stations, was the man on the spot for the opera broadcasts—the station's first announcer/program director. Evans had been one of those typical radio fanatics in high school in Chicago. He later worked summers on Great Lakes steamboats, studied for a while at the University of Illinois in Urbana, but then joined the navy, where he taught radio to hordes of young seamen. After the war he returned to Illinois to earn a degree, but lack of funds sent him back to the Great Lakes steamers to earn money. While working on the *Alabama* late in 1921, he tuned in on the broadcasts of KDKA. When he learned that Westinghouse was planning to open a similar station atop the Commonwealth Edison Building, he applied for and got a job with the station.

Since KYW was expecting to broadcast nothing but the opera, at least in the beginning, elaborate plans were laid to reproduce the music and the singing. Ten microphones were used. But Walter Chew Evans, acting as announcer and engineer, sat in a regular seat in the opera house, balancing his switching equipment on his knee. Evans may not have known much about opera when he began his duties, but he learned a great deal very quickly. He had to be immediately ready at any given moment to cut in or out whatever microphone was being played to at that moment. Different microphones were used for soloists and orchestra, and Evans had to become adroit in switching from one to the other as necessary.[3]

Broadcasting of the opera turned out to be a windfall to the Chicago Civic Opera Company, which had been in the doldrums. Perhaps Mary Garden had thought of this when she permitted broadcasting directly from the opera stage. Opera boomed in Chicago throughout the rest of the twenties. Not only were more people drawn to the opera house itself—that was doubtless what was really hoped for—but the unbelievable happened. The length and breadth of Chicago, everybody wanted to listen to the opera, and crude aerials went up on rooftops even in the bleak industrial parts of town. When the opera season began in the fall of 1921, it was estimated that there were only a thousand radio receivers in the Chicago area—most in the hands of longtime, die-hard amateurs. At the end of the opera season, in the spring of 1922, it was estimated that there were 20,000 sets in operation in the city. Those who couldn't assemble a set were trampling down the doors of department stores and radio shops to get their hands on a ready-made model so as to enjoy this unfamiliar pastime.

It would be too much to say that Chicago became culture-crazed overnight. And Westinghouse knew that when the opera season was over it would have to provide more diverse programming, which it did. This programming was pretty much like the programming at KDKA, at WJZ, and other stations around the country. But the success of opera in Chicago did not go unnoticed, either by radio executives or by musicians. Obviously, if opera could succeed in the Windy City, it could succeed elsewhere as well, and fears were banished that the general public would not tolerate listening to a "whole" opera, as opposed to selections or arias.

Back in Newark, at WJZ, Charles Popenoe had gotten the message from Chicago, and he began to hustle around to find an opera of his own to broadcast. Luckily, an opera company that had been out touring the country with Mozart's comic opera *The Impresario* returned to New York and was inveigled to come over to Newark to put on the entire opera over WJZ. The program aired on March 15, 1922, giving the New York metropolitan area its first taste of radio opera.

When the telephone company began its richly endowed commercial station, WEAF, a few months later, telephone research expertise would open up new vistas for classical music programming, especially in "remote" pickups, where broadcasts from symphony and concert halls could be sent into the airwaves. The first such remote broadcast was a performance of Verdi's opera *Aida* by the Metropolitan Opera Company, piped from the Kingsbridge Armory on November 11, 1922. The broadcast went off without a hitch, and, emboldened by its success, WEAF went on to broadcast the New York Philharmonic from the Great Hall of the College of the City of New York. Shortly thereafter, from the same hall, the college organist, Dr. Samuel Baldwin, began a popular series of Sunday afternoon recitals, the success of which determined the course of future musical programming at WEAF.

In spite of these and other triumphs, classical music broadcasting had to remain, at least for the next several years, pretty much of a novelty. It was still the era of the crystal set, after all, and quality tube sets were not yet widely available. It is hard to imagine that any real music lover or expert would have found radio music anything other than a squeaky distortion of cherished musical sounds. But the enthusiasm was there in spite of the difficulty of justifying it or explaining it.

One reason for rising expectations for radio as conveyor of music may have been the general dissatisfaction with technological developments in the phonograph field. The phonograph for many years had been the only means of disseminating music to mass audiences, yet little had been done in and for the field in the decade before the birth of radio broadcasting. Nor would much more be done in the next few years until the heat from the radio industry began to be felt in earnest. The American companies, most particularly the Victor Talking Machine Company of Camden, New Jersey, had become hidebound and unadventuresome and had made few improvements in any of their products.

One area where an advance should have been expected was the area of electrification. In 1922 there was no electric phonograph on the market. Victor was making the same old windup machine that it had been selling since shortly after the turn of the century. Nor was the company conducting any research in electrification. It was only after hearing that the Bell Labs were working on turning out an electrical turntable that Victor began to prick up its ears. In the end, Victor had to buy its electrical equipment from the telephone company.[4]

The Victor Company and its major competitors, Columbia and Brunswick, were charging 75 cents for their usual 10-inch popular records, an amount that seems extraordinarily high for those preinflationary times, especially recalling that the old 10-inch 78 rpm records played only about 4 minutes a side—enough for one popular dance tune. And they had charged even more back in 1910 for classical discs containing the voice of Enrico Caruso.

As things turned out, too, the 78 rpm record was a Procrustean bed for the phonograph industry when it came to competing with radio, especially where classical music was concerned. It took about five records to accommodate Beethoven's Fifth Symphony, and this was a perpetual nuisance to the music lover—think of no electric turntable, and no such thing as a record changer. The record industry lost out tragically in the classical music field during the 1920s and did not recoup its losses until the general availability of the long-playing record in 1948.

Until 1924 the phonograph industry could take some comfort in knowing (and reminding its customers) that the quality of sound on records was much higher than that of the radio. The radio sound was said to be "tinny," and there were those dreadful twin nuisances, fading and interference. What good was the transmission of a voice of some great soprano or tenor if the better part of an aria faded off into nothingness, or was interrupted by the sound of an ocean liner's whistle? We can all sympathize with Thomas Edison's annoyance when he heard "his" phonograph records being played over WJZ in 1921. "If the phonograph sounded like that," he told Tommy Cowan, "nobody would buy it."

But all of a sudden things changed drastically. In 1924 Edwin Armstrong's Superheterodyne Radiola was on the market, RCA was turning out all-tube sets by the thousands, and the radio sound was coming across loud and clear. Instead of offering an inferior sound to the phonograph, the radio now sounded infinitely better—at least to those who had the latest model sets. Not even the strongest partisan of the phonograph industry could doubt that deep trouble was at hand.

However, even though the radio of the middle twenties had surpassed the phonograph in sound reproduction, it was still a long way from being able to faithfully represent the tonal qualities of music. The difficulties were numerous, and for a while they seemed insurmountable.

Musical tones and overtones, for example, can be described in scientific terms as sound waves which vibrate at certain frequencies. These can be expressed in cycles per second (cps). Consider the music of the piano. Its lowest tone vibrates at about 27 cps, and its highest at about 4,000 cps. In a symphony orchestra the lowest frequency would probably be that of the double string base, about 40 cps. The highest tones that are clearly audible are probably the upper harmonics of the violins and oboes—about 16,000 cps. In the 1920 phonograph, and in early radio receiving sets, the upward limit of faithful reproduction was about 2,000 cps, and under 200 cps the tones could be scarcely heard. Actually, the defect of not being able to reproduce faithfully the two upper octaves (4,000 to 16,000 cps) was not catastrophic since only certain overtones were eliminated in the main. Yet these overtones are what gave a particular musical instrument its characteristic tone quality, and without them there is obvious distortion of tonal values.

Solutions to these problems were not entirely satisfying throughout the late 1920s, and technical improvements came slowly over the next several decades. A good deal of improvement came about in the thirties when so-called high fidelity stations were allowed to use sidebands to augment their transmissions, accommodating musical tones having frequencies up to 5,000 cps. But truthfully, even by the time of World War II, it is doubtful that many people in the United States were in possession of receivers adequately responsive to frequencies below 100 cps (G on the bottom line of the base clef) or higher than 3,500 cps (A in the fourth octave above middle C). The problem continues to be a nagging one today.

Another persistent problem, about which very little was done until after World War II, was in the area of dimension or perspective. Early radio music was strictly what is called monaural. In an auditorium or concert hall we hear with two ears, and we hear sounds coming to our ears from several directions. In early radio transmission all the sound was channeled through one microphone which eventually reached one loudspeaker, resulting in a considerable diminution of perspective. Experimentation with binaural sound systems did not really materialize commercially until well after World War II.

Nevertheless, for all of radio's faults, classical music was one area where radio would have a decided advantage over the phonograph. A radio program could play an organ concerto or a piano sonata, or indeed an entire symphony without a break, without the vulgar necessity of turning over a breakable shellac disc every four minutes. The pressure was on as early as 1923, although the phonograph industry was not really tragically damaged until 1927–28, at which time it went into a tailspin from which it did not recover for almost a decade. By 1929 the Victor Talking Machine Company had been bought by the Radio Corporation of America and suffered the indignity of having its vast Camden, New Jersey, plant converted to the making of radio sets. The recording business recovered in the late 1930s with the help of jukeboxes and disc jockeys, but for a time, in the depths of the depression, it appeared that phonograph manufacturing in the United States might completely vanish.

The decline in classical phonograph records was particularly cruel. For dance records, band music, shorter pieces, the decline was not immediate. After 1925 there arose a strong demand for hillbilly music on discs, and this demand never really died out. But it was obvious, as early as 1924, that if radio were to cultivate the area of classical music it would become a hands-down winner in any race with the phonograph. Radio had the better sound, it had the continuity, and it even had strong partisans in the musical world anxious to see radio music succeed.

Soon, too, classical music programming got attention from commercial sponsors, with high-calibre musical ensembles finding support as early as 1922 and 1923. On March 15, 1923, the Gimbel Brothers Department Store in New York began a regular weekly program of fine music over WEAF, one of the earliest sponsored programs. Not to be outdone by this cultural step forward, the very same day rival station WJZ scheduled a broadcast of *Tannhäuser* from Lexington Avenue Theatre in New York.

There was a healthy trend toward highly professional programming of light classical music by the mid-twenties. The most ambitious musical program at this time was probably the "Victor Hour," later called the "RCA Victor Hour." The program premiered on WEAF in 1925 and featured its own orchestra, the Victor Salon Orchestra. Regular performers on the show were John McCormick and Lucrezia Bori of the Metropolitan Opera, and other guest performers appeared from time to time, including Frances Alda, Reginald Werrenrath, and Emilio De Gogorza, all singers, and violinist Rene Chemet. Shortly after the debut of this show, a number of other classical music "hours" appeared on the radio: the Goodrich Silver Cord Orchestra, and programs sponsored by Cities Service, Philco, Brunswick, and the Edison Company.

But it was the establishment of NBC in 1926 that gave the greatest impetus to the spread of quality musical programming. The reason is obvious: While a single station located in Denver, New Haven or even Chicago would be hard put to offer any kind of regular series of live musical programs and to pay the bill for the rights and performers, a large network capable of sending a musical program from a concert stage in New York to every part of the country was an altogether different matter. Now sponsors would stand delightedly in the wings, and performers who might once have doubted the quantity or quality of the radio audience quickly lost their skepticism and were ready to sing over the radio and even sign on for regular appearances with a radio orchestra.

At the time of its founding in 1926, NBC was strongly committed to the mission of bringing classical musical programming to the masses, and it was determined to serve as a cultural benefactor whether through sponsored or sustaining programs. All of the early announcements from company headquarters stressed NBC's devotion to music and the desire to make this segment of its offerings the keystone of its public effort. Matching word to deed, the National Broadcasting Company laid elaborate plans to build resources in the musical field. Opened almost immediately was a music library, containing both sheet music and recordings. At New York headquarters, studios both large and small were fitted up to accommodate every kind of traditional musical assemblage. The company hired musical production and continuity staffs; it hired radio technicians with special expertise in acoustics and in the transmission of musical sound; it sought to bring into its own employ musical groups of various sizes—string quartets, glee clubs, bands and even full-scale orchestras.

Above all, they sought out true believers, men of music who would lend their time and talent to the cause of broadcasting. Of all the believers, none outranked the man NBC chose as its musical advisor and educational consultant: Walter Damrosch. For those still alive who remember the 1920s, the name of Walter Damrosch probably still continues to be identified with the cause of classical musical broadcasting. Damrosch was a man with strong prejudices, and he believed that he had found the medium whereby musical culture could be spread to the vast American continent, to millions of American citizens in isolated locations, most of whom had never heard a string quartet, an oratorio or a symphony.

At the time he became NBC's music consultant, Damrosch was the dean of American orchestra conductors, having conducted the New York Symphony Orchestra for many years. Damrosch was German born, his father the famous Leopold Damrosch who came from Breslau in the 1870s and founded the New York Symphony Society and the New York Oratorio Society. Walter Damrosch, born in Breslau in 1862, followed his father to the new world in 1871, eventually taking up the baton himself at the time of his father's death in 1885. In 1892 Damrosch founded the New York Symphony Orchestra, whose conductor he remained until he took up his duties with NBC in 1927.

Damrosch may not have been one of the world's great conductors, but he was certainly one of the world's great musical educators. He perceived his mission as one of upgrading the quality of musical culture in America. He had been at it for years — long before radio made its appearance. As far back as 1897 he had been supervisor of music education classes in the city of New York, and in connection with his work as a conductor he popularized a series of children's concerts and was a willing lecturer and speaker on musical topics to the young. Damrosch was active in all aspects of the musical life in America — certainly one of the nation's musical statesmen. It was he who prevailed on Andrew Carnegie to build the magnificent musical hall in New York City that still bears its benefactor's name.

With Damrosch's missionary zeal it is little wonder that he was one of the first to become interested in the educational possibilities of radio. In 1924 Damrosch delivered a manifesto over the radio from Carnegie Hall at the time of one of his Beethoven concerts, expressing publicly for the first time his strong belief that radio was to be the medium that would bring music into all American homes. Damrosch repeated the same theme numerous times in the next few years and, suiting the deed to the word, allowed his orchestra to perform before the radio audience on numerous occasions. It was not surprising, then, that when NBC asked him to be its musical impresario in 1927 he willingly relinquished his position as conductor of the New York Symphony, which the following year was merged with the New York Philharmonic Orchestra. The opportunities to reach out across the land were simply too great to resist.

Shortly after taking over as musical advisor at NBC, Walter Damrosch began a regular series of symphony concerts. He is perhaps best remembered today, however, as the originator of a series of music appreciation broadcasts that began in October 1928. First known as the RCA Educational Hour, the program later came to be called the NBC Music Appreciation Hour. By the early thirties it is estimated that six million American schoolchildren were regularly listening to Walter Damrosch on the network hookup. The NBC Music

Appreciation Hour was piped directly into classrooms, and many schoolchildren who had never heard of Beethoven or Haydn were greeted by Damrosch's hearty and avuncular greeting: "My dear children . . . ."

When CBS entered the picture in 1927 it became clear that this upstart was willing and anxious to run a good race with NBC in all areas in spite of its meagre resources. And one area in which it hoped to compete dramatically was the area of music. Conductor Howard Barlow assumed an advisory position at CBS comparable with that of Walter Damrosch at NBC.[5] But Barlow had little desire to pontificate on matters musical; his main concern was to put a good orchestra on the air. And he did. A twenty-three-piece orchestra was assembled and became the nucleus of what would be known as the CBS Symphony Orchestra. It is very significant that the very first program broadcast over the Columbia Phonograph Broadcasting System on the afternoon of September 18, 1927, was a concert by the Barlow orchestra.

To leave no doubt that CBS was aiming for the heights, the main offering of that evening's schedule was a performance of the opera *The King's Henchman* by Deems Taylor and Edna St. Vincent Millay. Singers from the Metropolitan Opera performed at the studio with the CBS orchestra, Howard Barlow conducting.

None of this means to suggest that classical music would remain the dominant feature in network programming; an explosion in all sorts of radio programming was just around the corner, and in the thirties the demands on broadcast time for popular sponsored shows would reduce the proportion of radio time given over to classical music. In 1927 CBS could afford to give over a whole evening to *The King's Henchman*, whereas in prime time a decade later such a thing would probably have been unthinkable. There were popular classical music shows on the networks during the thirties and forties, but usually no more than a half-hour's duration in prime time evening hours. Howard Barlow, for example, continued throughout these years and on into the television era with his "Voice of Firestone" program, but for most of those years it was a half-hour show.

Nevertheless the networks continued to have faith in classical music programming, and eventually many artists who once scoffed at the idea of radio moved over to the new medium. There were some who had been well disposed from the time of their early exposure to radio. Leopold Stokowski was favorably disposed. Edwin Franko Goldman, the famous bandmaster, had been touting the virtues of radio for nearly as long as Damrosch. John Charles Thomas, the celebrated baritone from the Metropolitan, began his long radio career in the 1920s. World famous performers like Jascha Heifetz, Ignace Paderewski and Sergei Rachmaninoff, whose high standards (and high fees) might once have barred them from the new medium, were eventually talked into going on the air.

In the early years of radio, almost anyone would (and did) offer to sing over the radio, and much of what was offered from the classical repertoire was unmistakably bad. But toward the end of the twenties radio began attracting some fine singers, a few of whom were already star attractions, others whose fame would be spread by this new medium. Madame Ernestine Schumann-Heink was already internationally acclaimed as the most famous contralto in history when she came to radio in her sixties. But radio brought to the attention of a much wider public such singers as Richard Crooks, Grace Moore, Barbara Maurel, James Melton, Gladys Swarthout and Lawrence Tibbett.

A new breed of conductor would arise — the radio conductor, whose name would not be associated with some great civic symphony but almost exclusively with radio itself. Howard Barlow was, of course, one. Donald Voorhees was another. Andre Kostelanetz began his long career in the mass media as an assistant to Howard Barlow in the late twenties. Some conductors of established orchestras moved over to the new medium and gave up an inferior or troubled career elsewhere. One such was Alfred Hertz, who gave up an exasperating situation as conductor of the San Francisco Symphony to become a full-time radio conductor. Hertz was best known for his Standard Symphony Hour, which endured throughout the thirties.

In time radio would attract even bigger names. The biggest catch was surely Arturo Toscanini, who at the end of the twenties was conducting the New York Philharmonic Orchestra. By the mid-thirties Toscanini was tiring of the whirlwind concert season and allowed himself to be drafted as conductor of a new NBC orchestra created specifically for him. NBC also built the magnificent Studio 8-H in the RCA Building in Rockefeller Center in New York, the most acoustically advanced studio of its kind at the time.

It is true that throughout the twenties and thirties radio was not technically equipped to do full justice to classical music. But help was on the way from a number of quarters, and the next decade would see some breakthroughs of enormous importance. Major Edwin Armstrong's last great contribution to radio was the development of frequency modulation (FM), and FM radio held out great promise for musical programming in the thirties. FM radio waves have two important advantages for musical programming: They are relatively static free, and they offer the possibility of much wider audio frequency bands (200 kilocycles, as opposed to the 10 kilocycles of the standard-wave stations). The wider band, of course, made possible more faithful reproduction of the frequency range of musical sounds.

RCA introduced FM in 1934 over station W2XF, using an experimental transmitter atop the Empire State Building in New York. By 1942 there were 25 licensed commercial FM stations in the United States, and when that development had to bow to the war effort that year, it is estimated that there were some 350,000 FM receivers in operation.

Even without FM there was a clamor throughout the thirties for "high fidelity," and "hi fi" became the byword of the day. Station WQXR also began operation in New York in 1934, and was specifically licensed for wider bands that would allow a fuller range of musical tones to be produced over the air. Admittedly, in 1934 there were very few receivers made in America ready to take advantage of this augmented transmission power. Most radio receivers in American homes in 1934 were probably capable of receiving only between 100 to 5,000 cycles. But the impetus was there, and the

Evening Concert Music Programs
Network Offerings — 1929

Concert-format programs heard on radio networks during January 1929; evening hours only. Adapted from: A Thirty-Year History of Programs Carried on National Networks in the United States, 1926–1956, *Department of Speech, Ohio State University, 1956.*

Program	*Network*	*Sponsor*
Atwater Kent Hour	NBC-Red	Atwater Kent
Chicago Civic Opera	NBC-Blue	Baulkite
Cities Service Concert	NBC-Red	Cities Service
De Forest Audions Band	CBS	De Forest Radio
Firestone Concert	NBC-Red	Firestone Tires
Halsey Stuart Concert	NBC-Red	Halsey Stuart
Kolster Radio Hour	CBS	Kolster Radios
La Palina Concert	CBS	La Palina Cigars
La Touraine Concert	NBC-Red	La Touraine
Major Bowes Capitol Theater Concert	NBC-Red	*
Maxwell House Concert	NBC-Blue	Maxwell House
Midweek Hymn Sing	NBC-Red	*
New York Philharmonic Orchestra	CBS	*
National Symphony Orchestra	NBC-Red	*
Old Company Program	NBC-Red	Old Company Coal
Palmolive Hour	NBC-Red	Palmolive Soap
Philco Hour: Jessica Dragonette	NBC-Blue	Philco Radios
Roxy Symphonic Concert	NBC-Blue	*
Savannah Linets Band	NBC-Blue	*
Stetson Parade	NBC-Red	*
Seiberling Singers: James Melton	NBC-Red	Seiberling
Sonora Hour	CBS	Sonora Radios

*Sustaining Program

post–World War II period saw tremendous surges in reception technology that in time would make possible high fidelity transmission of a very high order.

The development and persistence of stations like WQXR boded well for the future in other ways as well. When the years of network radio faded into the background, the radio industry would settle into a pattern of specialization in which individual stations set a particular pattern for programming. Accordingly the radio of the present day has classical music stations, newstalk stations, country and western stations, rock and roll stations, etc. So in time it was possible to overcome the great time restraints that were a burden to classical music programming in the years between 1930 and 1950. A station devoted entirely to classical music would at last be free to devote hours to the longest symphony or an entire opera, or even a cycle of Wagnerian operas.

There were severe limitations on what could be done with and for classical music on the radio of the 1920s. But in spite of all the limitations there was never the slightest hesitation to move forward and do the best that could be done with the existing state of the art. The great accomplishments of the post–World War II era are all firmly rooted in the convictions and desires of broadcasting pioneers, the early men like Fessenden and De Forest, whose feeble signals carried "sweet melody broadcast" into the airwaves.

13. The Sounds of Popular Music

No decade in American history was witness to more eruptive change in popular music than the decade of the 1920s. These changes were all eventually reflected in radio programming, although for a few years the radio industry moved forward timidly and haltingly as a purveyor of popular fare. Owners of the early radio stations tended to be conservative and were extremely hesitant to offer any music to the public that might be objectionable, or which might be construed as pandering to low and vulgar tastes. Jazz, for example, surely the most forceful and innovative musical form of the age, had a difficult time getting a hearing over the airwaves until late in the decade. Everybody was calling it the jazz age — but listeners to the radio before the mid-twenties might have been inclined to doubt that such a musical form existed.

All this should not mean to suggest that nothing but classical music was being heard on the radio in the early twenties. As we already know, there were technical and acoustic impediments to classical music during this time, and before the coming of the networks, broadcasts of a symphony orchestra or opera were, with rare exceptions, special events and isolated cultural curiosities. Still, since music consumed by far the largest portion of the broadcast day in the early twenties, it is a matter of curiosity what this music was. If not classical, not jazz, then what?

Well, of course, it was popular music, or perhaps we had better say that it was familiar or "respectable" music. It was the kind of music that would have been played or heard in middle-class homes since the turn of the century and perhaps before. It was recital music. It was the music that one would expect to hear at any fashionable afternoon tea, in hotel dining rooms or salons. Radio historian Erik Barnouw liked calling it "potted palm music," as apt a term as any. The most typical musical program on the radio during the early twenties was a lady soprano singing to the accompaniment of the piano — most likely some plaintive aria or simple song.

Doubtless recital music of this sort meant "culture" to Americans for many years. It was a solid part of the middle-class environment and apparently had been so for a long time. Even before the Civil War, English novelist Anthony Trollope, on a tour of North America, commented on the prevailing characteristics of American musical taste. He observed that every American hotel drawing room contained a "forlorn lady" singing and playing the piano. There was nothing like it anywhere in Europe. In every respectable American establishment female voices "rang and echoed through the lofty corners and around the empty walls."

A survey of all programming at WJZ between May and December 1923 shows the pattern of things as they must have existed everywhere in radio at that time. The largest number of musical programs during this period (and musical programming was about two-thirds of the total) fell into the following categories:[1]

Classification	Number of Programs
Soprano Recitals	340
Piano Recitals	266
Orchestras	196
Popular Song Programs	126
Violin Solos	125
Tenor Recitals	109
Baritone Recitals	98

As to the kind of music involved in these recitals, we can be sure that it was genteel, part of the standard repertoire of approved but not overly challenging favorites that any music conservatory student would be expected to master. Erik Barnouw excerpts the program log of WFAA in Dallas, for Thursday evening, October 10, 1922, which might well be considered typical for stations around the land at that time:

Baritone Solo
   "Vision Fugitive" from Herodiade — Massenet
   Recitative, "I Rage, I Melt, I Burn"; "Air Ruddier Than the Cherry,"
      from *Acis and Galatea* — G.F. Handel
   "Blow, Blow, Thou Winter Wind," words from *As You Like It* — J. Sarjeant
   Edward Lisman. Accompanist, Miss Whitaker.

Piano Concerto
   "Bourrée" — Louis Duillemin
   "Pavane" — Louis Duillemin
   "Gigue" — Louis Duillemin
   Mr. and Mrs. Paul Van Katwijk

Soprano Solo
   "The Birthday" — Woodman
   "Mi Chiamano Mimi," from *La Bohème* — Puccini
   Mrs. R.H. Morton, Lyric Soprano[2]

As to the quality of such music we have few living testimonials. In all likelihood it was almost uniformly mediocre, the sort of thing that every red-blooded American boy would instinctively sneak out of the back

door to avoid hearing during his mother's afternoon teas. It possessed the faint
tinkle of culture without any real taste or inspiration behind it. But it is what
passed for "refined music" in America for a hundred years.

Obviously music of this sort did not really appeal to mass musical tastes.
What it appealed to was the radio industry's lust for respectability and social
conformity. The compulsion was to convince the public that radio was a high-
toned medium of communication, and recital music was surely an easy route
to that end. And an inexpensive route as well, since third-rate amateur sopranos
were always available in large numbers and were more than willing to do their
screeching free of charge. Clearly, though, popular taste had been moving in
other directions for many years, and when radio truly became a mass medium
it would have to minister to those tastes—indeed, as the twenties progressed
there were certain chinks in the armor of the respectable but banal salon music.

First of all, numerous strains of commercial popular music had been
around for quite some time in the United States—probably since the 1890s.
Some of this would have even seemed old-fashioned by 1920, or would have
been accepted as old-fashioned by those who were young when the twenties
began. There were sentimental songs and ballads like "After the Ball Is Over,"
"Only a Bird in a Gilded Cage," "In the Good Old Summertime," "Sweet
Adeline," "In the Shade of the Old Apple Tree," "Let Me Call You
Sweetheart," and "Down By the Old Mill Stream," all of which were written
between the turn of the century and World War I. Most of these songs were
products of Tin Pan Alley and were fashioned for use on the vaudeville stage.
Most of them had found their way onto phonograph records and were sold in
millions of copies to the many who never enjoyed the privilege of witnessing
a vaudeville performance.

As old-fashioned as this kind of music had become by the early twenties
(old-fashioned but hardly moribund, for such songs can still be heard in the
1980s in clubs, lodges, pizza parlors and for that matter on TV) it was certainly
still "popular" and could be safely offered to radio listening audiences in programs devoted to music. A fair number of such programs slipped through the
veil of potted palm music as the WJZ survey shows.

Also respectable and commonplace in the early twenties were songs from
operettas and that new American musical form, the musical comedy. Radio
listeners could be expected to enjoy the compositions of Gilbert and Sullivan,
Victor Herbert, Franz Lehar, Rudolph Friml, Sigmund Romberg, E.Y. Har-
burg, Jerome Kern and others clearly identified with the musical stage. They
could be expected to jump for joy over the still lingering sounds of George M.
Cohan's patriotic numbers that enjoyed phenomenal popularity during the
war years: songs like "You're a Grand Old Flag," "Over There," and "Yankee
Doodle Boy."

Similarly, a certain amount of time could be granted to band music—the
marches of John Philip Sousa, for example. Early radio occasionally presented
live music from such bands. Edwin Franco Goldman, the New York bandmaster who offered free concerts to the multitudes "on the mall," became a
strong exponent of radio and performed over the air many times. Like Walter

Damrosch, he served as a self-appointed cultural ambassador for quality music. And Goldman's band, being a concert band, brought high-calibre musical fare to the radio at a time when it was not widely available nationwide.

But it was really dance band orchestras that the young wanted to hear, and these, too, were heard on radio from the beginning, although on a limited scale, and in spruced-up presentations. The young wanted played on the radio the same sorts of tunes that they were accustomed to hearing on phonograph records, but strong restraining hands kept things within safe bounds, steering clear of the most provocative and scandalous dance numbers of the day. Nonetheless, there was dance music in the early twenties; even Frank Conrad had played dance tune recordings to his small Pittsburgh loyalists before KDKA went on the air. Of course one could hear waltzes and fox trots, and one could hear touch-of-ragtime tunes like Irving Berlin's "Alexander's Ragtime Band." By the early twenties the kind of dances done by Vernon and Irene Castle, once thought to be somewhat scandalous, were now considered safe and respectable, as was the kind of syncopated dance music played in dance halls of the prewar period. There were some new bands, though, especially those containing music for the "sinful" saxophone, that would have been as much condemned on the radio as they were by parents who had to endure recordings of them emanating from Junior's room.

Jazz was still a forbidden word in radio in the early twenties, and very little of it went out over the airwaves; it eventually entered surreptitiously, and of course it would eventually change the whole complexion of radio programming. But it was not jazz itself that changed the face of popular music; it was rather the general drift of programming in the middle twenties, especially as sponsors and commercialism entered the picture. Radio music was to change, but not by revolution.

The truth is that the radio programmers found out by trial and error what the public liked, and what sounded good over the radio, and they were, after all, just as anxious to please as they were to uplift. So in the process of experimenting with many kinds of musical programming, they eventually found out what programs appealed to the widest audiences and the most diverse tastes. Radio audiences were vocal; they let their prejudices be known, and shortly a distinctly radiophonic musical style emerged.

A fine example of the emerging radio musician was Vaughn De Leath, popularly known as the "First Lady of Radio." In her many early appearances over WJZ while it was still in Newark, De Leath proved that she had discovered a style that appealed to radio audiences yet lay firmly within the precincts of propriety as then laid down. De Leath was a buxom, homey sort of lady, a typical product of the American heartland, having been born in the largely German community of Mt. Pulaski, Illinois (her real name was Leonore Vonderleith). She was also a thoroughly professional musician and even a composer, whose first composition was published when she was a girl of 13. Her experiences with radio went back to the pre–KDKA era when Richard Klein, Lee De Forest's sales manager, persuaded her to sing over the air on Station WXG. After several performances on the De Forest station, and before the "entertainment features" were banned by a government inspector, De Leath sang a number of songs over the radio, for which she received the first substantial quantity of radio fan mail.

One of those who remembered De Leath's 1916 success was Tommy Cowan, WJZ's aggressive announcer, who brought the popular lady back to the enlarged radio audience of 1922. De Leath was even more popular the second time around, and it is perhaps her success at this time that won her the sobriquet "First Lady of Radio." It was not simply that De Leath was a good singer with an appealing voice, but that she offered a combination of informal, relaxed conversation mixed with musical numbers. It was the total personality, the feeling of *Gemütlichkeit*, that made De Leath popular. She used a low-key approach, probably at some variance from the cold and aloof sopranos who pierced the night air in the early days.

De Leath also contributed to the art of radio singing a style that would turn out to have considerable impact. She virtually invented the technique of singing known as "crooning," a style prompted not so much by the desire to reach a specific audience as by the technical requisites of early radio. Singers, and especially some of the sopranos, had a tendency to blow the tubes on the transmitters and bend the pin in the meter, so announcers were forever moving the microphone away or urging singers to show restraint. De Leath, always willing to please, decided to adopt a soft, gentle, cooing approach that immediately became her trademark and an incentive to other popular singers. Today, of course, we associate crooning with the male singers who came to radio a few years later—especially Rudy Vallee, Lanny Ross and Bing Crosby—but the style was really pioneered by Vaughn De Leath in 1921. (In later years De Leath willingly accepted the honor of having invented the style, but she never liked being called a crooner.)

There is some reason to suspect that De Leath first used a crooning style or something like it when she first broadcast for De Forest in 1916. In her first broadcast she sang Stephen Foster's "Old Folks at Home," and shortly thereafter received a fan letter pronouncing, "You have inaugurated a new form of song which, no doubt, will be very popular."

The thing which made Miss De Leath popular, no doubt, and perhaps prompted Tommy Cowan to use her over and over again at WJZ, was that she projected a total radio personality—a soft and easygoing manner which contrasted sharply with the "mike-frightened" recitalists of the day. Clearly in this period of the middle twenties radio was struggling to discover mannerisms of its own and a means of ministering to mass taste. And the tendency was to offer music that would dovetail with the highly personal approach being used by the newly successful announcers—men like Graham McNamee and Norman Brokenshire.

The principal route to establishing popular music on the air was through mixed acts, song and patter routines, the early forerunners of what later became the radio "variety show." To give people the kind of music they wanted to hear you had to do it in a way that could be justified as simple light fare, and this was best done through a modification and toning down of traditional

Top: Billy Jones (left) and Ernie Hare, a much-loved song and patter duo who intro-
duced the sort of light fare that evolved into the radio variety show. (Photo courtesy
Culver Pictures.) Bottom: Vaughn De Leath, often called "The First Lady of Radio,"
became a popular favorite over WJZ in 1922 and is credited with inventing the singing
style known as "crooning." (Photo courtesy University of Illinois Library.)

vaudeville routines. The first and perhaps best remembered of these mixed acts was the team of Billy Jones and Ernie Hare, who were making regular appearances over WJZ in the fall of 1921—a routine that contained comedy and musical segments in roughly equal proportion.

Jones and Hare were typical vaudevillians, and their musical tastes ran the gamut of numbers that would have been sung on the vaudeville stage, with the more rakish and suggestive numbers omitted. They offered both comic songs and sentimental ballads, including all the expected confections of Tin Pan Alley. The Jones and Hare show began with regular theme for easy identification, and it became one of the best-known radio themes of the twenties. Old-timers will recall the words of the pattersong:

> How-do-you-do, everybody, how-do-you-do;
> Don't forget your Friday date,
> Seven thirty until eight;
> How-do-you-do, everybody, how-do-you-do!

Jones and Hare were as much alike as Tweedledum and Tweedledee. They were born on the same day of the month (Jones in New York City and Hare in Norfolk, Virginia), and both of their mothers had the same maiden name, although apparently they were no relation to one another. They were the same height and the same weight, had the same round and pudgy appearance. Some people professed that it was not possible to tell the two apart. Altogether a striking combination for what was once popularly known as a "harmony team." The two first came together when orchestra conductor Gustave Haeschen invited them to a recording session and asked them to sing a duet to enhance the value of a record he was making. Liking the result themselves, the two teamed up, and were successful as a team in New York by the time Tommy Cowan went on his first talent hunt to fill up the evening hours at WJZ.

In their early days at Newark, Jones and Hare sang ballads and sentimental tunes, and told jokes of the kind then published in railway timetables, seed catalogues and family magazines. They were decidedly mellow, genial, homespun, and above all tepid and inoffensive. Altogether the act was an excellent expedient for radio in the middle twenties, unused as yet to paying out large sums for a full-scale variety show with its numerous secondary performers, orchestras and top-flight announcers. In the beginning the duo acted as their own announcers, and throughout most of the twenties sailed along with only a single piano accompanist.

Still the show was enormously popular, and when sponsors entered the radio scene a few years later, it was acts like Jones and Hare that sparked their interest. Starting in 1923 Jones and Hare—now heard on WEAF—became known as the "Happiness Boys," because they were sponsored by the Happiness Candy Stores. Later on, with shifting sponsorship, they became the "Interwoven Pair," the "Best Food Boys" and the "Taystee Loafers."[3] The success of Jones and Hare gave rise almost immediately to a number of very similar song and patter programs, including the "Cliquot Club Eskimos," the "Gold Dust Twins," and the "Ipana Troubadours."

The kind of music heard on the "Happiness Boys" and similar programs would eventually lead to a much wider range of possibilities for popular music, and of course it would also eventually lead to the larger-scale "variety show" of the late 1920s, such as "The Fleischmann Hour" with Rudy Vallee. By that time American popular music was clearly much more in command of its own destinies than it had been when radio began in 1920.

One of the reasons for this, obviously, was that some of the earlier forbidden forms of music finally managed to push their way into daily programming. Jazz, naturally, was the principal bugaboo, that which had been soundly condemned, but which finally wormed its way into the holy sanctum of the airwaves. When the decade began, the playing of jazz would not have been deemed possible, but its immense popularity in the twenties could not be denied, and it was inevitable that it would creep in through one door or another.

The slowness of jazz in penetrating the genteel bastions of early radio was partly due to the fact that it was new to the national scene. As we know today, jazz originated in New Orleans, where it was once almost exclusively the province of Negroes in that city and a few other Southern cities. By World War I, jazz had made its way northward, at first to Chicago, and then to other Northern cities. The word "jazz" became something of a forbidden pop word of the subculture by the time the war broke out, and the vast majority of Americans had little knowledge of the word or the style of music to which it referred. At this time, when the word appeared in newspapers it was variously spelled jass, jazz, jasz, jaz, jatz, and jascz. Even to this day the origins and meaning of the word are obscure.

There were many moralistic objections to the playing of jazz on the radio in the early 1920s, but milder forms of dance band music did appear, and all of the major dance bands were managing to intrude a little jazz here and there. At first it was jazz that was softened, toned down to make it respectable, but listeners were wildly enthusiastic nonetheless. One of the earliest dance bands to make a strong impact on the radio was that of Vincent Lopez, who since the war had built something of a reputation as a "society" band leader, playing in semifasionable hotels in New York. Lopez had heard the so-called Original Dixieland Jazz Band and copied some of its tricks, although toning them down somewhat for his own appearances.

But the touch was there, and people found themselves dancing to jazz music when they least expected it. Lopez was a friend of Tommy Cowan, first announcer and program director of WJZ, and as early as the fall of 1921 Cowan brought Lopez and his band before the microphone at the Westinghouse plant in Newark. The first occasion was as a replacement of another act that cancelled at the last minute. Lopez and his group went over to Newark and performed for an hour and a half—all just for the fun of it, since radio wasn't paying in those days. But Cowan assured Lopez that all this would change: "There'll come a day soon when we'll both get paid—plenty. Wait and see."

Lopez did wait and he did see. He and his orchestra became one of the most popular fixtures on early New York radio. In that first concert in Newark he began by playing "Anitra's Dance" to a fox-trot tempo, but in time he managed to pass off some slightly livelier numbers. When the program was over, WJZ's undermanned and inadequate switchboard lit up like a Christmas tree, and in the days that followed, the mailman staggered under the weight of the hundreds of letters that came to the station expressing approval of this kind of programming. A phone call even came in from as far away as Washington, D.C.—in fact from Joseph Tumulty, Secretary to President Harding, expressing delight in the program.

Cowan and Lopez knew that they had hit upon a good thing. The only trouble was that Lopez was under contract to appear regularly at the Pennsylvania Grill in New York, and E.M. Statler, owner of the Pennsylvania Hotel, was not keen on Lopez and his band taking time off to traipse over to Newark to sound off over this newfangled device. Lopez, who was impressed by the enthusiastic response to the first broadcast, asked Cowan if he couldn't possibly get some kind of telephone hookup directly to the hotel so that two birds could be killed with one stone: The Lopez band could play before a live audience *and* a radio audience at the same time.

Alas, this was easier said than done, since AT&T, with its own jealous interests to protect, was not being too cooperative in such ventures. But the idea was so appealing that Cowan eventually managed to obtain a Western Union line to the Pennsylvania Grill, and regular band concerts were emanating from the grill before the year 1921 was over. When the series began, Lopez went on the air and explained to the radio audience that the program would be on the air every Friday evening from the Pennsylvania Grill, and that people could listen over their radios, or if they preferred, come down to the hotel to dance and watch the radio show in progress. Within an hour the telephone at the hotel had brought reservations for every table next Friday night, and calls kept coming in the following day. What's more, by noon the following Friday all the rooms were sold out in the hotel as well. Several hours before the first program, Seventh Avenue and several of the side streets were thronged with people still hoping that it would be possible to get into the show.

All of this changed the attitude of an astonished E.M. Statler. "Vincent," he said, "I couldn't build business up like this in a thousand years of hard work. You did it in an hour. I think radio has some real possibilities."

Within a year a number of other bands were to appear on radio and would also meet with this same spectacular success, although during this period the only bands invited to appear on the radio were others of these "respectable" ensembles. Perhaps the best known of those who tried to make jazz respectable for average middle-class audiences was Paul Whiteman, who also made an early appearance on WJZ—in 1922. Whiteman earlier turned down the idea of appearing on the radio, believing that nobody was listening except for a few kids tinkering with crystal sets. The success of Vincent Lopez in those broadcasts from the Pennsylvania Grill changed his mind.

Whiteman, even more than Lopez, was making a strong pitch for respectable jazz with classical devices and overtones, and he was able to do it with the skill of a conservatory-trained musician (Whiteman had at one time played

Jazz was a taboo on radio in the early twenties, but in the hands of a few classically trained masters like Paul Whiteman (shown here in 1923), it quickly gained national recognition and began wafting over the airwaves. (Photo courtesy Library of Congress.)

first viola in the Denver Symphony Orchestra). Later he found himself the leader and organizer of dance bands, and as early as 1919 he had supplied a number of these for posh hotels in California. Later he came East for an engagement at the swank Ambassador Hotel in Atlantic City, and his rise to nationwide fame was meteoric. For his engagement at the Ambassador, Whiteman brought with him his "hot" cornet player Henry Busse (a German who just barely spoke English) and his sophisticated arranger Ferde Grofe, who was just as keen on bringing classical devices to jazz as Whiteman was himself.

Whiteman brought respectability to jazz in more ways than one. While still in California he established the practice of actually writing up the parts for his musicians. Up to this point jazz playing was mostly completely improvised and wayward in execution. A group of players would just take up some melody from the pianist, and then develop melodies, counter-melodies and harmonies as they went along. Ferde Grofe, with his classical music background, implemented some rules of orchestration from his spot at the piano, and with his skillful arrangements managed to raise the "legitimate" (sometimes called sweet or straight) kind of jazz playing to a popular and respectable art.

As most everyone knows, the zenith of Whiteman's success in wedding jazz and classical forms came in 1924 when Whiteman commissioned George Gershwin to write a serious jazz composition for his orchestra — the result being the celebrated "Rhapsody in Blue," first performed at Aeolian Hall in New York on February 12, 1924. This composition made world celebrities of Whiteman, Gershwin and Grofe (who orchestrated the piece), and they enjoyed tours throughout the world where they were greeted as potentates and conquering heroes. Respectability? After "Rhapsody in Blue" there wasn't much talk about that anymore! Even the Prince of Wales sat in on drums in the Whiteman Orchestra on one of his American visits.

Paul Whiteman and his orchestra remained a regular feature on radio for a quarter of a century. What is perhaps more important, the Whiteman sound eventually made jazz respectable enough that jazz sounds influenced a whole generation of radio band leaders — men like Guy Lombardo, Ozzie Nelson, Ted Weems and Rudy Vallee. By the late twenties jazz was as much a part of everyday programming on radio as it would be in the thirties and forties. Yes, it was the jazz age, as F. Scott Fitzgerald called it, and by the last of the twenties radio had caught up with the age.

Admittedly, though, jazz took a long time making the grade in radio, and generally before 1925, at which time jazz records were being heard by the millions, there was very little jazz going out over the airwaves. At the time of the broadcast of Mozart's *Impresario* in 1922, William W. Hindshaw, who introduced the program to the audience, made a point of attacking the unhealthy and immoral influence of jazz, and the importance of keeping musical culture pure and unsullied. Stations that played jazz before 1925 were denounced, especially when they seemed to believe in it. In 1924 two brothers, Ralph and H. Leslie Atlas, started a radio station from the basement of their home on Sheridan Road in Chicago. The two were considered to be eccentric, and their station was denounced when it was found that the brothers wanted to make a specialty of playing jazz on a regular basis. The station was WBBM, later moved to the Broadmoor Hotel, and today the principal CBS station in Chicago.

Jazz was not the only musical form which had to buck its way forward in the radio world of the 1920s. It was a decade when forms were rapidly changing and developing, and there were musical forms which held a prominent position at the end of the decade that literally didn't exist at the beginning. One such form was country music, which in the 1920s was almost universally known as hillbilly music, although sometimes it was called "old-time music." There were, of course, older traditions of music from the South and from the hill country, with banjo pluckers and guitar strummers, but when the decade of the twenties began no musicians of this kind were professionalized: There were no country records and no country hits.

When commercial hillbilly music first hit the radio it met a much more gracious reception than jazz, primarily perhaps because its first appearance was on stations in the South, where there was a natural craving for the form, but also (and this was true a short time later when the music was played for city slickers in the North) because there was a long tradition of folk music behind it, which gave it an aroma of heartland respectability and folksiness. But before about 1922 hillbilly music was almost exclusively the province of amateurs, although occasionally a favored performer would get paid for appearing at county fairs, church picnics and other local gatherings. Shortly, however, record companies — always on the lookout for new types of recording material — began to make recordings of some of this local folk music, and they were amazed to find that there was a strong demand for it, not only in the regions where it was already commonplace but elsewhere around the country as well.

It was only natural when radio stations began appearing in the South that a certain amount of local music would be requested, so that what we now call country music was heard pretty early on radio stations in that part of the country. Possibly the first radio station to play country music was WSB in Atlanta, Georgia, a station owned by the *Atlanta Journal*, which went on the air on March 16, 1922. This station began with a 100-watt transmitter, but in several months a 500-watt transmitter was installed. Within a few months of its inaugural the station was featuring the music of several folk performers, including the Rev. Andrew Jenkins, a blind gospel singer, and Fiddlin' John Carson, already well known to many in Georgia because he had put on many performances during Georgia political campaigns.

Probably the first radio barn dance to appear on radio was on WBAP in Fort Worth, Texas, on January 4, 1923. WBAP, which formerly had been offering the usual fare of popular — semiclassical and sacred — music, began an hour-and-a-half program of square dance music led by an old-time fiddler and Confederate veteran, Captain M.J. Bonner. In those early, unregulated days, WBAP's signal could be heard as far away as New York, Canada and even Hawaii. Certainly it could be heard very well in Texas, the South and the Midwest, and the popularity of the program convinced numerous other stations to have their own country music or square dance programs. By 1925 many such programs were on the air.

The decade of the 1920s saw the birth of two of the most enduringly popular radio shows of record, "The WSM Grand Ole Opry" of Nashville, Tennessee, and "The WLS National Barn Dance" of Chicago. The first program of the "Grand Ole Opry" began on November 28, 1925, at the National Life and Accident Insurance Company's station WSM (the call letters stood for We Shield Millions). The program was started by George Hay, popularly known as the Solemn Old Judge. Hay introduced on this first program an 80-year-old dirt farmer known as Uncle Jimmy Thompson, who claimed that he knew more than one thousand fiddle songs. Uncle Jimmy started to play some of these songs, and at the end of an hour he proclaimed loudly, "Fiddlesticks! A man can't get warmed up in no one hour. This show has got to be longer." And so it became longer, eventually being expanded to four hours

on both Friday and Saturday evenings. The show captured longevity records
in more categories than one, finally becoming the nation's oldest radio program as it had once been the longest.

"The WLS Barn Dance" in Chicago was for many years the biggest and
most influential country music program, and in fact it had priority over "The
Grand Ole Opry." It began on April 19, 1924, over WLS (a station owned by
Sears, Roebuck & Company, thus the letters stood for World's Largest Store).[4]
WLS had only gone on the air a week before inaugurating this first barn dance
program, but the station immediately saw that it had a hit on its hands. The
first program came from a small mezzanine of the Sherman Hotel and consisted of a group of country-style fiddlers who were really supposed to be second fiddle (as it were) to the hotel's main attraction, the Isham Jones Dance
Band. The station was startled to find in the next few days that the Barn Dance
program attracted hundreds of letters, all asking for more fiddle or square
dance numbers.

In the early years, "The WLS Barn Dance" (only when it became a network
show was the name changed to "National Barn Dance") had a somewhat
different flavor from the music at the Opry. Chicago wasn't as familiar with
hillbilly music, so the show featured a wider variety of sentimental pop tunes,
"heart songs," and old-fashioned music with a countrified flavor. Many of the
early stars of "WLS Barn Dance" had little or any connection with country
music. There was an Irish tenor (Bill O'Connor), and the Maple City Four
Quartette. Organist Ralph Waldo Emerson played such songs as "Silver
Threads Among the Gold." One of the best-loved performers at the Barn
Dance was Grace Wilson, professionally trained as a contralto. But Miss Wilson
gamely broadened her style to embrace nearly every style of music popular in
the 1920s. She joined the Barn Dance in 1924 and stayed for 36 years, intro-
ducing such songs as "In the Shade of the Old Apple Tree" and "Bringing
Home the Bacon," the last being one of her all-time favorites for which she
regularly received thousands of requests.

In the mid-twenties, the Barn Dance had another powerful attraction in
the person of George Hay, the Solemn Old Judge, who came up from Memphis Station WMC to be a regular announcer on WLS—this before his invention of the Grand Ole Opry. Hay announced the Barn Dance, of course, but
he did a great deal of general announcing, and for years gave WLS station
breaks. He used a locomotive whistle for these breaks (down in Memphis he
had used a whistle from a Mississippi steamboat that he called a "hushpuck-
ing"). "WLS Unlimited" became his trademark, and listeners long
remembered his colorful station breaks—"WLS, the Sears Roebuck Station,
Chi-CAW-Go."

Another distinction for the Barn Dance a few years later was the show's
longtime identification with the Eighth Street Theatre, located on the edge
of Chicago's Loop. Here over the years millions of visitors would stand in line
to be part of the studio audience. The crowds were so large that admission had
to be charged, making it the only radio show for which admission was regularly
charged. The Barn Dance began broadcasting from the Eighth Street Theatre

on March 19, 1932, and by the time of the last broadcast there on August 31, 1957, there had been close to 3 million paid admissions to the show.

Radio lifted many a country singer to stardom. There was Uncle Dave Macon, born way back in 1870, and long billed as the oldest banjo picker in Dixie. Uncle Dave came to stardom through the vehicle of the Grand Ole Opry. The same thing happened to Bradley Kincaid, a Kentucky lad who migrated to Chicago with the intention of attending the YMCA College there, but shortly found himself singing on the Barn Dance, where he rose to stardom.

Popular music in all its forms was showing rich development in the late twenties, and by this time the restrictive barriers came tumbling down throughout the land. People were now allowed to hear on the radio everything they wanted to hear, including jazz, although by the decade's end jazz was giving way to swing music and to pop music of a rather eclectic variety. It was only natural, then, that pop music stars would arise in radio to capture the national circuits and appeal to audiences of all ages and cultural backgrounds. The stars of the future would probably have digested a number of different styles by the time that they took to the airwaves. Such, for example, would be true of Bing Crosby, whose long radio career began on the CBS Radio network in 1931. As a boy out of Spokane, Washington, Crosby was drawn to jazz, had bought the records of the Mound City Blowers and had absorbed their techniques. He was enthralled by the vaudeville singers of the day and the latest Tin Pan Alley numbers popularized by some of them, most especially his hero Al Jolson. Later on he was to fall naturally into the radio-born style of crooning, and with his magnificent vibrato he became the greatest crooner of them all.

As the decade of the twenties came to an end, and with an unparalleled diversity of popular musical styles acceptable not only to the general public, but to sponsors who were paying to put radio shows on the air, radio began to have its own assemblage of musical stars — those who had gotten to the top almost entirely through the medium of radio, and whose talents and gifts fitted that medium. Most of them had grown up with one of the prevailing styles of popular music — Bing Crosby and Mildred Bailey, for example, served an apprenticeship with Paul Whiteman — but their popularity was likely due to their own creative approaches to the radio style.

A perfect example of the rising generation of radio talents at the end of the twenties was Rudy Vallee, the proverbial college kid who never grew up, but who nonetheless was perceptive and intelligent enough to put together the first big hit variety show in radio. Vallee had been born in Island Point, Vermont, in 1901. He went to Yale, where he formed his own band and played the saxophone for parties and dances. Following all the musical fads of the mid-twenties, Vallee became Joe College incarnate — the boy with the raccoon coat, always at the center of some uproar, always cheering on the football squad. Vallee never seemed to outlive his craving for brunettes and things that come in bottles.

Vallee had a brush with radio as early as 1922, when he was only a freshman at Yale. He was asked to go into an old deserted loft of the A.C.

Rudy Vallee had performed over the radio during his student days at Yale in the mid-twenties, but his greatest contribution to radio (and later television) was his inauguration of the "variety show" in its modern garb. (Photo courtesy NBC.)

Gilbert Building in New Haven, where there was a primitive microphone into which he was supposed to play a few solos. In 1927, after graduating from Yale, he went to New York, where he played solos for $14.00 a week — the only guarantee offered him by Vincent Lopez, then running a musical talent office. Later on he joined several other ensembles and enjoyed regular employment for the next two years. In 1929 he had put together a group called Yale Collegians, a term that must have had enormous appeal, although of dubious accuracy. But it was while playing at the Heigh Ho Club on East 53rd Street in New York that big-time radio finally caught up with Vallee.

The Heigh Ho Club had been a regular engagement for Vallee for a number of weeks, at the beginning of 1929, when his agent talked a small radio station into broadcasting from the Heigh Ho Club. This station was WABC (later WCBS), shortly to become the flagship station of CBS in New York. On the day of the first show, a gentleman from the station showed up at the club and informed Vallee that because the station had no money to pay an announcer, Vallee himself would have to announce his own show and introduce his own numbers. The station representative was certain that this would throw terror in Vallee's heart as it usually did with new radio performers, but without batting an eye, Vallee agreed to go on acting as the show's host and announcer. At the Heigh Ho Club the German doorman, with a long officer's coat, would call out to arriving customers, "Heigh Ho," so Vallee decided to begin his program by saying, "Heigh Ho everybody, this is Rudy Vallee announcing and directing." The "Heigh Ho everybody" greeting became Vallee's opening on his later long-running variety network show, "The Fleischmann Hour."[5]

Rudy Vallee had already been a crooner and a "vagabond lover" of the kind that had been popular in early radio, but when his network show was unwrapped before a nationwide audience in the fall of 1930, a wholly new idea in programming was revealed—the true variety show. Not only did Vallee sing and announce his own songs, as he had from the early programs from the Heigh Ho Club, he also introduced a variety of other performers who blended and contrasted with his own style. A typical Vallee show might feature a little crooning or varied numbers by the host, but also the appearance of a comedian—say, Eddie Cantor, Fanny Brice or Ed Wynn. Sometimes he would have a dramatic actor like Maurice Evans or Lionel Barrymore. This format contrasted favorably with the "variety" shows of the day, which offered little real diversity of styles in their performers and less in the way of characteristic style or format. They were threaded together mechanically, as tiresome sequences of set numbers. Most earlier attempts made the mistakes of including an interval of serious or classical music followed by jazz or popular numbers. Vallee reached for the large popular audience, with a light and frothy format.

Just as important, though, Vallee would have what people liked to call a genuine radiophonic voice. Some called it sex appeal, and believed that Vallee had a kind of voice appeal on the radio similar to Rudolph Valentino's visual appeal on the silver screen. A journalist of the day commented: "By the divine accident or miracle that makes art nearer religion than science, the voice that starts its strange journey at the microphone hardly more than banal fills the air at its destination with some sort of beauty." Such were the magical transformations of radio.

There were also to be some major female musical stars at the end of the twenties. Kate Smith, "the Songbird of the South," made her radio debut in 1929. Kate Smith projected a mood of homespun motherhood—she was a girlish 22 years old in 1929, but somehow she projected that motherly feeling from the start. Smith opened each broadcast with "Hello, everybody," and closed with "Thanks for listenin' . . . and good-night folks." Thoroughly unintellectual, Kate Smith loved football, speedboats, anything and everything

Light Musical Programs
Network Broadcasts—1929

*Musical programming in evening prime-time network radio as of January
1929. Adapted from:* A Thirty-Year History of Programs Carried on National Radio Networks in the United States, 1926–1956, *Department of
Speech, Ohio State University, 1956.*

Program	Network
Musical Variety	
A & P Gypsies	NBC-Red
Armstrong Quakers Orchestra	NBC-Blue
Automatic Disc Duo	NBC-Blue
Ce-Co Couriers	CBS
Champion Sparkers	NBC-Blue
Cliquot Club Eskimos	NBC-Red
Coward Comfort Hour	NBC-Red
Dictograph Orchestra	NBC-Red
Dixie Circus	NBC-Blue
Evening in Paris	NBC-Red
Freed Eismann Orchestradians	NBC-Blue
Forhan's Song Shop	NBC-Red
Fox Fur Trapper's Orchestra	NBC-Red
Gold Strand Orchestra	NBC-Blue
Guy Lombardo Orchestra	CBS
Happy Wonder Bakers Quartette	NBC-Red
Hudson Essex Challengers	NBC-Blue
Ingram Shavers Orchestra	NBC-Red
La Palina Smoker	CBS
Lucky Strike Dance Orchestra	NBC-Red
Michelin Hour	NBC-Blue
Prophylactic Orchestra	NBC-Red
Roxy and His Gang	NBC-Blue
Vitaphone Hour	CBS
Whittal Anglo-Persians	NBC-Blue
Wrigley Revue	NBC-Blue
Light Music	
Aunt Jemima	CBS
Black Rock Boys	CBS
Breen & De Rose	NBC-Blue
Brome & Llewellyn	CBS

Enna Jettick Melodies	NBC-Blue
Jeddo Highlanders	NBC-Blue
Jones and Hare	NBC-Red
Lehn and Fink Serenade	NBC-Blue
Landt Trio	NBC-Blue
Neopolitan Nights	NBC-Blue
Peerless Reproducers	NBC-Red
Pickard Family	NBC-Blue
Raybestos Twins	NBC-Red
Smith Brothers: Trade & Mark	NBC-Blue
South Sea Islanders	NBC-Blue
Stromberg-Carlson Sextette	NBC-Blue
Sylvania Foresters	NBC-Blue
Utica Jubilee Singers	NBC-Blue
Vicks Vaporub Quartette	CBS

Hillbilly Minstrel Shows

Dutch Masters Minstrels	NBC-Blue

---

that smacked of the plain and ordinary. A gourmand, she recommended to her listeners a Southern dinner of fried chicken, baked squash and peppermint ice cream. Smith had begun her career as a theatre comedienne, but on radio she exuded a square and straight-laced sincerity. So sincere and convincing was Smith that she could advertise cigars and have a typical female listener convinced that cigars were mellow and inoffensive.

Another phenomenally popular female star of the late twenties was Jessica Dragonette, who gave up the concert stage to appear on the Cities Service Concert, offering light and semiclassical music. The striking blond Dragonette was always in strong demand for personal appearances. During one of her tours, 150,000 people turned out to hear her in Chicago's Grant Park. In Minneapolis she was mobbed by 15,000 fans during a blizzard. Dragonette remained a major radio star until the late thirties when she retired after a spat with her sponsors. Some of her fans were so outraged that they resolved to boycott radio until she returned. There is no doubt that she had a lovely and beguiling radio voice.

Eventually the musical fare on radio would be influenced by factors other than star quality. With the program day wildly expanding in the late twenties, and with many nonnetwork stations needing musical programming, it was inevitable that many program managers would eventually turn to the expedient of canned music to fill up the long hours. By the end of the twenties the playing of the music on phonograph records was once again coming into favor. The practice was by no means a new one, of course, since phonograph records had been played back in those very early days at KDKA. And there would be increasing pressures on the radio industry from record companies, from musicians and performers' unions to pay for this piracy—a disagreeable relationship that had to be hammered out over a period of many years.

For a while many radio stations skirted the law and even pretended that recorded programs were live performances. There was a station in Paterson, New Jersey, for example, which claimed to have a live Paul Whiteman, and the announcer even carried on imaginary conversations with Paul himself as he was about to give the upbeat, even though the program consisted merely of Paul Whiteman records. Of course this kind of practice could not have persisted, but it was proof of the inevitable dependence of radio on the products of its one-time arch enemy, the phonograph.

By the middle thirties radio was to see the permanent enshrinement of the functionary known as the disc jockey, that is, an announcer of popular musical programs that consist solely of the playing of phonograph records, with the inevitable chatter and commercial interlude. It is generally agreed that the disc jockey idea came to flower in 1935 when Martin Block started playing records on station WNEW in New York—a program that came to be known as "The Make-Believe Ballroom." Actually the disc jockey phenomenon (although not known by that name) was already apparent in the late twenties, especially on the West Coast, where several stations were playing records on a regular basis before the stock market crash. Station KMTR in Los Angeles may have had such programming as early as 1926.

What, after all, could you do to fill the time during those long hours—especially in the daytime? The early morning hours were a special problem. In 1929 in Chicago, on station KYW, an early morning disc jockey show featuring Miss Halloween Martin got off to a wildly successful start. Halloween Martin (so-called because she was born on that day in 1902) had come to Chicago from her native Texas to be a writer on home economics for the old *Chicago Herald Examiner*, which owned KYW. Martin, who had a college acting and dramatic background, was eventually put to announcing, and her sparkling and lively personality suggested to the station manager the idea of putting her on an early morning "wake-up" type of program. This program, eventually called "The Musical Clock" featured the time, temperature and weather—and the playing of phonograph records.

Generally Miss Martin picked her own musical selections. She experimented with everything musical from heavy classical to jazz, although she soon discovered that the early risers responded most favorably to light and lively music. "The Musical Clock" became enormously popular almost immediately, with thousands of letters pouring into the station. Miss Martin herself got the lion's share of the praise: "most pleasant voice we have ever heard on the radio," "don't ever allow anyone to announce anything but her," "adorable," and so on.

What these thousands may not have realized was that they were witness to the birth of a kind of radio program and style that would keep the medium going long after the radio stars had disappeared. When the great stars of radio's golden age were bumped off the airwaves by the menace of television, radio was still there. It was still there for pop music and for the sparkling voice. Programs like "The Musical Clock" continue to be the bread and butter of radio, and they show no signs of dying out. It is comforting to know that their existence is not new, that they go back to the first decade of radio, and their virtues were almost immediately evident to the listening audience.

14. The Expanding Broadcast Day

It may be something of a crude simplification to say that the coming of the networks in the mid-twenties immediately transformed radio into the kind of industry that is now remembered by Americans who lived through the thirties and forties. The network idea gave an electric jolt to radio finances, and vastly expanded the capabilities of the medium to offer superior programming, but actual results in the program field were slow and steady, not dramatic. There was no immediate leap forward to a daylong schedule of slick professional broadcasting. Even with its two networks, the Blue and the Red, and a near monopolistic hold on the national airwaves, NBC lacked the know-how and the resources to immediately transform broadcasting from its early timid and unadventuresome style.

Consider the great inaugural broadcast celebrating the inception of the 24-station Blue Network on November 15, 1926. In spite of its $50,000 cost, its roster of talent and its alleged audience of 12 million, the program was crude by standards that would become commonplace by the early thirties. The program offered a sampling of the best that was known to radio listeners in 1926: classical music presented by the New York Symphony and the New York Oratorio Society; singing by Mary Garden and Titta Ruffo; the dance orchestras of Vincent Lopez, Ben Bernie and George Olsen; the vaudeville humor of Will Rogers and Weber and Fields. But the continuity was stiff, formal and pretentious. Furthermore, such an extravaganza could hardly be followed up on a day-in, day-out basis.

Prime-time radio in the first few years after the founding of NBC continued to be largely bland and unexceptional. The modest expense and limited scale of programs like "The Happiness Boys" dragged other harmony and comedy teams to radio. Jones and Hare sound-alikes and look-alikes seem to have sprouted up everywhere. There were the "Sisters of the Skillet," not sisters at all but two roly-poly veterans of vaudeville named Eddie East and Ralph Dumke, as alike to one another as Jones and Hare, although a good deal fatter, having a combined weight of 500 pounds. Much of their humor was built around their experience as trenchermen. With somewhat stronger emphasis on humor of the "nutty" variety were (Ole) Olsen and (Chic) Johnson, who came to radio with long experience both in vaudeville and nightclubs. Among other groups which had avid followings in the post-network era were the "Cliquot Club Eskimos," the "Funnyboners," the "Do Re Mi Girls," the "A & P

Gypsies," "Roxy and His Gang," and the "Wrigley Revue." There seemed to be no end of duos in imitation of the Jones and Hare formula, indicating a copycat tendency that has infected both radio and television in the years since. There were Breen and De Rose, Lehn and Fink, the Smith Brothers Trade & Mark, Brome and Llewellyn, the Raybestos Twins.

Light fare of this sort during the first few years of network broadcasting was interlarded with strong doses of classical and light classical music, now usually provided by first-rate orchestras. During prime evening time in 1927–28 the NBC Red Network offered "The Atwater Kent Hour," "The Capitol Theatre Symphony," "The Cities Service Orchestra," "The Palmolive Hour," and "La France Orchestra." The NBC Blue Network had "The Ampico Hour of Music," "The Chicago Civic Opera," "The Maxwell House Hour" (with Richard Crooks), "The National Symphony Orchestra" (with Walter Damrosch), "The RCA Victor Hour" (with tenor John McCormick) and "The Stromberg-Carlson Hour." The fledgling Columbia network already had "The Columbia Phonograph Hour," "The Listener's Hour," "The New York Philharmonic Hour," "La Palina Concert" and "The Kolster Radio Hour."[1]

In general, radio still needed time-consuming programming in all fields of human experience and accomplishment. Gaps could be filled by educational talks, set political speeches, recitals, and when all else failed, the chit-chat of prolix announcers, nearly all of whom had mastered the art of ad-libbing for an hour or more without pause. The radio stars of the period tended to be those who could pull and stretch the hour with any ready-to-hand material. Typical of those who flourished in the late twenties was Tony Wons, who got his start at WLS in Chicago and later moved to CBS. Using an intimate style, and whispering a mere inch from the microphone, addressing himself primarily to a female audience, Wons offered a medley of verse, song and advice. It is estimated that by 1931 Wons had read as many as 100,000 poems over the air—a record no doubt, and one wonders if as many poems have been heard over the air in all the years since. Entertainers like Wons were doubtless as popular with broadcasting executives as they were with female listeners, since a potpourri of violin background music, homespun philosophy, and poems culled from countless anthologies and library collections could keep the long and unfilled evening hours somehow magically rolling by.

With the vast resources of the networks it was inevitable that more ambitious evening programming would very shortly be packaged and the desperate need for filling the gaps would subside. But there was more to the day than the evening hours, and soon the networks, indeed most large radio stations, would be challenged to fill the airwaves with sound from dawn to midnight, and perhaps beyond. In the middle twenties even the most prestigious stations, like WEAF in New York, did not broadcast all day long, but offered hours of silent time when it was thought that few people were listening. Quite typically a major station might sign on at 11:00 A.M. with some salon music, perhaps a talk about gardening or childrearing for the ladies, or some farm and weather information. At noon or one o'clock the station might fade out, only to resume once again at 4 P.M., perhaps with other "women's" programs or with a children's hour. Major programming would start at 6:00 P.M. and continue to 11:00 P.M. or midnight.

By 1930, however, most of the major stations had arrived at a full broadcast day (at least sunrise to midnight), gradually filling in the lacunae in the program log, sometimes with previously unheard-of styles of programming. Naturally mid-morning and mid-afternoon were tough to stretch, but in time even these were filled by sustaining or even sponsored programs of one sort or another.

On the other hand, some of the formerly neglected time periods were now discovered to have potential, and perhaps even the possibility of giant listening audiences. One such period was the early morning, once thought to be a wasteland. Truthfully, the early morning hours were not absolutely neglected even in the early days of radio. KDKA would occasionally attempt to reach early risers during its first few years, although mostly just for fun. But by 1934 the Pittsburgh pioneer station had a regular program of physical exercises with Spike Shannon. The exercise program idea spread quickly in the twenties, becoming something of a fad, and by the mid-twenties wake-up exercise programs of one kind or another could be heard in many parts of the country.

The notion of the early morning exercise program got a big boost in the New York area in 1925 when Bernarr Macfaddan, the eccentric millionaire physical culture nut, actually bought time on station WOR, then still having studios in Bamberger's Department Store in Newark. Editor of a magazine called *Physical Culture*, and also of the lurid tabloid *Daily Graphic*, which shocked New Yorkers with its nude spectacles and "composite" or faked photographs, Macfaddan was the first to pay for the morning time period. Macfaddan's program began at 6:45 A.M. and lasted until 8:00. Listeners could send for instructions and visual charts showing exercises which were done to musical accompaniment of piano, saxophone and violin. For a while Macfaddan himself led the exercise, and made full use of the opportunity to boost sales of *Physical Culture* and *Daily Graphic*. He also hoped to boost himself and his half-serious candidacy for the presidency on a platform of exercise, healthy bodies and free love.

Occasionally Macfaddan wouldn't show up or make it to Newark in time for the broadcast, and the show's engineer would take over as host and lead the exercises. The engineer, a young Englishman named John Gambling, had been a radio operator in the British merchant marine, had jumped ship after World War II, and had then found his way to WOR. Gambling would eventually take over the program when Macfaddan's interest flagged, and he remained in the early morning time slot at WOR for more than thirty years. The idea of calisthenics died out in the thirties on radio stations around the country, and by World War II there were very few early morning programs devoted to physical exercise. A different format gained the upper hand at WOR as elsewhere. John Gambling eventually moved to a music, chatter and time signal format that has mostly held sway in early morning radio since. For years Gambling's program, later called "Rambling with Gambling," featured a small studio orchestra—a subdued string ensemble rather than the blaring wake-up sound provided by Macfaddan. Gambling carried on a soft line of talk with the musicians, giving the time every three or four minutes for those doubting the accuracy of their alarm clocks. The Gambling show changed hardly at all over the decades, although in the late forties, because of disputes with the musician's union, the string orchestra was replaced by recorded music, making Gambling, like most of the wake-up broadcasters, a disc jockey.[2]

The idea of canned music during the early morning hours would not have been very popular in the twenties, and during much of the decade radio stations that did offer early morning programming filled the time with such things as calisthenics, health talks, agricultural news or sometimes the inevitable piano solo. The ideal or perhaps the most enduring approach to early morning programming was discovered not in New York, but in Chicago, where the remarkable Halloween Martin (see Chapter 13) took command of the early morning hours in KYW and dominated them in the Windy City until the mid-forties. Miss Martin played records, perhaps making her one of the nation's first real disc jockeys, and she did give the time. But more than that she offered her own sparkling personality and charm. At a time when women radio announcers were disappearing around the country—not to surface again in large numbers until the 1960s—Halloween Martin enraptured millions of Chicagoans with a beguiling and soothing voice.

There were other die-hards in the early morning field. Miss Martin had a competitor in Chicago—Norman Ross, who hosted a show on WMAQ for eighteen years (and who, like John Gambling in New York, was succeeded by a son of the same name). Longevity became the byword. In San Francisco Frank Cope's "Alarm Klok Klub" persisted on KJBS for nearly thirty years with hardly an alteration in format, and in the same time frame, 5 to 8 A.M.

Another time frame that now began to attract the attention of radio executives was the late-night period, after 11 P.M. or midnight. By the late twenties it was rapidly discovered around the nation that people didn't have a universal desire to turn off their radios at the accepted bedtime hour; rather, a nation of urbanites on varying work schedules would take comfort in radio sounds at almost any hour. Insomniacs were suddenly finding solace and companionship in soothing bedtime voices just as other large groups of listeners were depending on radio to jolt them out of bed in the morning. A wholly new kind of radio personality would arise to minister to this need—the announcer with the bedtime personality or bedtime voice, a tendency that continues to this day, as one learns by looking at advertisements in present-day radio industry magazines calling for announcers fitting into the category of "morning-voice announcer," or "evening-voice announcer," the latter being more soothing, more gentle, more soporific.

Before the decade of the twenties was over, numerous big city radio stations had late-night personalities who were among their most popular stars. There was George Hay, the Solemn Old Judge of WLS, Chicago; the Little Colonel of WSB, Atlanta; the Hired Hand of WBAP, Fort Worth; and Leo Fitzpatrick of WDAF's "Kansas City Nighthawks," who styled himself as the Merry Old Chief.

Because fewer stations were on the air during these late hours, and also because of the greater penetration of radio waves in the nighttime sky, many of these personalities earned fame and popularity far from their home cities. The "Kansas City Nighthawks" might be heard on the Pacific Coast or in Cleveland. Leo Fitzpatrick offered listeners membership cards in a society of "Nighthawks," in which two million people were said to have enrolled.[3] Whatever the truth about the listeners of these wizards of the nighttime sky, there can be no doubt that millions of Americans were lulling themselves to sleep or hugging their radios in dimly lit parlors to the dulcet and syrupy tones of these newly popular bedtime voices.

The hours of the day still most resistant to radio programming were the workday hours — late morning and mid-afternoon — but slowly these times also began to fill up. In the days before portable radios, the vast majority of daytime radio listeners were female, so that daytime radio was given over almost exclusively to household hint programs, talk programs devoted to child care, educational issues, canning, food prices, cooking, recipe swapping and the like. By their very nature, most of these programs were of local origin, but by the 1928–29 season, the three networks were offering expensively produced, and sometimes even sponsored, programs for a feminine audience. The NBC Red Network had "The National Home Hour" with Betty Crocker, the "Radio Household Institute" and "Teeth, Health and Happiness." The Blue Network had a daily cooking talk by Mrs. Julian Heath, "The Forecast School of Cookery," "The Farm and Home Hour" and a health talk program with Dr. Royal S. Copeland. CBS had the Ida Bailey Allen homemaker's program, and "Tomorrow's Baby" with Mary Norris. There was little variety in morning programming, with sometimes an attempt to blend advice-giving formats with light music. There was "The Jewel Tea Program," featuring recipes and household talks with interludes of music; there was "The Florida Citrus Music Program"; and seemingly a goodly number of programs that spread the music and patter formulas of evening fame to the daytime hours: "Jolly Bill and Jane," "The Parnassus Trio," and "Rastus and His Musical Menagerie."

Women's daytime radio had its personalities, not all of them female. One such was Eugene Field, perhaps the most successful morning radio personality of the after-breakfast time slot. Field, known as "Cheerio," was heard in New York at 8:30 A.M., capturing the "second-cup-of-coffee" housewife looking for a few moments to relax after the kids had gotten off to school. In roughly the same time period that was later to be commandeered in radio by Don MacNeill and his "Breakfast Club," and in the television era by the phenomenally popular Phil Donahue, Cheerio offered a blend of oleaginous advice and soothing music. Mimicking the style of Tony Wons, but with less conscious effort to make feminine hearts flutter — for it was not the hour for fluttering hearts — Cheerio read letters from his listeners and freely offered advice, with backdrop music supplied by an organ and the sound of singing canaries. NBC listed the program as "inspirational talk." Whatever the classification, Cheerio offered the most popular program of this time slot in the late twenties.

One major form of women's daytime programming that didn't see its birth in the 1920s was the serial drama, later contemptuously referred to as the soap opera. The soap opera burst suddenly on the scene in 1932, with programs like "Ma Perkins," "Myrt and Marge" and "The Romance of Helen Trent" beginning their long and successful runs at that time. There was very little network programming for women during the afternoon hours in the late twenties, most of the time slots reverting to local stations, where, doubtless, tea recitals and amateur sopranos continued to dominate these sluggish hours. Nonetheless, spadework was being done for the daytime serial during the evening hours, with a number of light love interest dramas making their debuts in the late twenties.

And the soap opera had other roots in the 1920s as well. Jim and Marion Jordan, later known to radio lovers everywhere as "Fibber McGee and Molly," claim to have originated the soap opera in a series called "The Smith Family," which made its debut over WJBO in Chicago in 1926. The Jordans, who were natives of Peoria, Illinois, got off to a slow start in vaudeville shortly after World War I (the couple were married in 1918), then moved into radio in 1925 doing singing commercials. They began airing their little domestic drama the following year. Actually "The Smith Family" was not like the soap operas of the next decade. It was not the lugubrious mixture of sex, misfortune and domestic crisis accompanied by solemn organ music that became standard fare in the thirties. But in another way "The Smith Family" was the forerunner of the classic soaps. It was a drama—albeit lightly and humorously treated—of small-town American life, a saga of unspectacular domesticity. If there was misfortune and mischance on "The Smith Family," it was clearly of the comic variety.

There were other natural forerunners of the soap opera in the late twenties, but they were not afternoon programs, and they, too, tended to be redeemed by a lighter touch, with only an occasional tincture of misfortune and unhappiness. These were the evening romantic dramas, of which there were a fair number on network radio by 1928–29. Among the programs of this sort going out over the networks by 1929 were "Famous Loves," "True Romances," "Polly Preston's Adventures," "Soconyland Sketches" and "True Story Hour."

Most of these women's dramas were evanescent and of low quality, but a few made a strong claim to substance and merit, and some became enormously popular as well. One such was "The Rise of the Goldbergs," which made its debut over NBC on November 20, 1929. It was a program somewhat hard to define by the standards of the late twenties, and perhaps even harder by the standards of later years. Written with considerable warmth and humor by the show's creator and star, Gertrude Berg, "The Rise of the Goldbergs" (the name was later shortened to "The Goldbergs") was sometimes likened to the "Amos 'n' Andy" series as a comic rendering of minority life. But without many overt gag lines, and with stories based on nuances of character, "The Goldbergs" could just as easily have been seen as serious domestic drama.

The show had its problems, though, and they were not due to the strangeness of the Yiddish dialect that must have been just as comical to mainstream American audiences as the Negro voice caricatures of "Amos 'n' Andy." In 1929 the classifications of program types had not yet hardened, and "The Goldbergs" was a once-a-week, 15-minute family comedy. On the other hand, since the humor was much more subdued than found in what we now call "situation comedy," broadcasters didn't quite know what to do with it. By 1934–35 the program was off the air on prime time. In 1935–36 it was back as daytime soap opera, but that categorization didn't really fit either since "The Goldbergs" never stooped to the usual soap opera staples: sex, misery, the other woman and implausible domestic misfortune. The program was a very normal domestic serial, ethnically colored to be sure (which supplied a touch of humor), but clearly put together with deft material that was worthy of prime-time display. The demotion of "The Goldbergs" to the ranks of the soaps was a misfortune,[4] but it was misfortune suffered by other shows which took to the air in the early thirties, like "Myrt and Marge" and "Vic and Sade." The latter program, written by Paul Rhymer, displayed literary merit, as did many of the programs that had their start at that time. Indeed, poet Edgar Lee Masters is said to have expressed the opinion that "Vic and Sade" presented the best American humor of its day. Nonetheless, this program also eventually joined the ranks of women's daytime drama.

So the soap opera of afternoon fame had its beginnings in a small core of somewhat more respectable and meritorious evening dramas for women, most of which passed away during the early 1930s. However, whatever bad can be said about the profusion of soaps that took to the air in 1932–33, there is no doubt that they achieved something that was probably undreamed of when network broadcasting began in the mid-twenties: They neatly filled up those long and abysmally slow afternoon hours.

Another kind of daytime audience which began to receive strong attention in the late twenties was the growing number of young listeners. Programs for children were not exactly new, since pioneer stations like KDKA and WJZ offered occasional "children's hours" or "bedtime stories" in the early twenties. But, as with women's programming, the number and quality of the programs increased at the end of the decade. For obvious reasons, most of the children's programs went on the air in the late afternoon and early evening, the hours when children were home from school.

Most of the children's programs of the late twenties were geared to the younger child, perhaps in the first few years of school. The boys' adventure stories of the "Jack Armstrong" variety were still a few years off and would not begin thrilling the nation's youngsters until 1932. The parade of children's programs began with shows like "Let's Pretend" (originally called "The Adventures of Helen and Mary"), and "The Singing Story Lady" with Ireen Wicker. Wicker, who changed the spelling of her name from Irene to Ireen because an astrologer told her that it would bring her good luck, certainly found luck on the radio, since her program continued for many years during the medium's golden age. Hers was one of the enchanting voices of radio both as singer and storyteller, a quality of sound seldom duplicated in the post-radio years.

Another great folk hero of radio made his appearance in the late twenties, and this was Don Carney, familiarly known as "Uncle Don." The "Uncle Don" show made its debut on WOR in New York in September 1928. Except for one brief year (1938–39) it was never a network radio show, but for many years during the thirties and forties it was said to enjoy the largest listening audience in the New York metropolitan area, with millions of youngsters addicted to the program. "Uncle Don" was heard from 6:00 to 6:30 P.M., and the program continued in that same time slot for nearly 21 years, its style and content varying hardly a jot during all that time.

"Uncle Don" was a mixture of original stories and songs, advice, personal messages, birthday announcements and other features with direct personal appeal. Uncle Don, a spellbinder if there ever was one, played the piano and sang his own concoctions, such as "Hello nephews, nieces, mine," sung to the tune of "My Caroline." He followed this up with a little nonsense verse which nearly all his listeners knew by heart:

> "Hibbidy gits, has hah,
> Rainbow, ree, Sibonia
> Skividee, hi-lo-dee,
> Horney-ka-dote, with an alikazon,
> Sing this song with your Uncle Don."

Uncle Don proceeded to tell stories about typical good little boys and girls such as Susan Beduzen and Willipus Wallipus, or about naughty children (and these seem to have existed in profusion) such as Slackerminds, Talkabouts, Meanwells and Stuckups. A much-loved feature of the program came when individual listeners were named over the air, usually because Uncle Don had been clued in by a parent on the occasion of a birthday or some other special event. Being informed in advance, Uncle Don would be able to say that if little Johnny Jones of Scarsdale would look behind the sofa or in the closet he would find something special hidden there. For a while Uncle Don also had a Sunday morning program in which he read the funny papers over the air, another of his many practices later picked up by other hosts of children's programs.[5]

The idea of the children's program spread around the country, with numerous "uncles" and "aunts" taking to the airwaves. But there were many variants of the formula, some finding their own distinctive techniques for reaching the hearts of the young. In Chicago at the Sears station, WLS, there were the "Lullaby Twins," Ford Rush and Glenn Rowell. The two complemented each other nicely; Rowell was short, chubby and cheerful, Rush was taller and more reserved, with a pleasing baritone voice and at least some of Uncle Don's magic. The "Lullaby Twins" were innovative, and the show's format was changed from time to time. One of the early projects was a make-believe "Woodshed Theatre" in which selected children (called "actots") put on their own plays. Listeners — mostly children of course — could get "reserved seats" by mailing two pins to WLS. Thousands of pins arrived, doubtless more than Sears, Roebuck & Company knew what to do with.

By the late 1920s then, radio broadcasting was beginning to assume the form that it would take for the next several decades. Slowly but inexorably the broadcast day was filled up with specialized programming: women's daytime programs, children's programs, early morning wake-up programs, sleepytime programs, and many other staples known to the listening masses of the next generation. Nonetheless, some kinds of programming that later became shining stars in the firmament of radio were still almost nonexistent in the late twenties.

News was still a deficient area in late twenties radio. Very few regularly scheduled news programs appear on the logs of the major networks in 1930, making it clear that neither NBC nor CBS had any strong commitment to news programming at that late date. At a time when the networks had already spent millions on musical programming, building up music departments and libraries, there was no such thing as a "news department," a news staff, or even a newsroom. There was no such thing as nightly news, five nights a week, although the program logs of the period show occasional news commentators doing news analysis one or two days a week. In the fall of 1929 H.V. Kaltenborn was delivering a news commentary on CBS at 6:30 on Monday evening, and Lowell Thomas would shortly appear with his nightly show; not until 1932, however, did any kind of decisive and permanent trend appear in this direction.

A listener from the next generation sampling the wares of late twenties radio would have found the biggest deficiency of the period to be in the evening prime time. Classical and light classical music programming still dominated the evening hours in 1930; the great mainstays of prime-time radio were still around the corner. The great comedy shows and their stars—men like Ed Wynn, Fred Allen and Jack Benny—were a few years in the future. The situation comedy had been born, of course, but the number of offerings was trivial. So, too, with the many thriller and detective stories that would crowd the airwaves during evening hours in the next decade. Meagre attempts had been made at prestigious and informative drama on the radio, but all of them were sporadic and irregular before 1930. The great days of a distinctive dramatic imagination as applied to the radio medium were as yet undreamed of; the talents of men like Norman Corwin, Orson Welles and Arch Oboler had not yet taken fire.

But great changes were in the offing as the twenties came to an end. Advertisers were very quickly discovering the riches of the new medium, and the sales genius of some network executives like William Paley at CBS were finding ways to wed this toothpaste or that cigarette to this or that bright new talent.

Then as the depression deepened, and as the vaudeville theatres fell dark, radio received a windfall of stars now ready to give their all for the medium of radio. Many of these would have been scoffers a few years previously, or would, at the very least, have regarded radio as a decidedly inferior form of entertainment. By 1932 Ed Wynn, sponsored by Texaco, was on the air as the "Fire Chief," broadcast before a live audience, and the true era of radio comedy began. Sponsors like Lucky Strike, Maxwell House, Chesterfield and Chevrolet opened up their purses as stars began falling from the vaudeville tree and into the waiting arms of radio. There were Eddie Cantor, Jack Pearl, Al Jolson, Fred Allen, Jack Benny, Burns and Allen, the Marx Brothers, Col. Stoopnagle, Howard and Shelton. The lively years of radio entertainment were about to begin.

Prime-time radio of the late twenties was thin in comparison to the mounting excitement of the 1930s. The old song and patter teams prevailed, and the variety programs like "Collier's Hour" and "The Eveready Hour" were stodgily rooted in the cradle of early radio. Still, by 1929 it was clear that those working in the business were entering the ground floor of a vast new entertainment industry. It was all just a matter of finding a show or two that would break things wide open. The advertisers were eager, the studio executives open to every suggestion. The medium was there; all that was needed now was to find a way to reach the millions with a big hit.

Curiously, the hit show that would transform radio into the leader of the entertainment industry was not the devising of Madison Avenue. It was not the skillfully planned work of radio men in the executive suite. Indeed, it did not even arise from the centers of network power in New York. Rather, radio broadcasting skyrocketed to national prominence on the basis of an accidentally discovered comedy skit called "Amos 'n' Andy," which began inauspiciously in Chicago and then, with incredible swiftness, wormed its way into the national consciousness and into the hearts of Americans everywhere.

15. *"Amos 'n' Andy"*

"Amos 'n' Andy," a fifteen-minute comedy show which went on the air over Chicago's WMAQ in 1928, would alter the face of radio forever. No longer would there be doubts that radio entertainment was really a commercial success and not just a fad of the 1920s; no longer would the minions of Madison Avenue have to wait and see. Now even the once-contemptuous movie moguls of Hollywood would believe that the home entertainment medium of radio could be a deadly competitor for mass audiences and for performing talent. And as far as the American people were concerned, there was now a persuasive reason why it was simply impossible to get along without owning a radio set or sets.

It would probably not be an exaggeration to say that during the height of its popularity in the early thirties, "Amos 'n' Andy" was so phenomenally successful that its total command of the airwaves would never be duplicated in the entire history of broadcasting—radio or television. It is believed that in the years of 1931 and 1932, "Amos 'n' Andy" reached as many as 40 million listeners; fully one-third of the population of the country tuned in on the program.

It is said that President Coolidge insisted that all activities at the White House come to a stop while "Amos 'n' Andy" was on the air. The telephone company claimed that calls declined sharply during the fifteen minutes the show was on the air (from 1930 to 1932, this was between 7 and 7:15 P.M.). In the summer months, almost anyone strolling down the streets of innumerable American towns could hear the sounds of the program wafting from window after window as he ambled along, and it might have been possible for this pedestrian to listen to the entire episode without going indoors.

Everywhere things ground to a halt at 7 o'clock. Drugstore proprietors refused to wait on customers while the program was in progress. Motion picture theatres installed radio loudspeakers in their lobbies, and sometimes stopped whatever picture was being shown so that their audiences could listen to the fifteen-minute show. Of course most Americans listened while eating dinner; thus the show became a favored social event around the dinner table.

"Amos 'n' Andy" was the brainchild of two men who had been in radio since 1925, Freeman F. Gosden and Charles J. Correll. Gosden and Correll conceived the show, wrote the scripts and acted all the parts—not only the title roles of Amos and Andy, but the secondary roles as well. It was an amazing *tour de force*, unparalleled anywhere in the annals of broadcasting history, and one which surely would have been impossible in the radio of the next generation. "Amos 'n' Andy" was a Negro dialect show, based on the lives of two naive Negroes living in the black community of the South Side of Chicago, cut off from their roots in the rural South, lost and perpetually confused in a complex world beyond their understanding. Their feeble attempts to come to grips with the buzzing and blooming confusion of city life were the root of the show's comedy and provided endless opportunities for new script ideas.

Gosden and Correll had gotten their start in radio as a harmony team but shortly drifted into a comedy dialect routine, which they had been working on in one form or another ever since becoming friends and collaborators in 1919. Dialect and blackface routines had been popular in vaudeville and were featured by various production companies that toured the country. Some of them were exceptionally good. Gosden and Correll were gifted comedians who fell into this kind of routine with gusto and freewheeling abandon.

Of the two, only Gosden — a Southerner born and bred — possessed an intimate acquaintance with Negro speech patterns. But Correll, who had grown up in Illinois, had travelled extensively in the South, and soon fell easily into the dialect voices which the two actors had used in many routines since the beginning of their partnership.

Freeman F. Gosden was born in Richmond, Virginia, in 1899. A genial extrovert, he was on the stage almost as soon as he could walk; at the age of ten he had entered a diving contest in Annette Kellerman's diving and swimming show. From earliest childhood he had enjoyed doing imitations of people he knew, and he took delight in all forms of mimicry. Growing up in Richmond, Gosden was raised by a black nurse. The Gosden household also harbored a Negro boy named Snowball, and in later years Gosden admitted that his close friendship with Snowball gave him much of the material and inspiration for the characters of Amos and Andy. By the time he was a teenager, Gosden became an expert at Negro dialect stories, and he learned to play the banjo, which made him adept at any kind of Southern-atmosphere routine. During World War I he was a navy radio operator, and after his release he worked for a time selling automobiles and later as a salesman for the American Tobacco Company. The call of the stage was irresistible, however, and in 1919 he got a job with the Joseph Bren Producing Company, which staged amateur talent shows for clubs, schools, fraternal organizations and church groups. It was while working for the Bren organization that Gosden met his future partner, Charles Correll.

Correll had been born in Peoria, Illinois, in 1890, and thus was the older of the two. Like Gosden, he had been drawn to show business since his earliest boyhood. In the basement of his home in Peoria, he and a friend staged plays and charged the kids in the neighborhood five pins for admission. When the circus came to town he sold lemonade, and he worked as an usher in a local theatre. Correll's father was a stonemason and hoped to teach the trade to young Charlie, but nothing pulled the lad in that direction. He studied the piano and for a while worked in silent movie houses as the improvising piano player; on the side he made use of every opportunity to learn all about show business, from singing to dancing.

In 1918 Correll got a job working for the Bren Producing Company and shortly was promoted to stage director, assigned to touring throughout the South putting on productions, hiring local talent, arranging for costumes, music and scenery. It was in August of 1919, while directing a home talent show for the Elks Club in Durham, North Carolina, that Correll met his future partner, Freeman Gosden. The two took to each other immediately and formed a friendship that was to last until Correll's death in 1972.

For a number of years, Gosden and Correll worked both together and apart as producers for the Bren Company, mostly following circuits in the South. They got together frequently for larger productions, Gosden rehearsing the performers and sometimes acting as the end man in a minstrel show, Correll acting as stage manager—in charge of costumes, scenery, playing the piano, or conducting the orchestra if there was one.

In 1925 the pair was assigned to the Bren Company's home office in Chicago as executives. Correll managed the firm's show division; Gosden, the circus department. At this time, the two were sharing an apartment, and they spent endless hours discussing what kind of show business acts they could invent for themselves. They sang harmony songs in their apartment, with Correll playing the piano and Gosden the ukulele.

Around this time Chicago was becoming a beehive of radio activity, and the rapidly growing stations were desperate for performers. A friend suggested that the two give radio a try, and they did a program at WQGA.[1] This program turned out to be a lot of fun because they just did the kinds of singing that they were doing in the evening around their apartment. Later they were offered a spot at station WEBH, which then had a small studio in the Edgewater Beach Hotel. They didn't get paid, but they were offered a free Blue Plate Special at the hotel's dining room. Technically they were supposed to do a late evening show six nights a week, but they got so involved with radio and with WEBH that shortly they were doing announcing and other chores. In spite of their quickly growing popularity, they kept their daytime jobs with the Bren Company, suspecting—like so many others—that radio was just a flash in the pan.

After a few months at WEBH the two were offered a job at the ambitious station WGN, drawing the magnificent sum of $250.00 a week. Here they continued a nightly harmony routine—a mixture of lively song and chatter, very similar to that which prevailed in radio at the time. But Gosden and Correll, with their vast experience, were a bit better than most amateurs being coaxed into radio for free, and they soon had a considerable following. They finally decided to leave their jobs with the Bren Company so as to devote themselves full time to radio.

Still, there were so many harmony teams in radio that WGN suggested that Gosden and Correll come up with some new kind of radio show. Henry Selinger, the station manager, keeping in mind that his station was owned by the Midwestern newspaper giant the *Chicago Tribune* ("the world's greatest newspaper"—thus the call letters, WGN), asked the pair if they would be interested in doing an adaptation of a popular family comic strip, "The Gumps." "The Gumps" was being serialized by the *Tribune* and was a big moneymaker. Gosden and Correll liked the idea of dramatizing a comic strip, but they had never played parts similar to the main characters in the strip. Also, being bachelors, they didn't think that they would be good at writing material for a family-type situation comedy, so they declined the suggestion.

The challenge was there, however, and shortly afterward they proposed a different kind of program to the station—a program using characters with which they were much more familiar. It was a program built around the lives of two black men, Sam and Henry, who had left the South and moved to Chicago in search of work. The idea would be a topical one for Chicago in the mid-twenties, since, in the wake of World War I, a great many Negroes had moved to Chicago from the deep South, most of them living in run-down neighborhoods just south of the Loop.

In spite of the fact that blackface routines were then very common in vaudeville, WGN management didn't immediately take to the idea; they were hoping to develop a skit that would promote one of the *Tribune*'s already existing comic strips. Finally, though, they agreed to give the show a try, and "Sam 'n' Henry" went on the air on January 12, 1926. The date is an important one historically, since this was to be the first serialized situation comedy on radio. Sam and Henry were characters very much like Amos and Andy would later be; the locale was changed somewhat when the program moved to another station two years later, but the humor and underlying philosophy were similar on both shows.

"Sam 'n' Henry" was not an immediate hit, and after a few weeks Gosden and Correll were starting to think of something else. But the program manager asked them to stick it out a little longer, and ever so slowly, a regular audience started to build. The program's continuous story line began to attract listeners anxious to find out how Sam and Henry would get out of their latest scrape, and what kind of trouble they would get into next. The show aired at 10:10 P.M. six nights a week, with Bill Hay, WGN's easygoing sales manager, acting as the show's announcer. Hay opened the show with the words "10:10, WGN, 'Sam 'n' Henry.'" The little skits that followed were all written and acted by Gosden and Correll.

"Sam 'n' Henry" continued on WGN until the end of 1927 for a total of 586 episodes. By this time the program had won a large following in the Chicago area, and Gosden and Correll were receiving requests to record the program for other stations around the country. WGN, however, was not anxious to give the program up for syndication, and the two performers waited for their contract to run out at the end of the second year, at which time they signed with station WMAQ, owned by the *Chicago Daily News*. Eager to get the program, WMAQ was willing to accept the idea that it be sold to other stations outside Chicago.

When Gosden and Correll moved over to WMAQ they could no longer use the title "Sam 'n' Henry" because that title was owned by the *Chicago*

Tribune. The *Tribune* had no intention of giving it up to a station owned by its rival, the *Daily News*, so a new title had to be found. At first Gosden and Correll thought of using Jim and Charlie, but by the time the new program went on the air on March 19, 1928, the names had been changed to Amos and Andy. Right from the start the program was sent to a number of other stations outside Chicago, all desperately looking for fresh program material to spice up their broadcast day.

The syndication was achieved by means of two standard 12-inch 78-r.p.m. phonograph records (this was before 16-inch 33-r.p.m. discs made this kind of transmission a simple affair). The two discs for the show made five-minute segments, around which the local announcer read an opening, commercials and a sign-off. Gosden and Correll called the system their "chainless chain," but it was, nonetheless, the first syndicated program in radio.

By the summer of 1929 the program was becoming popular wherever it was heard, and executives at NBC were anxious to get into the act. Rather than compete with Gosden and Correll's own syndicate, the fledgling network offered the team a lucrative contract to go out over the entire NBC network in the summer of 1929. The program was first heard nationwide over the NBC Blue Network beginning August 19, 1929. The "Amos 'n' Andy" national craze was now only a few months away.

Basically the characters of Amos and Andy were quite similar to Sam and Henry, although there were a few obvious differences. Amos Jones and Andrew H. Brown hailed from Atlanta, Georgia, instead of Birmingham, Alabama, but had also left the South to seek their fortunes in Chicago. Amos and Andy, like Sam and Henry, found themselves lost in an urban maelstrom not of their own making, and usually beyond their comprehension. Shortly after arriving in the city, they acquired a broken-down automobile with no top, which they believed made them businessmen. They established the "Fresh Air Taxicab Company of America Incorpolated."

In an early book dealing with the series, Correll and Gosdc.. gave an explanation of the two characters, whose personalities differed from one another, yet dovetailed so marvelously:

Amos: Trusting, simple, unsophisticated. High and hesitating in voice. It's "Ain't dat sumpin?" when he's happy or surprised and "Awa, awa, awa," in the frequent moments when he is frightened or embarrassed.... Andy gives him credit for no brains but he's a hard earnest worker and has a way of coming across with a real idea when ideas are most needed. He looks up to and depends on—

Andy: Domineering, a bit lazy, inclined to take credit for all of Amos's ideas and efforts. He's always "workin on the books," or "restin his brain," upon which, according to Andy all of the boys' joint enterprises depend. He'll browbeat Amos, pick on him, but let anyone else pick on the little one—then look out.[2]

In addition to the interaction of these confused but lovable characters, and their vain attempts to eke out a living, much of the action in the early episodes of the show revolved around a South Side rooming house, and another character called the Kingfish, who claimed to preside over a brotherhood called the Mystic Knights of the Sea. The Kingfish was such a dominant character that in later years one may have had occasion to wonder why the show was not called "Amos, Andy and the Kingfish." The Kingfish (George Stevens was his real name) was played by Freeman Gosden. Indeed, all of the parts in the early days were played by the two actor-writers, even the women. (Actually there were only one or two women in the story, and their appearances were usually kept to a minimum at the distant end of a telephone line.)

In 1928, when the program began, the WMAQ studios were located in the Merchandise Mart in Chicago, and the show was broadcast from there. Shortly after, when the show began airing over the entire NBC network, the broadcast time was changed to 7 P.M. by popular demand, and it remained in that time slot for a number of years. Gosden and Correll had an office in the Palmolive Building (now Playboy Building) in Chicago, where they wrote every word of the script. This was no mean feat at a time when there were six fifteen-minute shows a week. Usually the show for that day was written the same morning or afternoon, often requiring three hours of work. There was no rehearsal, because the writers thought that rehearsing would kill the spontaneity of the dialogue. On the other hand, every word of the show was scripted; there was no ad-libbing. "We read every word we ever said," Correll later admitted. But there was a lot of discussion and much give-and-take in the scripting sessions.

The studio in the Merchandise Mart was furnished like a living room, with a fireplace and overstuffed chairs. No one was allowed in the studio to distract the actors (in any case, in 1929, the "live" audience was unheard of in radio studios). The actors sat across from one another, and read from the scripts, but avoided looking at each other for fear that they might break out laughing while delivering the lines. They would adjust their position with reference to the microphone depending on what character they were doing. When Correll was impersonating Andy, he spoke in a low voice about one inch from the microphone. In impersonating Amos, who had a high-pitched voice, Gosden sat about two feet from the microphone. To do other characters the actors used different tones and different locutions and locations. Gosden did two of the show's most important secondary characters, the Kingfish and Lightning. Correll played Henry van Porter, Brother Crawford, and most of the white characters when called for. There were no sound effects men in those days, so the actors produced those also, although they were usually kept to a minimum. But both men were capable of making animal sounds, and would come to the studio prepared to reproduce the sound of breaking glass, objects being dropped, etc.

The humor of "Amos 'n' Andy" was based on character. The fact that the principals of the skit were black was somewhat incidental. It happens that the black parts fitted the talents and backgrounds of Gosden and Correll, but a similar show might have been built around any characters set down in an

Charles J. Correll (left) and Freeman H. Gosden — "Amos 'n' Andy." Their program, more than any other, put radio into competition as a national entertainment medium. No program, before or since, captured the commanding "audience share" enjoyed by "Amos 'n' Andy" at the height of its popularity in the early 1930s. (Photo courtesy of NBC.)

environment beyond their comprehension. Similar comedy could have been developed out of Irish or Polish immigrants in New York, or about country bumpkins coming to the big city anywhere for the first time. In the days of its greatest popularity there was only the smallest complaint that the show was built around stereotyped Negro characters. Gosden and Correll kept "Amos 'n' Andy" on the radio until 1960, and at no time during the show's long run was there strong opposition to the show's racial portraiture. There was slightly stronger opposition to the television version of the show beginning in the early fifties, featuring an all-black cast.

"Amos 'n' Andy" seems to have appealed to all kinds and classes of people, rich and poor, simple and educated. Most black listeners seem to have been every bit as amused by the show as the whites. This was probably partly due to the fact that all of the central characters were human, likeable and sympathetically rendered. If the writers were using them for evoking laughter, they were making fun *with* them, not *of* them. Gosden and Correll loved the characters they had created, and sometimes when playing the parts they would find themselves weeping. Gosden, whose lot was to play the simple, loveable

Amos, once remarked that "I feel so sorry for that poor ignorant fellow." Doubtless the masses who enjoyed the daily misfortunes of Amos and Andy did so because they saw something of themselves in the characters, something of the universal human condition. They perceived the poignant and tender as well as the comic.

To be sure, a great deal of the humor was provided by the use of Negro dialect and outrageous distortions of the language. Dialect humor was popular and widespread in 1930, and there was little if any objection to it in radio days; indeed, ethnic accents and speech oddities were extremely common in radio broadcasting down to 1950. Gosden and Correll raised their dialect treatment to a high art: Not only did they render the slurred speech of the Southern Negro, but they used the characters' lack of education as an opportunity for all kinds of word play—malapropisms, spoonerisms, mispronunciations of common words and phrases. The character of Andy was supposed to be more intelligent and sophisticated than Amos and some of the other regulars, and he accordingly tried to swamp his inferiors with big words and impressive-sounding locutions. Yet he was only a jot better informed than the others, and mostly intimidated them by bluster and a bossy, boastful manner. Shortly after the stock market crash in 1929, Andy took pains to explain the "repression" to Lightnin':

Andy: Well, Lightnin', 'course I would like to give you a job but de bizness repression is on right now.

Lightnin':   Whut is dat you say, Mr. Andy?

Andy: Is you been keepin' yo' eye on de stock market?

Lightnin':   Nosah, I ain't never seed it.

Andy: Well, de stock market crashed.

Lightnin':   Anybody git hurt?

Andy: Well, 'course Lightnin', when de stock market crashes, it hurts us bizness men. Dat's what puts de repression on things.

A whole lexicon of new words could have been made up from the "Amos 'n' Andy" program, and many of these coinages entered the language and became part of everyday American usage. There were phrases like "I'se regusted," "Ain't dat sumpin," "Holy Mackerel" (Kingfish's favorite expression swept the country and remains part of the language today), "Ow, wah! Ow, wah!" "Check and double check." Sometimes words and names of individuals were mispronounced in ways that probably would not have been found in the speech of even the most poorly educated Negro: "incorpolated," "J. Ping Pong Morgan," "Charles Limburger" (for J. Pierpont Morgan and Charles Lindbergh); in other cases Gosden and Correll used ever-so-slight mispronunciations for comic effect: sitchiation, sumpin, etc. The rendering of these pronunciations was so flawless and consistent that many listeners believed that the actors were Negroes speaking their own natural dialect.

"Amos 'n' Andy" remained a popular radio program for three decades.[3] But in its heyday, "Amos 'n' Andy" was a national craze the likes of which we have not seen since. The program revolutionized radio comedy; more importantly, it gave birth to commercial broadcasting as we know it today. In the early days of network broadcasting, lining up sponsors for radio shows was a painful and mostly unrewarding labor. While "Amos 'n' Andy" was still being enjoyed in the Chicago area during 1929, executives of the Lord and Thomas Advertising Agency convinced one of their accounts, the makers of Pepsodent toothpaste, that they would do well to sponsor "Amos 'n' Andy" on a nationwide hookup. When the program took to the NBC Blue in the summer of 1929, it was sponsored by Pepsodent. Almost immediately the toothpaste manufacturer began noticing dramatic increases in its sales.

This development was not lost on other potential sponsors. By 1930, sponsors descended on the networks like a plague of locusts, whereas only a year before hardly a one could be found willing to put hard money on the line. Whereas advertisers were formerly not sure that people listened to the radio, the phenomenal success of "Amos 'n' Andy," and the meteoric rise in Pepsodent sales, made everybody with anything to sell anxious to have a popular radio show of his own. By 1930, NBC began charging sponsors $3,350 an hour for prime time on the Blue Network, and $4,980 an hour for prime time on the Red Network. All of the networks, even the struggling infant, CBS, were suddenly rocketed into the big time.

As the dark clouds of the depression settled during the early thirties, radio in all commercial aspects was rapidly providing a financial bonanza, and a great deal of this success can be attributed to the almost incredible popularity of "Amos 'n' Andy." The "Amos 'n' Andy" fad drove thousands of listeners out to buy radio sets—people who otherwise would not have seen the need to have a radio of their own. The great dream that prompted Westinghouse to open a commercial broadcasting station back in 1920—the possibility of selling millions of radio receivers to a vast public—suddenly became a reality.

Too, with the depression era in full swing, masses of people lacked the money to go out for dinner or to a nightclub. Staying home became an obligatory form of relaxation, but one that could now be made enjoyable by the purchase of an inexpensive radio. And in the "Amos 'n' Andy" era radios did become markedly cheaper, easily within the reach of everybody's budget. In 1930 most of the radios sold were large console models, but the depression spurred the manufacture and sale of low-priced table models. By 1933, nearly 75 percent of the radios on sale were cheaper table models. For example, in 1933 RCA was selling its popular Cathedral Set at $19.95 (so called because the receiver's design resembled a small cathedral). Around this same time General Electric was selling its own compact model radio—AC-DC Model K-40—for $17.95. The International Radio Corporation of Ann Arbor, Michigan, was making a pocket-sized radio called the Kadette Jr. for sale at only $12.50.

While "Amos 'n' Andy" can't be credited with singlehandedly building radio in the late twenties and early thirties, it would be hard to find any more powerful single influence in those years. It was a time of adversity for all, and these two struggling urban Negroes symbolized the nation's plight and perhaps even did something to relieve it. Somehow the program represented to millions the spit in the eye that laughter gives to adversity, the kick in the pants that common sense gives to all stuffy idealisms. "Amos 'n' Andy" was a skillfully written and acted situation comedy that could continue to be the envy of radio and television writers in a slicker and more sophisticated age. The appeal of the series, both as human drama and as comedy, was universal and profound. After his visit to the United States in the early thirties, the celebrated British master of comic drama George Bernard Shaw was asked what he found most memorable about the new world. He responded, "There are three things which I shall never forget about America—the Rocky Mountains, Niagara Falls, and 'Amos 'n' Andy.'"

16. Radio Reprise

By the early 1930s there could be no doubt, if there had been any before, that radio was a glittering star in the firmament of the American entertainment industry, now offering an outright challenge to the moguls of Hollywood. As the legitimate stage was cruelly diminished by the sagging economy of the depression years, and as vaudeville stages fell dark, radio became a great haven for every kind of performing talent. Comedians like Fred Allen and Jack Benny would forsake vaudeville by 1932 and would begin their long but eventually successful quest to find a unique style of radio entertainment — a style that had roots in the older forms of comedy but shortly would be recognized as a distinctly new form of popular art.

The depression was the making of radio in more ways than one. Smaller incomes, recession, deflation, meant that more Americans had to watch their pocketbooks and spend more evenings at home before the fireplace. Now they would sit before the radio. So now at last it happened that a very high percentage of Americans, even in remote areas, owned one or more radio sets. The price of sets plummeted, with small table models quickly replacing massive living room consoles as the high-demand items. By 1932, all of the major manufacturers were making these small and inexpensive models that were financially within nearly everyone's reach. These little boxes became not only household utilities, as David Sarnoff had once dreamed they would; they became a solace and comfort in the nation's darkest hour.

Of course as radio rapidly became a mass medium on a grand scale, it attracted its fair share of scoffers and detractors. There would be those who would see the quality of programming falling — surrendering to the baser goals of commercialism. There would be those who would say that the original ideals of broadcasting had been lost in a morass of trivial entertainment aimed at the lowest common denominator. Some would complain that the government-owned stations of Europe were able to hold their heads high while American radio sank into a quagmire of the cheap and the tawdry. Of course, skepticism of the cultural value of radio was inevitable, and it was hardly new in the history of radio. Even in its first few years many cultural critics were complaining that there was little of value on the air. Perhaps there is even something inherent in all the electronic media that spurs this kind of skepticism. The telephone had its early detractors — those who believed that Mr. Bell's invention would be a national time-waster. Still earlier, Ralph Waldo Emerson had scoffed at the telegraph, observing that it might be a fine thing technically, but expressing doubt that anything of any importance would go out over it:

> The light outspeeding telegraph
> Bears nothing on its beam.

The same thing would be said many times over about radio by those who espoused the gloomy point of view. But for all its weaknesses, radio would have a largely beneficial effect on American life. It provided a great national matrix, a kind of cultural ground, a center of shared harmonies. There was something in the fact that we as a people, inhabiting a vast continent that often seemed to keep us apart, could find in the popular medium of radio some shows and personalities that we could laugh at together, enjoy together. Radio gave us a common point of reference that no other form of entertainment, no print media could hope to do.

If there were complaints that the mammoth radio industry was filling up the broadcast day with trash—inferior drama, soap opera, kiddie boxtop shows—there can also be no refuting the fact that radio would continue to minister to higher cultural needs as well. When the 1920s began, only a small fraction of the American population had ever heard the performance of a symphony orchestra, and had little hope of ever hearing one; yet radio now made it possible to hear such orchestras on a regular basis. By the early 1930s RCA was building its great skyscraper at Rockefeller Center in New York, and this contained among other things the marvelously engineered hall, Studio 8-H, from which would be heard NBC's own orchestra under the baton of the great Arturo Toscanini.

Starting in the early thirties, too, Saturday afternoons would find millions of Americans glued to their radios to hear the weekly broadcast from the stage of the Metropolitan Opera in New York, with the legendary Milton Cross at the microphone. Stations like New York's WQXR were now beginning to experiment with high-fidelity broadcasting, and in 1934 NBC began experimental FM broadcasting which in time would prove a boon to audio transmission of classical music.

By the early 1930s, too, it was clear that radio was to play other major roles in the betterment of the national life. Radio had golden opportunities to be a purveyor of information and public opinion, clearly an essential function in the preservation of any democracy. Radio news became an important part of American culture, especially after the Munich crisis of 1938, a role continued by television news in the years since the eclipse of network radio. Radio had been perceived to be a tool of great political importance ever since the early 1920s, but the 1930s saw the first of our real media presidents—Franklin Delano Roosevelt—who wooed the American public with several distinct radio styles, each of them seemingly models of perfection. Roosevelt employed with equal effectiveness an intimate radio delivery in his fireside chats as well as a traditional platform style of oratory with a silver-throated eloquence that passed through the microphone with exemplary dramatic polish. No one could doubt that forever after, the electric media and not the stump or the city armory would be the true arena of presidential politics.

If radio gave American politics the style and audience that we know today, it did even more for the common speech and for the native idiom. The polished tone and perfect modulation of the American radio announcer have had a great deal to do with the development and preservation of more refined and dignified American speech patterns. Radio could not, and has not, obliterated regional speech patterns—the hillbilly or Brooklyn accent, the sounds of the tidewater country or of the Boston common—but it has given us a standard of excellence and an American sound that suits us as a people: formal but not affected, literate but not stuffy. In the golden age of radio we knew how good American English was supposed to sound because we heard it on the radio, and with all good luck, picked a great deal of it up for our every-day conversation. The art of the spoken word has sadly been somewhat neglected in the television era, but not entirely, since radio came first and led the way to euphonious vocal sounds.

When television began to take over the vast network audiences in the early 1950s and radio was firmly but gently eased aside, it was believed by many that radio might well die, or at the very least be relegated to some stagnant backwater. Interestingly that has not happened. Radio has had its ups and downs since the early 1950s, but on the local level it has remained strong, and with the large numbers of channels open to radio broadcasting, radio has been able to enjoy a flexibility and a spontaneity that is denied to television with its ponderous commercial commitments, its costly and limited airtime. After more than 60 years of broadcasting, radio remains very much alive.

Naturally, radio continues to be a strong conveyor of musical programming, and the improvements in FM and high fidelity since World War II have proven that radio is the ideal medium for the transmission of classical music. Commercially, of course, radio continues to thrive as a communicator of all the musical forms—rock and roll, country and western, pop—in all of their manifestations and blendings. With its considerable latitude and flexibility, radio has been much freer than television to experiment with all of the musical forms and to lead and develop all the trends of the day.

And radio continues to have talk! Many people believe that talk makes the world go round, and certainly humans have an insatiable appetite for it. Doubtless this explains the very many radio stations in America which feature talk twenty-four hours a day—sometimes it is called "newstalk" in the trade. Such a format would have once been thought impossible, but in the so-called "post-radio" era, nothing that people like is impossible. With technologies developed in the last few decades many radio stations are also able to involve their audiences in intimate ways through telephone call-in shows, where citizens may express opinions over the air on matters of public import or simply matters of touching human concern.

There are many people who can tolerate the disembodied sound of radio at times of the day when they cannot endure the flashing light of the television screen; thus there are many who will listen religiously to a morning radio wake-up show who would not dream of turning on the television at that hour. Others are kept from loneliness by a tiny portable radio stashed under their pillows — the strains of classical music perhaps, or the chit-chat of the local announcer as he listens at midnight in his darkened studio to some phoned-in elegy on a lost dog or stray cat.

Somehow or other, and obviously in strange ways, not entirely comprehended and even misunderstood by media wizards like Marshall McLuhan, radio continues to harbor great possibilities for human intimacy not claimed by television. One thinks back to the early days of radio when men like Norman Brokenshire and Graham McNamee received thousands of fan letters and cards from people who did not think of them as an entertainment elite, but just as good friends. Maybe there is something about a soothing or charming voice that makes the fellow behind the mike a friend. Whatever the case, radio seems to have its own domain, its own kingdom, and there presently seems to be little likelihood of it being lost in the scheme of things.

Whatever doubts might have been expressed by skeptics back in the 1920s, when radio was new and sounds had to be plucked by the cat's whisker from the fertile night air, radio has grown up to be something big and unexpected and wonderful. It has in fact conferred many more blessings on society than even its most enthusiastic supporters of the early days could have hoped. Radio's charms may have been something of a mystery in the beginning; they may be something of a mystery today; but that they will continue to exercise their spell over us, few can doubt.

Notes

1. KDKA

1. For a more detailed account of Marconi's life and professional career, see Degna Marconi's *My Father Marconi*. Also more recent accounts, *Marconi: Father of Radio*, by David Gunstan, and *Marconi*, by W.B. Jolly.

2. De Forest; *Father of Radio*, p. 238. For a more recent assessment of De Forest's career, see I.E. Levine, *Electronic Pioneer Lee De Forest*, New York: Messner, 1964.

3. *Father of Radio*, pp. 269–71.

4. For a full account of Armstrong's career see Lawrence Lessing's *Man of High Fidelity: Edwin Howard Armstrong*.

5. The name of the corporation was changed to "RCA Corporation" on May 9, 1969. Presumably, with radio now taking a back seat to television, the letters RCA no longer stand for anything!

6. Quoted in Gleason L. Archer, *History of Radio*, p. 112.

7. For an account of the beginnings of KDKA, see Gleason L. Archer, *History of Radio*, pp. 201–4.

2. The Radio Rage

1. Popenoe continued to be manager of WJZ when it moved to New York, and when it was taken over by RCA in 1923. When the National Broadcasting Company was established he became its treasurer, which position he held until his death in 1928.

2. Quoted in Gleason L. Archer, *History of Radio to 1926*, p. 218.

3. Quoted in Erik Barnouw, *A Tower in Babel*, p. 85.

4. AT&T had actually been carrying on broadcasting experiments before 1922. The company had a series of earlier experimental stations: 2XB in the headquarters building on West Street in New York, begun in 1919; 2XF at Cliffwood, New Jersey, and 2XJ at Deal Beach, New Jersey, both broadcasting in 1920. For details, see: William Peck Banning, *Commercial Broadcasting Pioneer: The WEAF Experiment*.

5. The American Telephone and Telegraph Company eventually bowed out of radio broadcasting, selling Station WEAF to the National Broadcasting Company on November 1, 1926. WEAF then became the anchor station of the NBC Red Network, and naturally one of the premier radio stations in the United States.

3. Up from the Crystal Set

1. Banning, *Commercial Broadcasting Pioneer*, pp. 22–25.

2. Consoles were available in the early 1920s, but were not produced in large numbers until widespread use of A-C tube sets in 1927.

3. For details of which, see Gleason L. Archer, *Big Business and Radio*, pp. 229–30.

4. *The Rise of the Radio Announcer*

1. In its experimental stage the station's call letters were WBAY.
2. See Brokenshire's autobiography, *This Is Norman Brokenshire*, 1959.
3. Quoted in H.L. Mencken, *The American Language, Supplement Two*, p. 34.
4. *Ibid.*, p. 35.

5. *A Million Sets Are Sold*

1. A small number of sets were also made for RCA by the Wireless Specialty Apparatus Company.
2. As quoted in Gleason L. Archer, *Big Business and Radio*, p. 16.
3. *Broadcasting, 1939 Yearbook*, p. 11.
4. *The Radio Industry*, p. 254.

6. *The Beckoning Hand of Advertising*

1. Quoted in Gleason L. Archer, *Big Business and Radio*, p. 31.
2. British radio remained essentially a government monopoly until the 1950s, at which time a commercial alternative was permitted.
3. AT&T Press Release, Jan. 26, 1922.

7. *The Wavelength Wars*

1. Quoted in Barnouw, *A Tower in Babel*, p. 180.
2. Frost, *Education's Own Stations*, p. 4.

8. *The Birth of Radio News*

1. There was a third nominating convention in 1924, and it was an important one. The Conference for Political Action nominated Wisconsin Senator Robert M. LaFollette for president. LaFollette put together one of the most successful third party efforts in history, receiving nearly 5 million votes. The conference that nominated him was not covered by the mini-networks.
2. Brokenshire, *This Is Norman Brokenshire*, pp. 48–49.
3. Quoted in Archer, *History of Radio to 1926*, pp. 346–47.
4. Thomas stayed with NBC for sixteen years and then returned to CBS, where he remained until his last broadcast on May 14, 1976.

9. *Sportscasting in the Twenties*

1. Phillips Carlin would eventually give up announcing for management; he later became Program Manager for WEAF and Eastern Program Manager for NBC.

2. For a more extensive account of McNamee's early career as announcer and sportscaster, see his *You're on the Air* (New York: Harper & Bros., 1926).

10. Networks

1. Station KSD had begun operations in June, 1922, and was one of the most powerful in the nation. It was equipped with a Western Electric transmitter and it was said to be the first station in the country to operate on 400 meters.

2. These terms actually went back to 1923, when telephone company long-lines engineers were drawing up layouts for future possible broadcasting lines connecting stations. To distinguish one layout from another, colored lines were drawn; thus there was a red layout, a blue layout, a purple layout, and so on. The names took on a popular and later an official significance at the start of NBC operations in 1926.

3. NBC was owned 50 percent by RCA, 20 percent by Westinghouse and 30 percent by General Electric.

4. Not, however, on the West Coast. NBC now had to go about the task of acquiring a West Coast network of stations.

5. Paley, *As It Happened, A Memoir*, pp. 32–33.

6. CBS kept its headquarters at 485 Madison Avenue for thirty-five years, eventually taking over most of the building. In the mid-1960s they moved to their own modern skyscraper at 51 West 52nd Street.

11. The Educational Stations

1. Probably the first educational station to be licensed for general broadcasting, although this is not absolutely certain, was KFOO at Latter-Day Saints University in Salt Lake City, Utah, which received its license in December, 1921. It was far from the first educational station in operation, however; there were a number of experimental stations in or near college campuses before World War I. As to KFOO, it made serious efforts to broadcast lectures and concerts in 1923 and 1924, and in October 1922 became the first station to broadcast the organ of the Mormon Tabernacle. But the station was closed by the federal government in 1927.

2. Of course commercial stations also gave serious thought to the educational use of radio in the twenties. KDKA made plans for educational programming as early as 1920. Lessons in accounting were broadcast over WJZ in 1923. A series of programs called "The Little Red School House" was broadcast over WLS in Chicago. Using the available commercial stations, New York University became a pioneer in educational broadcasting with its "Air College" as early as 1923. So great were the demands for these services in the New York metropolitan area that NYU actually established a Department of Broadcasting under Professor Henry Cook Hathaway.

3. Barnouw, *A Tower in Babel*, p. 61.

4. This was the typical pattern in the universities during the 1920s when the stations were still considered "experimental." More usually, in the years since, they have been operated as independent units or by Departments of Broadcasting, as opposed to Departments of Electrical Engineering or Physics.

5. Frost, *Education's Own Stations*, p. 472.

6. *Ibid.*, p. 148.

7. *Ibid.*, p. 120.

8. *Ibid.*, p. 3.

12. *Classical Radio Music: The Cultural Windfall*

1. De Forest, *Father of Radio*, p. 225.
2. *Ibid.*, p. 351.
3. Barnouw, *A Tower in Babel*, p. 89.
4. The Victor Talking Machine Company finally got an electric phonograph on the market in time for the Christmas trade in 1925.
5. Howard Barlow was born in Mt. Carmel, Illinois, on the Wabash River, and began his musical career as a choirboy in the local Methodist Church. Later his father bought him a brass trumpet from Sears and Roebuck, which eventually led him to form his own band. He subsequently attended the music school at Columbia University and in 1927 was the music director of the Neighborhood Playhouse in lower Manhattan.

13. *The Sounds of Popular Music*

1. Goldsmith and Lescarboura, *This Thing Called Broadcasting*, pp. 99–100.
2. Barnouw, *A Tower in Babel*, pp. 126–127.
3. Jones and Hare had an eighteen-year career in radio. The team broke up at the time of Ernie Hare's death in 1939. Billy Jones died the following year.
4. In 1928 WLS was sold to *Prairie Farmer*, the great Midwestern farm paper, which naturally was enthusiastic about all kinds of farm programming, including country music.
5. For Vallee's account of his break into radio, see his autobiography, *Let the Chips Fall*.

14. *The Expanding Broadcast Day*

1. See Summers, *A Thirty-Year History of Programs Carried on National Radio Networks in the United States, 1926–1956*.
2. The Gambling program continued in almost the same time slot in New York until Gambling's retirement in 1959. It continued thereafter with Gambling's son, also named John Gambling.
3. Barnouw, *A Tower in Babel*, p. 167.
4. Miraculously, though, "The Goldbergs" weathered the years and later had a successful run on television.
5. For an account of the life and career of "Uncle Don" Carney, see Bill Treadwell's *Head, Heart and Heel*.

15. *"Amos 'n' Andy"*

1. This was not strictly their first appearance on radio. On tour in New Orleans in 1920, the two had sung the popular song "Whispering" over an experimental station.
2. Gosden and Correll, *All About Amos and Andy*, p. 43.
3. Charles Correll died in 1972, and Freeman Gosden died in 1982.

Bibliography

A complete bibliography of radio, even early radio, would require a massive volume, and at the present time such a volume is lacking. The bibliography that follows, however, should be sufficiently complete for the ordinary reader to permit further explorations of the field of radio history. The bibliography consists of six sections: bibliographical sources; books and articles; unpublished material, including oral history collections and dissertations; government publications; periodicals; and broadcast archives. Each of these sections contains a brief note about the problems relevant to researching early radio in this area.

One recurring problem in constructing a bibliography of the early years of commercial broadcasting is that many of the available sources are contained in broader histories of radio or even of mass communication generally. I have attempted to include material that is relevant to early radio, and in a few instances this means including works that have small but pertinent reference to the early days—roughly the decade of the 1920s. On the other hand I have also attempted to exclude works that are almost wholly devoted to broadcasting history after 1930, including television. It has not always been easy to make close distinctions as to the specific relevance of a particular work, but the reader can make a reasonable assumption that the sections below will give him thorough guidance to available materials in the history of early radio.

Bibliographical Sources

There is no really complete bibliography of the history of radio, although the volume by McCavitt below is fairly complete and recent. The general reader may be reasonably content with the bibliographies contained in some of the standard histories of radio and mass communication, especially the works listed below by Barnouw, Czitrom and Lichty and Topping. Those searching the field would also do well to consult the indexes and bibliographical aids of *Journalism Quarterly* and the *Journal of Broadcasting*.

Barcus, F. "Bibliography of Studies of Radio and Television Program Content, 1928–1958." *Journal of Broadcasting*, 4, no. 4, Fall 1960.

Barnouw, Erik. *A History of Broadcasting in the United States*. Vol. 1, *A Tower in Babel: To 1933*. New York: Oxford University Press, 1966.

"Books About Radio." *Radio Broadcast*, September, 1922, pp. 441–2.

Cooper, Isabella. *Bibliography on Educational Broadcasting*. Chicago: University of Chicago Press, 1942.

Czitrom, Daniel J. *Media and the American Mind: From Morse to McLuhan*. Chapel Hill: University of North Carolina Press, 1982.

Journal of Broadcasting. Bibliographies on many topics; lists of theses and dissertations.

Journalism Quarterly. Contains extensive bibliographies of books and periodicals.
Lichty, Lawrence W. *World and International Broadcasting: A Bibliography*. Washington: Association for Professional Broadcasting Education, 1970.
_____, and Malachi C. Topping. *American Broadcasting: A Source Book on the History of Radio and Television*. New York: Hastings House, 1975.
Rose, Oscar. *Radio Broadcasting and Television*. Wilson, 1947.
Shiers, George. *Bibliography of the History of Electronics*. Metuchen, NJ: Scarecrow, 1972.

Books and Articles

The following is an extensive list of books and articles which were either written in the twenties or substantially relate to the development and experience of radio in the early days. It should be noted that in addition to these sources there are also a great many resources of a more ephemeral nature—promotional material, brochures, picture books—which go a long way to give a full and colorful picture of early radio. A great deal of this material is not available in libraries, but is nonetheless of considerable value. (The next section, "Unpublished Material, Oral History Collections, Dissertations" lists a fair number of these items.)

Abbott, Waldo. *Handbook of Broadcasting*. New York: McGraw-Hill, 1941.
"About the Radio Round Table." *Scientific American*, 127, December, 1922, pp. 378–379.
Aitken, Hugh G.J. *Syntony and Spark: The Origins of Radio*. New York: Wiley, 1976.
Allen, Fred. *Treadmill to Oblivion*. Boston: Little, Brown, 1954.
Allen, Frederick Lewis. *The Big Change: America Transforms Itself*. New York: Bantam, 1952.
_____. *Only Yesterday: An Informal History of the 1920s*. New York: Harper & Bros., 1957.
Allport, Gordon W. *The Psychology of Radio*. New York: Harper & Bros., 1935.
American Broadcasting. *An Analytical Study of One Day's Output of 206 Commercial Radio Stations*. Ventura, CA: Ventura Free Press, 1933.
Andrews, Robert Douglas. *Just Plain Bill: His Story*. New York: McKay, 1935.
Archer, Gleason L. *Big Business and Radio*. New York: American Historical Company, 1931.
_____. *History of Radio to 1926*. New York: American Historical Company, 1938.
Armstrong, Edwin H. "The Story of the Super-Heterodyne." *Radio Broadcast*, 1924, pp. 198–207.
Arnold, Frank A. *Broadcast Advertising: The Fourth Dimension*. New York: Wiley, 1931.
Aylesworth, Merlin H. "The Listener Rules Broadcasting." *Nation's Business*, September, 1929.
_____. "Men, Mikes and Money." *Collier's*, April 17–24 and May 1–8, 1948.
Bacher, William A. *The Treasury Star Parade*. New York: Farrar and Rinehart, 1942.
Baker, George F., Foundation, Harvard University. *The Radio Industry*. Chicago and New York: Shaw, 1928.
Ballard, William C. *Elements of Radio Telephony*. New York: McGraw-Hill, 1922.
Banning, William Peck. *Commercial Broadcasting Pioneer: The WEAF Experiment*. Cambridge: Harvard University Press, 1946.
Barber, Red. *The Broadcasters*. New York: Dial, 1970.
Barnes, Pat. *Sketches of Life*. Chicago: Reilly & Lee, 1932.

Barnouw, Erik. *A History of Broadcasting in the United States*. Vol. 1, *A Tower in Babel: To 1933*. New York: Oxford University Press, 1966.

_____. _____. Vol. 2, *The Golden Web: 1933 to 1953*. New York: Oxford University Press, 1968.

Beaumont, Charles. "Requiem for Radio." *Playboy*, May, 1960.

"Beginnings of Broadcasting." *IEEE Spectrum*, 1964.

Bellows, H.A. "Broadcasting: A New Medium." *Harvard Alumni Bulletin*, December 18, 1930, pp. 382–386.

Bensman, Marvin R. "Regulation of Broadcasting by the Department of Commerce, 1921–1927." In *American Broadcasting* by Lawrence W. Lichty and Malachi C. Topping. New York: Hastings House, 1975.

_____. "The Zenith-WJAZ Case and the Chaos of 1926–27." *Journal of Broadcasting*, 14, Fall, 1970, pp. 423–440.

Berg, Gertrude. *The Rise of the Goldbergs*. New York: Barse, 1931.

Berg, Molly, with Cherney Berg. *Molly and Me*. New York: McGraw-Hill, 1961.

Bickel, Karl A. *New Empires: Newspapers and the Radio*. Philadelphia: Lippincott, 1920.

Bickel, Mary E. *George W. Trendle: An Authorized Biography*. New York: Exposition, 1972.

Bliven, Bruce. "How Radio Is Remaking Our World." *Century*, 108, June, 1924, pp. 147–154.

_____. "The Legion Family and the Radio." *Century*, 108, October, 1924, pp. 811–818.

Boorstin, Daniel. *The Americans: The Democratic Experience*. New York: Random House, 1963.

Boucheron, Pierre. "News and Music From the Air." *Scientific American*, 125-A, December, 1921, pp. 104–105.

Bouck, Zeh. *Making a Living in Radio*. New York: McGraw-Hill, 1935.

Briggs, Asa. *The History of Broadcasting in the United Kingdom*. Vol. 1, *The Birth of Broadcasting*. London: Oxford University Press, 1961.

_____. _____. Vol. 2, *The Golden Age of Wireless*. London: Oxford University Press, 1965.

Briggs, Susan. *Those Radio Times*. London: Weidenfeld and Nicolson, 1981.

Brindze, Ruth. *Not to Be Broadcast: The Truth About Radio*. New York: Vanguard, 1937.

Broadcast Pioneers. *Historical Inventory and Industry Reference Library*. New York: Broadcast Pioneers, 1969.

Brokenshire, Norman. *This Is Norman Brokenshire*. New York: McKay, 1954.

Bruno, Harry A. "Meet WEBJ — First Radio Trolley Station." *New York Telegram Mail*, August 2, 1924.

Burlingame, Roger. *Don't Let Them Scare You: The Life and Times of Elmer Davis*. Philadelphia: Lippincott, 1961.

Burrows, A.R. *The Story of Broadcasting*. London: Cassell, 1924.

Buxton, Frank, and Bill Owen. *Radio's Golden Age*. Ansonia Station, NY: Easton Valley, 1966.

_____, and _____. *The Big Broadcast, 1920–1950*. New York: Viking, 1972.

Cantril, Hadley, and Gordon Allport. *The Psychology of Radio*. New York: Harper & Bros., 1935.

Carneal, Georgette. *A Conqueror of Space: An Authorized Biography of Lee De Forest*. New York: Liveright, 1930.

Carpenter, H.K. *Behind the Microphone*. Raleigh, NC, 1930.

Casson, Herbert N. *The History of the Telephone*. Chicago: McClurg, 1910.

Charnley, Mitchell V. *News By Radio*. New York: Macmillan, 1948.

Chase, Francis, Jr. *Sound and Fury: An Informal History of Broadcasting*. New York: Harper & Bros., 1942.

Chase, Gilbert. *Music in Radio Broadcasting*. New York: McGraw-Hill, 1946.

Cheerio (pseud.). *The Story of Cheerio by Himself*. New York: Garden State, 1946.

Chesmore, Stuart. *Behind the Microphone*. Nelson, 1935.

Chester, Edward W. *Radio, Television and American Politics*. New York: Sheed and Ward, 1969.

Chicago Tribune Radio Book: A Listener's Handbook. Chicago: Chicago Tribune, 1929.

Churchill, Allen. *Remember When*. New York: Golden, 1967.

Clark, David G. "H.V. Kaltenborn's First Years on the Air." *Journalism Quarterly*, Summer, 1965, pp. 373–381.

Codel, Martin (editor). *Radio and Its Future*. New York: Harper & Bros., 1930.

Cole, Barry, and Oettinger Cole. *Reluctant Regulators: The FCC and the Broadcast Audience*. Reading, MA: Addison-Wesley, 1978.

Colpitts, E.H. "The Future of Radio Telephony." *Scientific American*, 113, December 4, 1915, p. 485.

"Communicating Over Great Distances: The Invention of the Telegraph, Telephone, and Wireless Telegraphy." *Scientific American*, 112, June 5, 1915, p. 531.

Correll, Charles J., and Freeman F. Gosden. *All About Amos and Andy*. New York: Rand McNally, 1929.

Crabb, Richard. *Radio's Beautiful Day*. Aberdeen, ND: North Plains, 1983.

Crosby, Bing (as told to Pete Martin). *Call Me Lucky*. New York: Simon and Schuster, 1953.

Crosby, John. *Out of the Blue*. New York: Simon and Schuster, 1952.

Crosley, Powel, Jr. *Simplicity of Radio: The Blue Book of Radio*. Cincinnati: Crosley Radio Co., 1924.

Czitrom, Daniel J. *Media and the American Mind: From Morse to McLuhan*. Chapel Hill: University of North Carolina Press, 1982.

Danielian, N.R. *AT&T: The Story of Industrial Conquest*. New York: Vanguard, 1939.

Daniels, Jonathan. *The Time Between the Wars*. Garden City, NY: Doubleday, 1966.

Danna, Sammy R. "The Rise of Radio News." *Freedom of Information Center, Report No. 211*. School of Journalism, University of Missouri, November, 1968, pp. 1–7.

Danzig, Allison, and Peter Brandwein (editors). *Sport's Golden Age*. New York: Harper & Bros., 1948.

Darrow, Ben H. *Radio Trailblazing: A Brief History of the Ohio School of the Air*. Columbus, OH: College Book Co., 1940.

Davenport, Walter. "A Baritone Out of Work." *Collier's*, June 4, 1928.

Davis, Stephen. *The Law of Radio Communication*. New York: McGraw-Hill, 1927.

Dawson, Mitchell. "Censorship on the Air." *American Mercury*, 31, March, 1934, pp. 257–268.

De Forest, Lee. "The Audion—A New Receiver for Wireless Telegraphy." *Scientific American*, 64, Nov. 20, 1907, pp. 348–356.

_____. *Father of Radio: The Autobiography of Lee De Forest*. Chicago: Wilcox and Follett, 1950.

De Hass, Anton. *The Radio Industry: The Story of Its Development*. Chicago: Shaw, 1928.

Dewey, John. "Radio's Influence on the Mind." *School and Society*, 40, December 15, 1934, p. 805.

Dragonette, Jessica. *Faith Is a Song*. New York: McKay, 1951.

Dreher, Carl. *Sarnoff: An American Success*. New York: Quadrangle, 1977.

Dunlap, Orrin E. *The Story of Radio*. New York: The Dial Press, 1935.

_____. *Marconi: The Man and His Wireless*. New York: Macmillan, 1937.

_____. *Radio's 100 Men of Science*. New York: Harper & Bros., 1944.

_____. "Who Pays the Broadcaster?" *Popular Radio*, January, 1927, pp. 11–15; 94.

Dunning, John. *Tune In Yesterday: The Ultimate Encyclopedia of Old-Time Radio, 1925–1976*. Englewood Cliffs, NJ: Prentice-Hall, 1976.

Durstein, Roy S. "We're on the Air." *Scribner's Magazine*, 83, May, 1928, pp. 623–631.

Edelman, Murray. *Licensing of Radio Services in the United States, 1927–1947*. University of Illinois Studies in the Social Sciences, Vol XXXI (published Ph.D dissertation), Nov. 4, 1950.

Education on the Air. Yearbook of the Institute for Education by Radio. Annual, 1930–.

Edwards, Frank. *My First 10,000 Sponsors*. New York: Ballantine, 1956.

Eichberg, Richard. *Radio Stars of Today*. Boston: Page, 1937.

Eisenberg, Azriel. *Children and Radio Programs*. New York: Columbia University Press, 1936.

Elton, J. Hannaford. "Tomorrow in Radio." *Illustrated World*, 37, June, 1922, pp. 499–505.

Ericson, Raymond. "A Recollection of Richard Crooks." *New York Times*, March 27, 1966.

Evans, James F. *Prairie Farmer and WLS*. Urbana: University of Illinois Press, 1969.

Ewan, David. *The Life and Death of Tin Pan Alley*. New York: Funk and Wagnalls, 1964.

Felix, Edgar H. *Using Radio in Sales Promotion*. New York: McGraw-Hill, 1927.

Fessenden, Helen M. *Fessenden: Builder of Tomorrows*. New York: Coward-McCann, 1940.

Fessenden, Reginald Aubrey. "A Brief History of Wireless Telegraphy." *Scientific American*, 67, January 9, 1909, p. 18.

Fink, John. *WGN: A Pictorial History*. Chicago: WGN.

Firth, Ivan, and Gladys S. Erskin. *Gateway to Radio*. Macaulay, 1934.

Foster, Eugene S. *Understanding Broadcasting*. Reading, MA: Addison-Wesley, 1978.

Friedershoff, Burk. *From Crystal to Color, WFMB*. Indianapolis: WFMB, 1964.

Friedrich, Carl J., and Jeannette Sayre Smith. *Radio Broadcasting and Higher Education*. Cambridge, MA: Studies in the Control of Radio, 1942.

_____, and Evelyn Sternberg. "Congress and the Control of Radio Broadcasting." *American Political Science Review*, 38, October–December 1943, pp. 797–818; 1004–1026.

Frost, Stanley E., Jr. *Education's Own Stations*. Chicago: University of Chicago Press, 1937.

_____. "Radio: Our Next Great Step Forward." *Collier's Weekly*, 69, April 18, 1922, p. 3.

_____. "Marconi and His Views of Wireless Progress." *Review of Reviews*, 66, August, 1922, pp. 106–70.

Garis, Roger. *My Father Was Uncle Wiggily*. New York: McGraw-Hill, 1966.

Gelatt, Roland. *The Fabulous Phonograph*. Philadelphia: Lippincott, 1954.

Gernsback, Hugo. *Radio for.All*. Philadelphia: Lippincott, 1922.

_____. "The Broadcast Listener." *Radio News*, June, 1923, p. 1.

_____. "Fifty Years of Home Radio." *Radio-Electronics*, March, 1956.

Gilbert, Douglas. *American Vaudeville: Its Life and Times*. New York: Dover, 1963.

Godfrey, Donald G. *A Directory of Broadcast Archives*. Washington, DC, 1982.

Goldsmith, Alfred N., and Austin C. Lescarboura. *This Thing Called Broadcasting*. New York: Holt, 1930.

Greb, Gordon B. "The Golden Anniversary of Broadcasting." *Journal of Broadcasting*, Winter, 1958–59, pp. 3–13.

Green, Abel, and Joe Laurie, Jr. *Show Biz from Vaude to Video*. New York: Holt, 1951.

Gross, Ben. *I Looked and Listened: Informal Recollections of Radio and TV*. New York: Random House, 1954.

Gunston, David. *Marconi: Father of Radio*. New York: Crowell-Collier, 1965.

Gurman, Joseph, and Myron Slager. *Radio Round-Ups*. Boston: Lee & Shepard, 1932.

Harlow, Alvin F. *Old Wires and New Waves*. New York: Appleton-Century, 1936.

Harmon, Jim. *The Great Radio Heroes*. Garden City, NY: Doubleday, 1967.

_____. *The Great Radio Comedians*. Garden City, NY: Doubleday, 1970.

Harris, Charles K. *After the Ball: Forty Years of Melody*. New York: Frank Maurice, 1976.

Harris, Credo Fitch. *Microphone Memories*. Indianapolis: Bobbs-Merrill, 1937.

Head, Sidney W. *Broadcasting in America*. Boston: Houghton Mifflin, 1956.

Hedges, William S. "Radio—The New Education." *What's in the Air*, March, 1924.

_____. "Radio on the Road." *Motorview*, September, 1924.

Hettinger, Herman S. *A Decade of Radio Advertising*. Chicago: University of Chicago Press, 1933.

_____. *Radio: The Fifth Estate*. Philadelphia: American Academy of Political and Social Science, 1935.

High, Stanley. "Not So Free Air." *Saturday Evening Post*, February 11, 1939.

Hilbrink, W.R. *Who Really Invented Radio?* New York: Putnam, 1972.

Hill, Frank Ernest. *Listen and Learn: Fifteen Years of Adult Education on the Air*. American Association for Adult Education, 1937.

Hilliard, Robert L. (editor). *Radio Broadcasting: Introduction to the Sound Medium*. New York: Hastings House, 1974.

"Historical Synopsis of Principal Events in NBC's First Forty Years." *Radio-Television Daily*, May 10, 1966.

Hoover, Herbert. *The Memoirs of Herbert Hoover: The Cabinet and the Presidency, 1920–1933*.

Hornblow, Arthur. "Will Radio Hurt the Theatre?" *Theatre Magazine*, March, 1925, p. 7.

Hower, Ralph M. *The History of an Advertising Agency: N.W. Ayer & Son at Work*. Cambridge: Harvard University Press, 1939.

Husing, Ted. *Ten Years Before the Mike*. New York: Farrar & Rinehart, 1935.

Innis, Harold A. *Empire and Communication*. Oxford: Clarendon, 1950.

Jackson, Joseph H. "Should Radio Be Used for Advertising?" *Radio Broadcast*, November, 1922, pp. 72–76.

Jewett, Frank B. "Wireless Telephony." *Review of Reviews*, 59, May, 1919, pp. 500–503.

Jolly, W.B. *Marconi*. New York: Stein and Day, 1972.

Kaempffert, Waldemar. "Radio Broadcasting." *Review of Reviews*, 65, April, 1922, pp. 395–401.

Kahn, Frank J. *Documents on American Broadcasting*. New York: Appleton-Century-Crofts, 1973.

Kaltenborn, H.V. *Fifty Fabulous Years*. New York: Putnam, 1950.

_____. "On the Air." *Century Magazine*, 112, October, 1926, pp. 666–676.

Kaplan, Milton A. *Radio and Poetry*. New York: Columbia University Press, 1949.

Kaufman, Helen L. *From Jehovah to Jazz*. New York: Dodd, Mead, 1937.

Kinscella, Hazel Gertrude. *Music on the Air*. New York: Viking, 1934.

Kirshner, Allen, and Linda Kirshner (editors). *Radio and Television: Readings in the Mass Media*. New York: Odyssey, 1971.

Lackman, Ron. *Remember Radio*. New York: Putnam, 1970.

Landry, Robert J. *Who, What, Why Is Radio?* New York: George W. Stewart, 1942.

_____. *This Fascinating Radio Business*. Indianapolis: Bobbs-Merrill, 1946.

_____. "Wanted: Radio Critics." *Public Opinion Quarterly,* December, 1940.

La Prade, Ernest. *Broadcasting Music.* New York: Rinehart, 1947.

Lauder, Sir Harry. *Between You and Me.* New York: McCann, 1950.

Lavery, Don. "Back in 1926 When Radio Was the Big News Medium." *Chicago Daily News,* February 19, 1966.

Lazarsfeld, Paul F. *Radio and the Printed Page.* New York: Duell, Sloan & Pearce, 1940.

_____, and Harry Field. *The People Look at Radio.* Chapel Hill: University of North Carolina Press, 1946.

_____, and Patricia L. Kendall. *Radio Listening in America.* New York: Prentice-Hall, 1948.

_____, and Frank N. Stanton. *Radio Research.* New York: Duell, Sloan & Pearce, 1941.

Leamy, Edmund M. "Twenty-Five Years in Radio—Carlin Chuckles at His Memories." *New York World Telegram,* September 24, 1948.

Leatherwood, Dowling. *Journalism on the Air.* Minneapolis, MN: Burgess, 1939.

Lescaboura, Austin. "Radio for Everybody." *Scientific American,* 126, March, 1922, p. 166.

_____. "How Much It Costs to Broadcast." *Radio Broadcast,* September, 1926, pp. 367–71.

Lessing, Lawrence. "The Late Edwin H. Armstrong." *Scientific American,* April, 1954.

_____. *Man of High Fidelity: Edward Howard Armstrong.* Philadelphia: Lippincott, 1956.

Levenson, William B. *Teaching Through Radio.* New York: Farrar & Rinehart, 1945.

Levin, Harvey J. *"The Invisible Resource": Use and Regulation of the Radio Spectrum.* Baltimore: Johns Hopkins University Press, 1971.

Levine, I.E. *Electronic Pioneer: Lee De Forest.* New York: Messner, 1964.

Lichty, Lawrence W. "Radio Drama: The Early Years." *NAEB Journal,* July–August 1950, pp. 10–16.

_____. *World and International Broadcasting: A Bibliography.* Washington: Association for Professional Broadcasting Education, 1970.

_____, and Thomas W. Bohn. "Radio's March of Time: Dramatized News." *Journalism Quarterly,* Autumn, 1974, pp. 458–462.

_____, and Malachi C. Topping (editors). *American Broadcasting: A Sourcebook on the History of Radio and Television.* New York: Hastings House, 1975.

"The Long Arm of the Radio Is Reaching Everywhere." *Current Opinion,* 72, May, 1922, pp. 684–687.

Lott, George E., Jr. "The Press-Radio Wars of the 1930s." *Journal of Broadcasting,* Summer, 1970, pp. 275–286.

Lundberg, George A. "The Content of Radio Programs." *Social Forces,* 7, 1928, pp. 58–60.

Lutz, William W. *The News of Detroit.* Boston: Little, Brown: 1973.

Lynd, Robert S., and Helen M. Lynd. *Middletown: A Study of Modern American Culture.* New York: Harcourt Brace, 1929.

Lyons, Eugene. *David Sarnoff.* New York: Harper & Row, 1966.

McBride, Mary Margaret. *Out of the Air.* New York: Doubleday, 1960.

McCarty, Harold B. "WHA: Wisconsin's Radio Pioneer." *Wisconsin Blue Book, 1937.* Madison: State of Wisconsin, 1938.

McCavitt, William E. *Radio and TV: A Selected Annotated Bibliography.* Metuchen, NJ: Scarecrow, 1978.

MacDonald, J. Fred. *Don't Touch That Dial: Radio Programming in American Life, 1920–1960.* Chicago: Nelson-Hall, 1979.

McGill, Earle. *Radio Directing.* New York: McGraw-Hill, 1930.

McLauchlin, R.J. "What the Detroit News Has Done in Broadcasting." *Radio Broadcast*, June, 1922, pp. 136–141.

MacLauren, William Rupert. *Invention and Innovation in the Radio Industry*. New York: Macmillan, 1949.

MacLeish, Archibald. *The American Story*. New York: Duell, Sloan & Pearce, 1944.

McLuhan, Marshall. *Understanding Media*. New York: McGraw-Hill, 1964.

McMahan, Morgan E. *Vintage Radio*. Palos Verdes, CA: Vintage Radio, 1973.

McMeans, Orange E. "The Great Audience Invisible." *Scribner's Magazine*, March, 1923, pp. 410–416.

McNamee, Graham. *You're On the Air*. New York: Harper & Bros., 1926.

McNicol, Donald. *Radio's Conquest of Space*. New York: Murray Hill, 1928.

Malone, Bill C. *Country Music USA*. Austin: University of Texas Press, 1968.

Marconi, Degna. *My Father Marconi*. New York: McGraw-Hill, 1962.

Marconi, Guglielmo. "Origin and Development of Wireless and Telegraphy." *North American Review*, May, 1899, pp. 625–629.

Mattfield, Julius. *Variety Music Cavalcade: 1920–1961—A Chronology of Vocal and Instrumental Music Popular in the United States*. Englewood Cliffs, NJ: Prentice-Hall, 1966.

Maver, William. "Wireless Telegraphy: Its Past and Present Status and Its Prospects." *Annual Report of the Smithsonian Institution*, 1902, pp. 261–274.

Maxim, Hudson. "Radio—The Fulcrum." *Nation*, July 23, 1924, p. 91.

Mencken, H.L. *The American Language, Second Supplement*. New York: Alfred A. Knopf, 1948.

Midgley, Ned. *The Advertising and Business Side of Radio*. New York: Prentice-Hall, 1948.

Mills, John. *A Fugue in Cycles and Bells*. New York: Van Nostrand, 1935.

Mitchell, Curtis. *Cavalcade of Broadcasting*. Chicago: Follett, 1970.

Mix, Jennie Irene. "At Last—Great Artists Over the Radio." *Radio Broadcast*, March, 1925.

_____. "Good National Radio Programs Prove 'What the Public Wants.'" *Radio Broadcast*, May, 1925, pp. 62–65.

Morris, Lloyd R. *Not So Long Ago*. New York: Random House, 1949.

Morton, Robert A. "Regulation of Radio Telegraphy." *Scientific American*, March, 1912 (Supplement 23), pp. 180–181.

NBC: A History. New York: National Broadcasting Company, 1966.

NBC and You. New York: National Broadcasting Company, 1944.

Newsom, Iris (editor). *Wonderful Inventions: Motion Pictures, Broadcasting and Recorded Sound at the Library of Congress*. Washington, DC: Library of Congress, 1985.

Norris, Lowell Ames. "The World's First Radio Program." *Yankee*, December, 1965.

O'Brien, Howard V. "It's Great to Be a Radio Maniac." *Collier's Weekly*, September 13, 1924, pp. 15–16.

O'Brien, P.G. *Will Rogers: Ambassador of Good Will and Prince of Wit and Wisdom*. New York: Prentice-Hall, 1948.

Osgood, Dick. *WYXIE Wonderland: An Unauthorized 50-Year History of WXYZ Detroit*. Bowling Green, OH: Bowling Green Popular Press, 1983.

Page, Leslie J., Jr. "The Nature of the Broadcast Receiver and Its Market in the United States from 1922 to 1927." *Journal of Broadcasting*, Spring, 1960, pp. 174–182.

Paley, William S. *As It Happened: A Memoir*. Garden City, NY: Doubleday, 1979.

Passman, Arnold. *The Deejays*. New York: Macmillan, 1971.

Pastore, John O. *The Story of Communications: From Beacon Light to Telstar*. New York: Macfadden-Bartell, 1964.

"Patents: An Inventor's Vindication." *Newsweek*, October 30, 1967.

Perry, Armstrong. *Radio in Education: The Ohio School of the Air and Other Experiments*. New York: Payne Fund, 1929.

Poindexter, Ray. *Golden Throats and Silver Tongues*. Conway, AR: River Road, 1978.

Presbery, Frank. *History and Development of Advertising*. New York: Doubleday, 1929.

"The Problem of Radio Reallocation." *Congressional Digest*, October, 1928, pp. 255–286.

"Quin Ryan's Coffee Break." *Chicago Tribune*, March 7, 1969.

Radio—A Picture Story. Management in the Public Interest. Washington, DC: National Association of Broadcasters, 1945.

Radio as an Advertising Medium. New York: Metropolitan Life, 1929.

The Radio Boys on the Mexican Border. New York: Bunt, 1922.

Radio Broadcasts in the Library of Congress, 1924–1941. Washington, DC: Government Printing Office, 1982.

"The Radio Symphony." In *Radio Research*, edited by Paul F. Lazarsfeld and Frank N. Stanton. New York: Duell, Sloan & Pearce, 1941, pp. 110–139.

Reck, Franklin R. *Radio From Start to Finish*. New York: Crowell, 1942.

Reeves, Earl. "The New Business of Broadcasting." *Review of Reviews*, November, 1925, pp. 529–532.

Robinson, Thomas Porter. *Radio Networks and the Federal Government*. New York: Columbia University Press, 1943.

Rockwell, Don (editor). *Radio Personalities: A Pictorial and Biographical Annual*. New York: Press Bureau, 1935.

Roosevelt, Franklin D. *Selected Speeches, Messages, Press Conferences, Letters*. New York: Rinehart, 1957.

Rorty, James. *Order on the Air*. New York: Day, 1934.

————. "The Impending Radio War." *Harper's*, November, 1931.

Rothafel, Samuel L., and Raymond L. Yates. *Broadcasting: Its New Day*. New York: Century, 1925.

Rymer, Mary Frances. *The Small House Half-Way Up the Next Block: Paul Rymer's Vic and Sade*. New York: McGraw-Hill, 1972.

Sarno, Edward F. "The National Radio Conferences." *Journal of Broadcasting*, Spring, 1969, pp. 189–202.

Sarnoff, David. "Radio of Today and Tomorrow." *New York Sunday Herald*, May 14, 1922.

————. "The Freedom of the Air." *Nation*, April 10, 1924.

————. "Radio—As Told to Mary Margaret McBride." *Saturday Evening Post*, August 7 and 14, 1926.

————. "Development of the Radio Art and Radio Industry Since 1920." In *The Radio Industry*. New York: Shaw, 1928.

"Sarnoff: Dreamer of the Radio." *New York Herald Tribune*, September 27, 1936.

Schmeckelbier, Laurence F. *The Federal Radio Commission: Its History, Activities and Organization*. Washington: Brookings Institution, 1932.

Schramm, Wilbur (editor). *Mass Communications*. Urbana: University of Illinois Press, 1949.

Schubert, Paul. *The Electric Word: The Rise of Radio*. New York: Macmillan, 1928.

Seldes, Gilbert. *The Public Arts*. New York: Simon and Schuster, 1956.

Settle, Irving. *A Pictorial History of Radio*. New York: Citadel, 1960.

Shurick, E.P.J. *The First Quarter-Century of American Broadcasting*. Kansas City: Midland, 1946.

Siepmann, Charles Arthur. *Radio's Second Chance*. Boston: Little, Brown, 1946.

Slate, Sam J., and Joe Cook. *It Sounds Impossible*. New York: Macmillan, 1963.
Slide, Anthony. *Great Radio Personalities in Historic Pictures*. New York: Dover, 1982.
Smith, R. Franklin. "Oldest Station in the Nation?" *Journal of Broadcasting*, Winter, 1959–60, pp. 40–55.
Smith, Robert R. "The Origin of Radio Network News Commentary." *Journal of Broadcasting*, Spring, 1965, pp. 113–132.
Sokel, Bernard. *A Pictorial History of Vaudeville*. New York: Citadel, 1961.
Soule, George Henry. *Prosperity Decade, 1917–1929*. New York: Rinehart, 1947.
Spaeth, Sigmund. *History of Popular Music in America*. New York: Random House, 1948.
Spaulding, John W. "1928: Radio Becomes a Mass Advertising Medium." *Journal of Broadcasting*, Winter, 1963–64, pp. 31–44.
"Special Report: Four Decades of the NBC Network." *Broadcasting Magazine*, May 19, 1966.
Stearns, Marshall W. *The Story of Jazz*. New York: Oxford University Press, 1956.
Stevenson, Elizabeth. *Babbitts and Bohemians: The American 1920s*. New York: Macmillan, 1967.
The Story of WOR. Newark, NJ: Bamberger Broadcasting Service, 1934.
Strother, French. "The Unfolding Miracles of Wireless." *World's Work*, April, 1922, pp. 347–361.
Sullivan, Mark. *Our Times*. Vol. 6, *The Twenties*. New York: Charles Scribner's Sons, 1937.
Summers, Harrison B. *A Thirty-Year History of Programs on National Radio Networks in the United States, 1926–1956*. Columbus, OH: Ohio State University Press, 1958.
Swing, Raymond Gram. *"Good Evening" — A Professional Memoir*. New York: Harcourt Brace, 1964.
Taylor, Deems. "Radio: A Brief for the Defense." *Harper's*, April, 1933, pp. 554–563.
Taylor, Glenhall. *Before Television: The Radio Years*. New York: Barnes, 1979.
Tebbel, John. *David Sarnoff: Putting Electronics to Work*. Chicago: Encyclopaedia Britannica, 1963.
This Fabulous Century: 1920–1930. New York: Time-Life, 1969.
Thomas, Lowell. *Magic Dials*. New York: Polygraph, 1939.
Thurber, James. "Soapland." In *The Beast in Me and Other Animals*. New York: Harcourt Brace, 1948.
Treadwell, Bill. *Head, Heart and Heel*. New York: Mayfair, 1958.
Tyler, Tracy F. *An Appraisal of Radio Broadcasting in the Land-Grant Colleges and State Universities*. Washington, DC: National Committee on Education by Radio, 1933.
Tyson, Levering. *Radio and Education*. Chicago: University of Chicago Press, 1933.
Ulanov, Barry. *The Incredible Crosby*. New York: Whittlesey House, 1948.
"The Use of Radio in Education." *Jewish Chronicle*, March 5, 1926.
Vallee, Rudy. *Let the Chips Fall*. Harrisburg, PA: Stackpole, 1975.
Voice of Experience (pseud.). *Stranger Than Fiction*. New York: Dodd, Mead, 1934.
"Voice of the Twenties." *Time*, May 18, 1942.
"Voices from Radio's Past Record Its Birthpangs." *Tide Magazine*, August 13, 1955.
Wagner, Paul H. *Radio Journalism*. Minneapolis, MN: Burgess, 1940.
Wallace, John. "What We Thought of the First Columbia Broadcasting Program." *Radio Broadcast*, December, 1927, pp. 140–141.
Waller, Judith. *Radio: The Fifth Estate*. Boston: Houghton Mifflin, 1946.
Webster, Bethuel M., Jr. *Our Stake in the Ether*. Washington: American Academy of Air Law, 1931.

Wedlake, C.E.C. *SOS: The Story of Radio Communication*. New York: Crane, Russak, 1973.

Wertheim, Arthur. *Radio Comedy*. New York: Oxford University Press, 1979.

West, Robert. *So-o-o-o You're Going on the Air*. New York: Rodin, 1934.

_____. *The Rape of Radio*. New York: Rodin, 1941.

Whalen, Grover. "Radio Control." *Nation*, July 23, 1924, pp. 90–91.

White, Llewellyn. *The American Radio: A Report on the Broadcasting Industry in the United States*. Chicago: University of Chicago Press, 1947.

White, Paul. *News on the Air*. New York: Harcourt Brace, 1947.

"Who Will Ultimately Do the Broadcasting?" *Radio Broadcast*, April, 1923, pp. 524–525.

"The Wireless Telephone Tests." *Wireless Age*, November, 1915, pp. 111–116.

Wood, Clement C. *The Life of a Man*. Kansas City, MO: Oozhorn Publishing Co., 1934.

Wood, J. Howard. *WGN: A Pictorial History*. Chicago: WGN, 1961.

Woodfin, Jane. *Of Mikes and Men*. New York: McGraw-Hill, 1951.

Yates, Raymond F. "The Long Arm of Radio." *Current History*, March, 1922, pp. 980–985.

_____. "What Will Happen to Broadcasting?" *Outlook*, April 19, 1924, pp. 604–606.

Young, James D. "Is the Radio Newspaper Next?" *Radio Broadcast*, September, 1925, pp. 576–580.

Young, Otis B. "The Real Beginning of Radio." *Saturday Review*, March 7, 1964.

The Zenith Story. Chicago: Zenith, 1955.

Zolotov, Maurice. "Washboard Weepers." *Saturday Evening Post*, May 29, 1943.

Unpublished Material, Oral History Collections, Dissertations

A vast amount of material is available relating to early broadcasting, but a great deal of it is to be found only in specialized collections, in archives or oral history collections. No serious student of broadcasting can afford to neglect the riches offered by collections such as that of the Broadcast Pioneers History Project in Washington, D.C., the Columbia University Oral History Project (Radio Section) in New York, or the Mass Communications History Center of the Wisconsin Historical Society in Madison. The listings that follow relate in part to materials found in such collections. For the reader's convenience, when such collections are referred to, the following abbreviations are used:

(BP)	Broadcast Pioneers Project, National Association of Broadcasters, Washington, DC
(CU)	Columbia University Oral History Collection, New York
(NB)	National Broadcasting Company Library, New York
(WH)	Mass Communications History Center of the Wisconsin Historical Society, Madison

Alexanderson, E.F.W. Reminiscences. (CU)

"The American Amateur." List of 120 early radio announcers, published Buffalo, New York, 1926. (BP)

American Heritage. Book Section. "Pioneers Recall the Early Days of Radio." Incl. H.V. Kaltenborn, William S. Hedges, Lyman Bryson, E.L. Bragdon, Dorothy Gordon, Lawrence Ashley Hawkins, Donald G. Little, Herbert Hoover, Chester H. Long, Arthur Judson, Thomas H. Cowan, Walter C. Evans, Orestes H. Caldwell. (BP)

"Amos 'n' Andy." Letters, Clippings, Memorabilia. (BP)

Amrad. A manufacturer of radio equipment in the early 1920s. Interviews with company officials, engineers, etc. (BP)

Aylesworth, Merlin H. "The National Magazine of the Air." Speech at the Graduate School of Business Administration, Harvard University, 1928. (BP)

———. "Radio and the Press." Address delivered before the School of Public and International Affairs, Princeton University.

———. "What Makes the Wheels Go Round." Address over 53 stations of NBC, October, 1928. (BP)

Baker, Walter Ransom Gail. Reminiscences. (CU)

Barlow, Howard. Reminiscences. (CU)

Barnes, Patrick Henry. Reminiscences. (CU)

Barnett, Joseph M. Reminiscences. (CU)

Barton, Jane. "Radio Stars of Early Broadcasting." (BP)

Bauman, Ludwig. "Who's Who on the Air." 1932. (BP)

"Bell Telephone Hour: A Unique Chapter in Broadcast History." News File. (BP)

Bigger, George C. "A Broadcasting Service for Agricultural Colleges." Address, July, 1924. (BP)

———. "Facts on Radio Broadcasting (1920–1964)." WLBK, DeKalb, IL, May, 1964. (BP)

———. "History of the National Barn Dance on WLS." August, 1964. (BP)

"The Birth of Radio." Detailed descriptions of early studios and equipment. Westinghouse. (BP)

Bill, Edgar S. "What Radio Means to Farm People." Chicago, WLS, February 19, 1930.

Bontsema, Peter (Pete) H. "My Twenty-Three Years in Radio (1923–1946)." (BP)

"The Boy." Eleven Radio Talks over WBZ, Boston, 1929. (BP)

Bragdon, Everett L. Reminiscences. (CU)

Brainard, Bertha. Reminiscences. (BP)

"Broadcast Advertising in New England and New York. The WBZ-WBAZ Market." 1929. (BP)

"A Broadcast Novelty." Jim De Witt, Station KOIL, Council Bluffs, IA, 1926. (BP)

Broadcast Pioneer Bulletins. Serial, 1950–. (BP)

Bryson, Lyman Floyd. Reminiscences. (CU)

The Building of Radio City. Photos and Clippings. (BP)

Caldwell, Orestes Hampton. Reminiscences. (CU)

Cappa, Joseph D. Interview. (BP)

Carlin, Phillips. Miscellaneous biographical material. (BP)

———. Reminiscences. (CU)

Caton, Chester F. "Radio Station WMAQ: A History of Its Independent Years." Unpublished Ph.D. dissertation, Evanston, IL: Northwestern University, 1951.

"Cavalcade Program." First program to use rhymed announcements. NBC, 1929. (BP)

CBS Annual Reports. (BP)

Chester, Giraud. "The Radio Commentaries of H.V. Kaltenborn." Unpublished Ph.D. dissertation, Madison: University of Wisconsin, 1947.

Clark, Thomas Edward. Reminiscences. (CU)

Conrad, Frank. Tribute to Frank Conrad by David Sarnoff upon Conrad's receipt of 1940 Gold Medal of the American Institute of the City of New York. February 1, 1940. (BP)

Consadine, Bob. Clippings of a series on Willliam S. Paley. *New York Journal American*, May 23–30, 1965. (BP)

Cowan, Thomas H. Reminiscences. (CU)

The Crosley Story. Exhibits, 1969. (BP)

"David Sarnoff." Biographical sketch, RCA, 1945. (BP)

Davies, Edward A., and Jim Tisdale. "Philadelphia Pioneer Voice." Interview, September 2, 1964. (BP)

Davis, H.P. "The History of Broadcasting in the U.S." Address at Harvard University, April 28, 1928. (BP)

"Daytime Hours Sell." New York: NBC, 1933. (NB)

De Forest, Lee. Interviewed by Gordon R. Greb, 1959. (CU)

_____. Transcript of De Forest Pioneers Meeting, New York, November 22, 1967. Contains an address by De Forest; remarks by Alfred Goldsmith, Raymond Guy, *et al.* (BP)

Dill, Clarence C. Interviewed by Ed Craney, 1964. (BP)

Director of NBC Personnel. February 1, 1929. (BP)

"Dr. Conrad and His Work." Westinghouse Press Release, June 27, 1942. (WH)

Du Mont, Allan. Obituary, *New York Times*, November 16, 1965. (BP)

Dunham, E.L. "Commercial Broadcasting." WNAC, 1925–26. (BP)

"Early Days of WOC—Davenport, Iowa." Tape, 51-page transcript. (BP)

Espenschied, Lloyd. "Recollections of the Radio Industry." (CU)

Evans, Walter Chew. Reminiscences. (CU)

"The Eveready Hour Book of Radio Stars." 1930. (BP)

Felix, Edgar H. Reminiscences. (CU)

Fessenden, Reginald Aubrey. Articles, Correspondence. (BP)

"The First Church Broadcast." Article from *Christian Advocate*, November 14, 1968. (BP)

"The First Forty." WCCO and early radio in Minneapolis-St. Paul. (BP)

Fritz, F.G. "Wendell Hall: Early Radio Performer." (BP)

Gambling, John B. Reminiscences. (CU)

Gammons, Earl. "The Twin Cities Story." 1964. (BP)

"Gentlemen Be Seated." Pamphlet, New York: NBC, 1930. (NB)

Goldin, J. David. Radio Catalogue—3774 items. (BP)

Goldsmith, Alfred N. "Highlights of Radio Broadcasting." Series of articles, 1925. (BP)

_____. "The Battle for Strong Broadcast Signals." April, 1933. (BP)

_____. Scrapbook—209 pages. (BP)

Greene, Robert S. "The Development of Narrative Technique in Radio Drama and Its Relationship to the Rise of News Broadcasting." Master's essay, 1958.

Greene, Rosaline. Reminiscences. (CU)

Gunzendorfer, Wilton. Reminiscences, 1960. (CU)

Guy, Raymond Frederick. Reminiscences, 1960. (CU)

Hager, Kolin. Reminiscences, 1960. (CU)

Hanson, Malcolm P. Papers, 1906–47. (WH)

Hanson, O.B. "The House That Radio Built." NBC: 1935.

Harkness, William E. Reminiscences. (CU)

Harrison, Henrietta. Reminiscences. (CU)

Hart, Fred J. Interviewed by Gordon B. Greb, 1962. (CU)

Hart, Herschell. Reminiscences, 1951. (CU)

Hedges, William S. Reminiscences, 1951. (CU)

"History of Radio Broadcasting and KDKA." Westinghouse, 1950. (BP)

"History of the Radio Club of America." Golden Jubilee Issue, 1909–1959. (BP)

Hoins, Jack. "The History of ABC." (NB)

Holland, Lawrence La Motte. Reminiscences. (CU)

Hoover, Herbert. Letter to Paul B. Klugh, re: "Hoover Conferences." November 15, 1925. (BP)

_____. Reminiscences. (CU)

Horn, Charles W. Address broadcast over KDKA, January 3, 1923. (WH)
_____. "Recollections of a Pioneer Engineer." (BP)
Hummert, Ann. "The Women's Daytime Serial." Lecture, Columbia University, January 11, 1939. (BP)
Husing, Ted. "My Eyes Are in My Heart." (BP)
_____. Obituary, *New York Times*, August 11, 1961.
"Important Dates and Facts in Radio Development, 1897–1922." American Radio and Research Corporation. (BP)
Janis, Eddie. Reminiscences. (CU)
Jansky, C.M., Jr. "The Beginning of Radio Broadcasting." Tribute to Dr. Earle M. Terry. (BP)
Judson, Arthur. Reminiscences. (CU)
Kaltenborn, H.V. Papers. (WH)
_____. Reminiscences. (CU)
Kintner, S.H. Address Delivered over KDKA, December 20, 1922. (WH)
"KNX-CBS Radio." Los Angeles: KNX, 1961. (BP)
Lasker, Albert Davis. Reminiscences, 1950.
"Let's Look at Radio Together." 60 pages, June, 1935. (BP)
Lichty, Lawrence W. "A Study of the Careers and Qualifications of the Members of the Federal Radio Commission and the Federal Communications Commission, 1927–61." Master's essay, Columbus: Ohio State University, 1961.
_____. "The Nation's Station: WLW." Ph.D. dissertation, Columbus: Ohio State University, 1961.
Linton, Bruce A. "A History of Chicago Radio Station Broadcasting." Ph.D. dissertation, Evanston, IL: Northwestern University, 1954.
Little, Donald G. Reminiscences, 1951. (CU)
Logan, Thomas F. "The Right Use of Broadcast Advertising." Address AAAA Convention, October 6, 1927. (BP)
McKee, June. Reminiscences. (CU)
"Making Pep and Sparkle Typify a Ginger Ale." New York: NBC, 1929. (NB)
Malone, Ted. Taped interview. (BP)
Marconi, Guglielmo. Miscellaneous papers, addresses, tributes. (BP)
Meyers, Walter E. Interviews, articles, correspondence. (BP)
Mosby, Arthur J. Taped interview. June 2, 1966. (BP)
NBC. Advisory Council Reports, 1927–35. (BP)
_____. Listing of Board Chairmen, Presidents from 1926–1969. (BP)
_____. Memorandum of minutes, Advisory Council, annual meetings 1927–. (NB)
NBC News Service. Description of NBC quarters in Radio City, September 22, 1933. (BP)
Nobel, Milton. "The Municipal Broadcasting System: Its History, Organization and Activities." Master's essay, New York: City College of New York, 1953.
"Norman Brokenshire." Obituary. (BP)
Paley, William S. "Early CBS History." *Broadcast Pioneer Bulletin.* (BP)
Payne, George Henry. "The Federal Communications Act." Lecture, Harvard University, May 14, 1935. (BP)
Perkins, Col. Ray. Interviews and clippings. (BP)
"Personalities at 711." Series to acquaint listeners with NBC staff. December 13, 1929. (NB)
Petry, Edmund. "The Origin of Bulova Radio Time Signals and Station Representatives." 7 pages. (BP)
Photographs of radio stars. Collection from the twenties and thirties supplied by Jane Barton. (BP)

Pickerell, Elmo. Taped interview, 1967. (BP)

Plant, Eldon M. Reminiscences, 1951. (CU)

Political Broadcasting. Miscellaneous clippings. (BP)

Ponting, Herbert. Reminiscences. (CU)

Popenoe, Charles B. "WJZ." (BP)

Pro Musica, Direction Cesare Sodero, Classical Music, NBC. 1930. (BP)

Pyle, Howard S. "Visiting the Ghosts of Radio." Radio Relay League. (BP)

Radio Drama Prize Competition. Schenectady, New York, WGY, 1923. (BP)

"Radio Enters the Home." New York: Radio Corporation of America, 1922. (NB)

RCA Annual Reports. New York, 1920–. (NB)

Robertson, Bruce. "Recollections of the Radio Industry." 1963. (CU)

"Roosevelt Inauguration Heard by World Over." NBC news release, March 4, 1933. (BP)

Ryan, Quin. Article on broadcasting's role in politics, 1920–1935. *Chicago Tribune*, July 12, 1964. (BP)

_____. "Reminiscences of WGN." (BP)

_____. Reminiscences on early sportscasting. *Chicago Tribune*, May 29, 1968. (BP)

Sarnoff, David. Miscellaneous papers, articles, letters, addresses. (BP)

_____. "Individual Radio—Radiolette." Exchange of letters with Alfred N. Goldsmith, 1922. (BP)

_____. "Radio and the Phonograph Industry—A Few Fundamentals." Article, 1922. (BP)

_____. "Development of Radio Since 1920." Lecture at Harvard University, April 16, 1928. (BP)

_____. "Radio Progress." Address, 1930. (BP)

_____. "Three Decades of Radio." November 18, 1936.

Singiser, Frank. "With the Joneses at the Shore." Script, WGY, 1928.

Sterling, George. "Government in Broadcasting, From the Post Roads Act of 1866 to 1934." (BP)

Thomas, Lowell. Taped interview with Doug Storer, March 15, 1968. (BP)

Toscanini, Arturo. Numerous articles and memorabilia. (BP)

Tyson, Edward Lloyd. Reminiscences. (CU)

"Voice of Firestone." Script of first program, December 3, 1928. (BP)

Wallace, Wesley Herndon. "The Development of Broadcasting in North Carolina, 1922–1948." Unpublished Ph.D. dissertation, Durham, NC: Duke University, 1962.

Waller, Judith. Reminiscences. (CU)

Wallington, James S. Taped interview, March 1, 1967.

Walters, Joseph. Reminiscences. (BP)

Warner, J.C. "History of Radio Corporation of America." 1937. (BP)

Watson, Paul G. "Early Vacuum Tubes." From *Electronics World*, December, 1964. (BP)

WBZ, Boston. Papers, memorabilia. 1921–1929. (BP)

WEEI, Boston. Miscellaneous clippings, inaugural program, September 29, 1924. (BP)

Weir, Austin. "The Prime Purpose of Radio in Canada." University of Toronto, 1933. (BP)

Westinghouse Magazine, Articles on KDKA anniversary, December, 1936. (BP)

Westinghouse News Service. Clip sheets, various dates. (BP)

Weston, Frank. "The Cliquot Club Eskimo Story." Taped interview. (BP)

WGK, Schenectady. Historical papers and memorabilia. (BP)

WGN, Chicago. Clippings, articles, biographies, memorabilia. (BP)

WGY, Schenectady. "Silver Anniversary of Farm Broadcasting over WGY." Illustrated booklet. (BP)

Whalen, Grover A. Reminiscences. (CU)
"What's the Right Word." A Dictionary of Radio, Television Electronics. RCA, 1952.
  (BP)
White, Robert E. Reminiscences. (BP)
Whitmore, Frank D. "Philadelphia's Early Radio Days." Collection of articles. (BP)
Wilmotte, R.M. "History of the Directional Antenna." February, 1957. (BP)
WJZ, Newark. Log, 1923–26. In unpublished NBC papers. (WH)
WJZ, Newark. Photos of first studio, October, 1921. (BP)
WMAQ, Chicago. Miscellaneous clippings. (BP)
Woods, Mark. Reminiscences, 1951. (CU)
WSM, Grand Ole Opry. History Picture Book. (BP)

Government Documents and Publications

Since the government of the United States has been deeply involved in regulating the means of electronic communication from the time of their first appearance, there is a considerable literature of government documents, congressional committee reports, serial publications and the like. Since regulation in all of its legal ramifications is a vast field, the number of individual documents relating to radio, even early radio, is a highly complex and specialized area of research. The documents listed below, in some cases serials, represent the principal sources of information relevant to the general treatment of the present work.

Federal Radio Commission. *Annual Reports, 1927–33*. Washington, DC: Government
    Printing Office. Reprinted by Arno Press.
_____. *Commercial Radio Advertising: Letter from the Chair in Response to Senate
    Resolution 129*. 72d Cong. Washington, DC: Government Printing Office, 1932.
Federal Trade Commission. *Report on the Radio Industry, in Response to House
    Resolution 548*. 67th Cong., 4th sess. Washington, DC: Government Printing
    Office, 1924.
U.S. Congress. *Communications Act of 1934 with Amendments and Index Thereto*.
    Washington, DC: Government Printing Office, 1934.
_____. House. Committee on Interstate and Foreign Commerce. *Regulation of
    Broadcasting: Half a Century of Government Regulation of Broadcasting and the
    Need for Further Legislative Action (McMahon Report)*. 85th Cong., 2nd sess., 1958.
    Washington, DC: Government Printing Office, 1958.
_____. _____. Committee on Merchant Marine and Fisheries. *Government
    Control of Radio Communication: Hearings Before the Committee*. 65th Cong., 3d
    sess., Dec. 12–19, 1918. Washington, DC: Government Printing Office, 1919.
_____. _____. _____. *Jurisdiction of Radio Commission: Hearings Before
    the Committee*. 70th Cong., 1st sess., Jan. 26–Feb. 14, 1928. Washington, DC:
    Government Printing Office, 1928.
_____. Senate. Committee on Interstate Commerce. *Commission on Communica-
    tions: Hearings Before the Committee*. 71st Cong., 1929–30. Washington, DC:
    Government Printing Office, 1930.
_____. _____. _____. *Radio Control: Hearings Before the Committee*. 69th
    Cong., 1st sess., Jan. 8–Mar. 2, 1926. Washington, DC: Government Printing Office,
    1926.
U.S. Dept. of Commerce. *Radio Service Bulletin*. Monthly, 1915–34; thereafter by
    Federal Communications Commission.

U.S. Dept. of the Interior. *Report of the Advisory Committee on Education by Radio*. Columbus, OH: F.J. Heer Printing Co., 1930.

Periodicals

Included below are the names of periodicals of a specialized nature which relate to the history of early broadcasting. Included are a few additional sources such as the *Journal of Broadcasting*, which were begun only in the post-radio age, but which nonetheless contain articles or other indexed references to early broadcasting. Many general magazines and other serials of the 1920s also contain articles dealing with radio. The reader may wish to check *Ulrich's International Periodicals Directory* as a guide to such publications.

Billboard. 1894–.
Broadcasting. 1931– (later combined with *Broadcast Advertising, Broadcasting-Telecasting*).
Broadcasting Yearbook. 1935–.
Journal of Broadcasting. 1957–.
Journalism Quarterly. By Association for Education in Journalism. 1924–.
The Marconigraph. 1911–13.
Old Timer's Bulletin. By Antique Wireless Association. 1959–.
QST. By American Radio Relay League. 1915–.
Radio Age. 1922–28.
Radio Art. 1923–29 (semi-monthly, then quarterly).
Radio Broadcast. 1922–30.
Radio Dealer. 1922–28.
Radio Digest. 1922–33 (irregular).
Radio Guide. 1925–26 (monthly); 1931– (weekly).
Radio News. 1919–25.
Radio Retailing. 1925–39 (monthly).
Radio Service Bulletin. 1915–34 (monthly).
Radio Stars. 1932–38.
Radio World. 1922 (weekly).
Variety. 1905– (weekly).
Variety Radio Directory. 1937–41 (annually).
Wireless Age. By Marconi, monthly, 1913–19; by RCA, 1919–25.

Broadcast Archives

There are very few complete recordings of broadcasts in the pre-1930 period. Before the appearance of the networks there was considered to be little reason for preserving complete radio broadcasts. By the late twenties, however, with shows like "Amos 'n' Andy" becoming extremely popular nationwide and sold in syndication, records of complete broadcasts began to proliferate. Obviously most pre-1930 recordings are of poor quality—at least the few that have survived. A number of years ago when Edward R. Murrow and Fred W. Friendly began their series "You Can Hear It Now," for Columbia records, they were able to offer recordings of old radio shows or highlights back to the inauguration of President Franklin D. Roosevelt in 1933. But when they later decided to do a record covering the history of the 1919–1933 period they had to rely almost completely on simulated dramatizations, using paid actors to

impersonate Calvin Coolidge or Herbert Hoover. They offered the singing voices of
Bing Crosby and Rudy Vallee as representative of the musical styles of the twenties, but
they used recordings of a later period for this.

Readers interested in learning of the whereabouts of recordings of early radio
broadcasts would do well to consult the book *A Directory of Broadcast Archives*, edited
by Donald G. Godfrey (Washington: Broadcast Education Association, 1983). Listed
below are the names and addresses of broadcast archives that contain recordings from
the early days, although it must be understood that not all of these contain significant
materials from the 1920s.

> Library of Congress
> Motion Picture, Broadcasting and Recorded Sound Division
> Thomas Jefferson Building, Room 1053
> Washington, DC 20540
>
> National Archives
> Motion Picture and Sound Recording Branch
> Washington, DC 20408
>
> Broadcast Pioneers Library
> 1771 N Street NW
> Washington, DC 20036
>
> Museum of Broadcasting
> 1 East 53d Street
> New York, NY 10022
>
> Radio Yesteryear
> Box C
> Sandy Hook, CT 06482
>
> Johnson Collection
> Bureau of Museums and Historic Sites
> Hall of Records
> Dover, DE 19903
>
> Radio-Television Division
> Northwestern University
> Evanston, IL 60201
>
> Yale Collection of Historical Sound Recordings
> Yale University
> New Haven, CT 06520
>
> Old Time Radio
> Golden Radio Buffs of Maryland
> 9506 Iroquois Avenue
> Baltimore, MD 21219

Most of these archives offer only restricted use of old recordings, although some
of the sources mentioned above offer tapes and records of old radio broadcasts for sale.

Radio Yesteryear and Old Time Radio are in this category. Interested persons might also wish to consult the spoken and dramatic section of the Schwann Long-Playing Record Catalog for a list of recordings of classical radio broadcasts, mostly from the golden age of radio.

Index

Page numbers in boldface indicate illustrations.

U

V

W